Modern Hotel-Motel Management Methods

Revised Second Edition

Modern Hotel-Motel Management Methods

Revised Second Edition

HERBERT K. WITZKY

Partner: Herbert K. Witzky & Associates
Professor: Fairleigh Dickinson University

Ahrens Series

HAYDEN BOOK COMPANY, INC.
Rochelle Park, New Jersey

Library of Congress Cataloging in Publication Data

Witzky, Herbert K
 Modern hotel-motel management methods.

 (Ahrens series)
 Bibliography: p.
 Includes index.
 1. Hotel management. 2. Motel management.
I. Title.
TX911.W58 1976   658'.91'64794   76-41755
ISBN   0-8104-9467-1

Witzky, Herbert K.

     1   2   3   4   5   6   7   8   9   PRINTING
    ───
       76 77 78 79 80 81 82 83 84   YEAR

Preface

Modern industry has gone through various stages of organization. During the 18th and 19th Centuries, at the time of the Industrial Revolution, the first stage consisted of efficient manufacturing methods. Today, the second stage is still in effect—mass production dependent on mass consumption.

The hotel and motel industries have also undergone similar revolutionary changes, particularly the second stage—a mass feeding concept that is reducing the number of skilled workers and artisans.

However, there is a constant change in public taste and desire that has been recognized by objective housing and feeding managements everywhere. The revolution is continuing, not just in terms of efficiency as thought by some, but in an understanding and acceptance of both production and consumption principles as applied to modern hotel and motel management.

This is not meant to say that the need for skills in our industry is declining. Rather it means that newer skills, even more complex and exacting than before, are needed. Their advent has called for the development of social, intellectual, and human skills at managerial and supervisory levels in this new era. Modern management and the professional manager have already been given increased status and prestige, new rewards in power, as well as direct and supplementary benefits and incentives which place the hotel and motel manager class at the head of all other industries today.

The pages that follow are the product of twenty-five years of work in varying responsibilities in operating, departmental, managerial, and top corporate levels, followed by consulting work for both individual and corporate entities. It represents the results of research and the application of tested and applied techniques as well as methods and concepts that have proved themselves in countless situations.

The idea for the book was conceived while I was a totally paralyzed quadreplegic at the Institute of Physical Medicine and Rehabilitation of New York University, headed by Dr. Howard Rusk — who, with Doctors Donald A. Covalt, Morton Marks, George Karantonis, and Jack Hofkosh, encouraged me in the development of new skills. Its execution was one life line to recovery; the other was and is my wife, who, in addition to typing many versions of the original material, has seen its development over the years and also the severest tests of its application.

Along the way have been many who have aided me in providing opportunities, first as employee and later as consultant. The first of these was Frank G. Wangeman, who gave me my start, of the Hilton Hotels Corporation; and Joseph P. Binns; the late Eugene C. Eppley, President of Eppley Hotels Company, and Honorary Chairman of the Board of Sheraton Hotels Corporation; G. David Schine, President of Schine Hotels; the late Byron C. Calhoun, former President of Intercontinental Hotels Corp.; Wallace S. Whittaker, former President then Chairman of the Board of Intercontinental Hotels Corp.; Roscoe C. Edlund of Rogers, Slade & Hill, wise counselor, teacher and friend; Robert H. Whalen, Vice President, Clermont Hotels, and early associate and friend; James V. Bennett, Vice President & Managing Director, the Ritz-Carlton Hotel in Boston, a great and extremely knowledgeable hotelman, true humanitarian, and friend; Robert P. Sonnabend, Chairman of Sonesta International Hotels Corporation; the late James D. Fuller, former Vice President of Bing & Bing Hotels and Properties; Robert Huyot, former President and Chairman, Inter-Continental Hotels Corporation; the late Paul L. H. Heine of the Brunswick Hotel in Lancaster, Pennsylvania; Cooky Rachelson of Cooky's Restaurants, New York; the late Fred L. Mino, managing partner of Horwath & Horwath; General John R. Beishline, former Department Chairman and Professor of Management, New York University's School of Commerce; and Peter F. Drucker, whose greatness as a teacher along with his deep and incisive thinking provided a turning point in my life as it has for many others. I also thank a very long list of principals in corporate and individual organizations who have employed me over the years as consultant. Obviously it is impossible to list all the friends and associates whom I have known and worked with side by side and to whom I wish to pay tribute. My principal associates have been and are George Kostakis, Herbert Rosenfeld, Peter Prevelige, George Sandland, John Boyle, William Hamilton, Tom Niven, Ken Nichols, and Art Hafstad.

Credit is due to the late Edith Sabra Dudley, a former long-time editor of the Hotel Gazette, to Rudolph C. Hiller, its publisher, and to Alan Bonds and Peter Zurita, Hayden Book Co./Ahrens Division, who gave invaluable assistance and advice on the presentation of the manuscript, and all of whose suggestions I employed, resulting in a greatly expanded version of this text.

Herbert K. Witzky

New Fairfield, Connecticut

Contents

Modern Hotel-Motel Management Methods

Revised Second Edition

Part I

Communications

1

Improving Business Writing

The problem of writing clear, direct, and readily understandable business communications is a major one in the conduct of business affairs. Adding to it are the different schools of thought on just how the writing is to be done.

One apparently simple approach just says that a letter or memorandum must be grammatically correct. For those who have been fortunate in developing sound grammatical construction this answer presents less of a problem. But the business of writing is not one of construction alone. It is readership that counts more. The person receiving the communication is expected to act or react according to the message it contains.

Any letter or communication that belabors the point, or one that *just does not read,* presents an obstacle. Textbooks often have that problem. One reads and reads and just does not seem to get anywhere. The textbook writer does not worry too much about readability because organization, facts, and an instructor are needed to explain the subject matter. Obviously, writing for the reader's convenience is the objective in business. Any mere collection of information will not be enough to get action, understanding, interest, and motivation at the other end.

Another school of thought, attributed to a highly diversified corporation with outstanding management, requires every communication to be written as simply as possible regardless of form. The idea here is to make certain that the message is understood by the reader as it was intended. Even strikeovers and misspelled words are forgiven if the message is clear and direct, leaving no questions unanswered in the mind of the reader.

Although it is highly desirable, business cannot expect to, or become involved with such things as whether or not one should end a sentence with a preposition, the use of split infinitives, or the question of syntax. The educational and intellectual levels of the work force in an organization are simply too varied to expect the rigid rules of English composition and grammar to be fully observed. Management is concerned with getting results through and with people, and, if for example, the use of a cartoon—as was the vogue quite recently—will aid in getting a message across and will get things moving, then that approach justifies the means. After all, the Chinese use word images in some 5000 unique characters that make up this terse, clear and picturesque language.

The communication problem is always present; management is fully aware of its dependence on written statements, policy interpretations and verbal instructions. There is almost complete dependence on the written word, and there is constant room for improvement. The damage that may be caused by misunderstanding in terms of wasted time, delays, etc., for lack of knowing what to do, is a matter of daily record.

Common Writing Errors

A close look at the problem as to what causes communications breakdowns reveals that the most common fault is the writing of gobbledygook, using difficult, impressive, unessential words and long sentences in addition to roundabout expressions and repetition.

Gobbledygook. Here is a common complaint. The Government has a notorious reputation for sending out material which is not only hard to follow, but also requires the reader to read and re-read the material, which may still result in misunderstanding. Here is a sample from the Tax Bureau:

> In the case of individuals other than farmers, if 80% of the tax (determined without regard to the credits for tax withheld on tax-free covenant bonds and for income and tax withheld on wages) exceeds the estimated tax (increased by such credits), and in the case of farmers, if 66⅔ percent of the tax (determined without regard to such credits) exceeds the estimated tax (increased by such credits), there shall be added to the tax an amount equal to such excess, or equal to 6% of the amount by which the tax so determined exceeds the estimated tax so increased, whichever is the lesser.

It is little wonder that errors in the payment of taxes run into the millions year after year. The well known writer Rudolf Flesch, and principal exponent of *The Art of Plain Talk,* which is also the title of a "must reading" book, has turned this cumbersome bit of confusion into understandable English as follows:

> If your estimate turns out to be less than ⅘ of the tax you will have to pay a fine. To figure out your fine, subtract your estimate from your whole tax and take 6% of the difference: the smaller of the two figures is what you will have to pay as your fine. By *tax* we mean here your tax regardless of your credits for tax withheld on bonds or wages. By *estimate* we mean your estimate to which we have added these credits. If you are a farmer, we cut ⅘ to ⅔ for you.

Long Sentences. No one has contributed more to the clarification of what makes the English language more readable than Dr. Rudolph Flesch. His formulas for defining sentence length in the order of difficulty, have been studied, appraised and then proved by proponents and exponents alike.

Average Sentence Length in Words

Very Easy	8 or less
Easy	11
Fairly Easy	14
Standard	17
Fairly Difficult	21
Difficult	25
Very Difficult	29 or more

It is apparent that the average reader will read easily sentences of 17 words or less. Great writing that is remembered seems to bear this out. The classic example, of course, is the King James version of the Bible, which is the best seller of all time. Written in prose, it is clear, direct and carries the reader forward easily.

Perhaps the words of Sir Winston Churchill serve best to illustrate simply the point being made. He says, "Short words are best and the old words when short are the best of all."

Difficult and Impressive Words. A lot of time is wasted by using long-winded, difficult words that are designed to impress but do not really inform. Instead, they confuse the reader and make it almost impossible to achieve any understanding. Here is a classic example which was prepared by the office of Civilian Defense during the last World War.

> Such preparations should be made as will completely obscure all Federal buildings and non-Federal buildings during an air raid for any period of time from visibility by reason of internal or external illumination. Such obscuration may be obtained either by blackout construction or by termination of the illumination. This will, of course, require that in building areas in which production must continue during the blackout, construction must be provided that internal illumination may continue. Other areas, whether or not occupied by personnel, may be obscured by terminating the illumination.

What confusion. The order in no way tells the reader what he should and must do during an air raid. When the President, Franklin D. Roosevelt read the above order, he immediately ordered and is quoted as having said:

> Tell them that in buildings where they have to keep the work going, to put something across the windows; in buildings where they can afford to let the work stop for awhile, to turn out the lights.

The very simplicity of the rewritten order is what is so striking and, therefore, effective. Obviously, no one could fail to understand the message and take appropriate action.

Unessential Words. Observing the simple rule above saves time and effort in writing, and makes the finished communication easier to read. Unessential words are also wasted words, such as *whereas, now therefore, as heretofore defined, alternative but, qualitative and quantitative,* etc.

Here is a sample from a policy memorandum:

> The forms are obsolete and should be consigned to the receptacles utilized in disposing of your daily accumulation of trash.

A rewrite simply says:

> Since the forms are obsolete, throw them away.

Instead of writing directly to a person, some communications are impersonal and indirect. This procedure often leaves the reader in doubt as to what he must do. Here is an example:

> It is suggested that the voucher be rewritten with the explanation that official business was performed on January 25th.

Why not come right out and say clearly and simply the following:

> Please rewrite the voucher and explain that you performed official business on January 25th.

Here are a few more examples of how to cut down on unessential words:

Before:
> You are hereby advised that your report should be sent directly to the Washington office as promptly as it is possible for you to complete it.

After:
> Your report should be sent to the Washington office promptly.

Before:
> Here is a copy that is attached hereto for your information and ready reference.

After:
> A copy is attached.

Before:
> It will be noted that all messages that are written and released by the Toledo office, ...

After:
> All messages from the Toledo office . . . .

Before:
> Your attention is hereby directed to Section 7a of the act which says . . . .

After:
> Section 7a says, ...

Words, words, words; many add up to two, three and four times the number needed; instead of clarifying they complicate. The struggle and wasted time of wading through them tries both patience and tempers.

Roundabout Expressions. This type of writing leaves the reader in doubt. Instead of strengthening the message, it is weakened by the use of roundabout words and phrases that cloud the message. Used throughout a memorandum, paper or letter, the effect is boring, tiresome and negative on the reader. Here are some examples:

Before:	*After:*
The office is of the opinion that	We believe . . . .
It is our understanding that	We understand . . . .

Before:	After:
Approval to the request was given by you on March 15th	You approved this request on March 15th.
The order is currently in the process of undergoing revision	The order is being revised.
The difficulties in the administration of . . .	Difficulties in administering . . . .

Simplification can also cover the substitution of simple words for phrases. This type of writing strengthens a sentence and provides a direct, clear image of what is being said. Here are some examples:

Before:	After:
with respect in	in
in connection with	by, in, for, etc.
despite the fact that	though
in view of the fact that	since, because
give encouragement to	encourage
make inquiry regarding	inquire
have need for	need
meets with the approval	approves

Repetition. Many people believe that repetition is a good thing. Of course, this depends on where and how it is used. In making a speech, repetition, if properly introduced, is effective and greatly aids in selling the message to the audience. From the standpoint of message retention in public speaking, it is a useful technique. Repetition can be used in business writing as in a summary sentence or repeating a point made in another sentence as a further explanation. But all too often the mistake is made of repeating within the same sentence. This only serves to confuse the reader. Here are some examples:

This will enable the states to get started sooner *than if they wait until some later date.*
The study is nearly completed *at the present time.*
As a matter of interest, we shall be interested in knowing . . .
Unemployment compensation *benefits.*

Obviously, the unessential words which would repeat the meaning have been italicized. A good rule to follow is to use only enough words to get your message and point across clearly and correctly.

Tips on Business English Usage

Drilled into every student of Business English and repeated in many textbooks, are six simple rules that apply to any type of business writing. The reader may wish to use the checklist to see how many *yeses* or *noes* are scored. The analysis which should follow is a helpful method of self-improvement in the business writing process.

1. *Completeness.*
   a. Does it provide all the necessary information?
   b. Does it answer all the questions that may be raised?

   If the communication is in answer to a request for information or a report prepared for review and which will lead to a decision, the writer must review its purpose. An effort must be made to determine whether all the facts have been covered and all the questions answered.

2. *Conciseness.*
   a. Are all the essential facts covered?
   b. Has care been taken to include only the essential words and phrases?

   This essential area is intended to limit the writer in covering only the essential details and to eliminate irrelevant and immaterial information.

3. *Clarity.*
   a. Is the language used written for the audience? Does it fit the reader in the simplest manner, enough to get the message across easily?
   b. Do the words used exactly express the thoughts?
   c. Is the sentence structure clear?
   d. Does each paragraph express one complete thought unit?
   e. Do the paragraphs follow each other in proper sequence?

   Obviously good organization makes for clarity. It cannot be achieved without proper control of facts and details, the result of presenting material to the reader in a regular sequence. A clear thought and outline helps in writing and aids clear presentation.

4. *Correctness.*
   a. Is the information accurate?
   b. Are the statements made true and in accord with policy?
   c. Is the writing clear in terms of freedom from errors in presentation, grammar, spelling and idiomatic expressions?

The most important aspects of correctness concern themselves with the accuracy of the statements made. While grammar and spelling are essentials, the style of writing should not be affected. Words are a part of human nature, therefore, expression should be natural and unaffected, free flowing and not stiff. The best writing comes easily and is the result of being prepared to write. Style is the result of experience and a solid framework of reference.

5. *Appropriateness of Tone.*
   a. Will the tone of the writing bring out the desired response from the audience?
   b. Is the writing free from antagonistic words and phrases that could offend the reader?
   c. Is the writing free from pompous, stilted, hackneyed words and phrases?

Tone is the most important part of a communication. It may be concise and to the point; and it may have all the essentials as to facts and necessary detail, but it may also be cold and unfriendly, thereby killing the very impression it may wish to convey. And, if it is intended to sell an idea or to make a request, it may fail completely because it lacks the very warmth and friendliness that it needs. Some writers of business communications believe in being brief and to the point, and they are afraid to show emotion or to express a friendly wish or greeting.

Attorneys and bankers are notorious for this type of thinking and writing. They are in the business of public relations, deal with and through many publics every day; yet to bring themselves to say *thank you* or *with friendliest greetings and good wishes* is a major concession.

Yet a personal visit with any of these persons may find them warm and sincere. As a professional group, the mantle of austerity has always fitted them well in the mind of the general public, yet banks in particular, are spending huge sums on lollipops, dolls, toys, give-aways and a smile. But the writing of a letter or business communication is still a cold, hard proposition.

6. *General Effectiveness.*
   a. Is it satisfactory or does it need revision?
   b. Is it passable but needs correction, thus insuring a better response?
   c. Will it pass in terms of readability?

Obviously this question of general effectiveness is a passing or failing test with a minimum of effectiveness level. Such test questions merely serve to indicate that revision and correction are as much a part of the writing process as the construction phase itself. One should never fear making a correction such as crossing out and adding information.

Theodore Roosevelt, before, during and after the presidency, thought nothing of making corrections directly on the original communication going out to the public. In doing this, it was his idea to let the reader know that the letter or memorandum, or the communication, was not routine but had actually been read and reviewed by him personally.

Tips on Planning Your Writing

Everything worthwhile in the way of writing is generally planned and sometimes is carefully outlined in advance. To the experienced writer this is a simple matter. But for the beginner, it often means drudgery, and saying *What shall I say?* and *How shall I say it?* Naturally, this depends largely on the purpose of the communication. The simplest rule to follow is to jot down your ideas as they come to you. Then, after you have exhausted your thinking, group the ideas together so that they are in sequence.

An introduction to a subject may mean to start immediately, wasting no words by beating around the proverbial bush. Plunging directly into the subject is the safest way to make a start. But one can start with an anecdote that leads into the subject.

Any start is difficult. The body is merely the development of the points that are to be made. The end is often a stumbling block. If it is a letter, it should end in a friendly way or a concluding sentence followed by a regular close. Other writing, such as reports, for example, may call for a summary and conclusion. But many reports find a summary and conclusion at the beginning as well as at the end. The report which follows merely seeks to prove the opening statement.

Good writing means good reading. People generally write in the style they are accustomed to read. As to skill, it is a matter of more reading and simply more writing. The two go hand in hand. Adding vocabulary by becoming acquainted with new words and their usage helps. Writing also means rewriting and a skill in saying what is meant as simply as possible.

One should beware of the statement *practice makes perfect*, a long outmoded and discarded theory. Practice, of course, does not harm when such practice observes proper procedures and methods. Good writing also means a good environment and good reading in whatever the field of interest may be. It does not include good speaking, for one does not write as one speaks. The only relationship between speaking and writing is really in terms of tone, feeling, and ideas.

Handling Business Messages

Here are some considerations for the writer of business communications that may prove helpful:

1. One should first carefully analyze the incoming message. Try to understand the reasoning behind a request or a reply. This helps in developing as complete as possible an answer. Make notes on the incoming correspondence and *underline* anything that pertains to the reply and will aid in its preparation.
2. Get a mental photograph of the reader. Picture him in his dilemma if there is one. At least, visualize the problem presented as well as the background of the subject under consideration. A quick superficial reply may result in trouble ahead. Many an executive has lost his position because of a hasty decision and what later turned out to be a half-baked reply.
3. Once the thought-out reply from penciled notes on the side of a letter or the back of an envelope is ready, it should be dictated. The purpose of the communication, once clear in the mind of the writer, has its greatest strength at that time. Any further delay could weaken the message, and cause it to lose its tone.
4. A mental outline, the result of experience and time, is usually sufficient, particularly for routine replies. Some believe in going to the extent of noting particular phrases and special words in their proper order. Each piece of writing is different. For some, a pat answer is all that may be required. Others call for individual treatment and care, particularly when the material and the idea are of a vital policy-making nature which may affect the future course of a function, person, or the very nature of the business itself.

Closing with a Biblical quotation may sum up the most important consideration in writing:

Except ye utter by the tongue words easy to be understood, how shall it be known what is spoken? For ye shall speak into the air.

I Corinthians XIV:9

2

Conferences and Meetings

The value of a good meeting was well expressed by Frank Abrams, a former President of the Standard Oil Company of New Jersey. He said: "It stands to reason that if you get five men together and one man is wrong, the mistake is going to be picked up; or if one man has a good idea, the others will contribute to it and develop it. And if they all have good ideas, what comes out may be better than the separate ideas together."

While this statement has considerable merit, it also has some factors which may cause anyone to question its value. Unfortunately people are not always inclined to contribute to others in either developing an idea or even in carrying it further in a discussion. Frankly, it all depends on the relationships that exist between people. If real teamwork is present and there is a common interest in the objective at hand, then a coordinated group effort is entirely possible and desirable. But if personal differences exist and there is not a real group spirit, then the effort and idea of having a group cooperatively contribute to an idea or pick up an error will fail.

There are basic factors, however, about conferences and meetings that require prior consideration. For example, there is not a person who has not sat through a conference or a meeting which proved to be a boring, futile, frustrating one, and even a complete waste of time. Practically anyone will agree that conferences are both necessary and useful in the normal conduct of business. Often used as problem-solving sessions, such types of meetings are not generally thought of as real conferences, but they are, if the elements of free discussion and participation are present. In fact, this type of meeting is frequently conducted in an informal manner such as the get-together luncheon or cocktail party which may or may not be followed by a dinner if warranted.

Solving problems by mutual discussion and review, or discovering and reviewing new ones and exploring other areas of interest, all serve to unify if not at least clarify their ideas, opinions and decisions.

Any type of meeting can be made interesting. But the truly successful one does not just happen. An investigation will always reveal that it has generally been well planned.

What Makes Meetings Interesting

If one were to hold a meeting on the subject of "What Makes a Meeting Interesting," the answers, as a recent survey showed, would come out something like this:

1. The discussion leader was sincere and believed in his subject.
2. There was enough of an opportunity for everyone to air his views.
3. It was apparent that every person who spoke up had something to say, and was made to feel he contributed to the meeting.
4. The meeting was informal; everyone seemed to be completely at ease.
5. Enough visual material was used during the meeting to make the discussion easy to follow.
6. All persons attending the meeting were prepared and knew when, where and about what the meeting would cover.
7. No lost time or painful pauses occurred; everything seemed to move without effort.
8. Enough amusing incidents entered into the discussion to make the total subject time interesting.

Quite obviously the one unifying thread running through the above comments is that the basic ingredients for insuring the success of a conference is prepared and organized participation. The more information in the form of facts, fresh ideas, opinions and thoughts that is presented by conferees, the more productive and resultful the meeting will be.

Just plain talking, of course, is to be avoided, as it is not particularly productive. Every meeting or conference must be guided and carefully run according to a schedule.

Meetings and Conferences Defined

A word about terminology. A meeting can be between two people or include thousands, but a conference is usually held among a more limited group, such as 10 or 20. The meeting and the conference may have similar objectives, both with an established purpose. However, the conference is more of a discussion and an exchange of viewpoints rather than an instructive type of get-together. Conferences are really self instructive in that the group members learn from one another. The leader of a conference may merely encourage discussion, but seldom personally answers questions. For this reason, persons of similar rank and experience who can mutually understand and respect each other's viewpoint are the best persons to attend a conference.

Generally a conference leader's responsibility covers the following five points as defined by the Personnel Development Division of General Foods:

1. To state the problem clearly and in such a manner that it arouses interest and starts discussion.
2. To keep discussion moving, to keep it on the subject, and to try to get *everyone* present to take part.
3. To bring out friendly differences of opinion; but to let the group settle who is right, not try to settle it himself.
4. From time to time, to summarize the conclusions reached thus far, occasionally asking for a vote when it is difficult to establish a consensus any other way.
5. To draw final conclusions and either to write these on the board or have a secretary take notes to be handed out later.

The Conference Leader's Job

A leader of a conference also has a job to do in laying out a careful plan that the meeting is to follow. The very informality of a conference might lead one to think that there is no plan or that none is needed. Actually the reverse is true; even more planning is required and even a higher degree of coordinating skill than in running a large meeting. In fact, the skills in terms of their relative weight may be entirely different for the meeting than for the conference.

A good conference leader should do four things:

1. A friendly relationship should be established at the start of the meeting. Complimenting the group on getting together, something

that is sincere, is a good way to begin. "We have called this meeting in order to get your help and counsel on . . ." (state the problem or reason) is a complimentary opening.

2. The group should be put at ease by making it clear that no one will be called upon for an answer. The timid person, seeing considerable discussion going on, usually finds himself contributing in due course. Just calling directly on someone may prove embarrassing to the person, leader, and the group. Of course, it depends on whether or not this is important in a business discussion. Failing to participate may show a weakness and result in loss of standing, even position, particularly if the person called on is responsible for knowing the subject being discussed.

3. A brief opening explanation on how the meeting is to be conducted helps to make clear that the success of the meeting depends on everyone taking part. A free, informal, "no-standing-up-when-talking" meeting should be stressed.

4. The most difficult and important part of the meeting is to raise the opening question in such a manner so as to get the discussion aroused. This can be a general statement giving the pros and cons, or it can be a review of the past, leading to the purpose of the conference. Sometimes it can be brought to a head by simply taking a count on who is for or against a question. This usually gets things going if nothing else will.

A conference leader should be tactful in not criticizing anyone for an opinion. He should also encourage honest differences of opinion to make certain that all sides of a question are effectively aired. Of course, differences will often occur. In such situations, only three methods are open to the leader—domination, compromise, or integration. The first is never a satisfying way that sits well with the dominated, whereas compromise may save face. However, the integration of the opposing ideas so that opposing sides each get what they want but perhaps in a different form, may work best of all.

For example, Wilson wants a window open and Harris wants it closed. Discussion reveals that Harris wants the window closed because it means a draft for him, but he has no objection to having fresh air. The difference is solved by opening a window in another room. This method of solving a difference is called integration; it requires skillful imagination and experience.

Other problems for leaders are controlling people who want to argue, those who want to talk too much, those who have a closed mind on a subject, and those who answer every question before anyone else has a chance to answer. All of these problems simply require getting other people to talk and contribute to the general purpose of the subject at hand.

Conducting the Interesting Meeting

While much of what has been said on conferences readily applies to meetings, there are some additional, generally applicable factors to be taken into consideration. A meeting may be made up of various levels of intelligence, education and rank. This presents one serious problem, but does require an overall appreciation of the audience's understanding and ability to participate in a general discussion.

Here is a guide that will aid anyone in running an effective, resultful meeting:

Preparation and Participation. Many meetings are called without sufficient notice, thus allowing participants little or no time to prepare themselves to effectively contribute to a meeting. Such failures to notify actually defeat the real purpose of a meeting.

Depending on the nature of the meeting, it is a wise policy to give a few days or even a week's notice to participants, enabling them to prepare themselves, gather their thoughts, ideas and whatever facts or thoughts they may need to insure their effective participation.

It is of primary importance also to let participants know clearly just what the subject under consideration will be. Being specific in this area, by stating the problems or policy matters to be discussed, clearly and directly, aids in securing the interest and the support of all who attend.

Issuing a brief memorandum announcing a meeting helps as do advance telephone calls. Sometimes a reminder call a few hours before the meeting is necessary. But in well seasoned organizations such follow up is superfluous.

Purpose. As already covered earlier in this chapter, stating the purpose, outlining the problems, and providing all necessary supporting detail to make certain all dimensions of the subject under discussion are clearly understood, and establishing the objectives that are to be attained as a result of the meeting, should be presented after making introductory remarks.

Pads, Pencils, and Facts. It is important either to have a recording secretary make a written and running record of the opinions and thoughts on the subject under consideration, or to do this chore personally.

One should continue the meeting by asking for opinions from those in attendance, on the problem or subject under discussion. Then gather and make a record of all the facts. Distributing pads and pencils at the start or before the meeting begins is helpful. A blackboard or paper easel is good for illustrative purposes. To assist the fact gathering process, it is a good idea to make any exhibits that are on hand readily available to the group. This will aid in making the meeting interesting and speed it along. Using a little showmanship and the merchandising of ideas, keep interest and discussion at a good response level. In fact, the more facts that are developed during the meeting, the better the results will be. Meetings are said to be successful only if they accomplish what they intended to do in terms of objectives and actual results.

Naturally the more cooperation and participation that can be developed during the meeting, the better the spirit and enthusiasm of the group will be. It is wise to avoid stopping discussion until all the available and essential facts have been developed and placed into the proper perspective.

Analysis. This important phase of the meeting technique concerns itself with encouraging the expression of group opinions and relating them always to the real issues under consideration. It is wise to pause as one proceeds and ask, "How do the facts affect the problem?" The more personal the interest is that is injected into the discussion, the greater will be the group contribution toward the effective solution of the problems under consideration.

Above all, one should avoid hurrying this very decisive evaluation process. As the facts begin to fall into a regular pattern, one should begin to frame the major and minor supporting ones. Then is the time for the development of specific suggestions and solutions, which will define the issues and point the way to objective decisions.

Mutually Agreeable Solutions. This is the critical area. The more agreement that is obtained along the way, the more effective the carrying out of the solution later on will be. This actually then, is the final test as to whether or not the meeting has been really worthwhile.

One should not be discouraged if different solutions are presented near the close of the meeting. This actually is a healthy sign. The chairman or leader of the group then has to direct the group into arriving at a solution that embodies the best ideas that have been expressed during the evaluation process.

As one proceeds, it wil be noted that there are always common denominators of agreement on every viewpoint. This lends itself to a summing up by the leader or chairman. The group may then move toward an agreement by simply having the leader ask for it. The major objective is to get a solution that has been democratically achieved and is really acceptable to the group.

Following Through. Very often meetings end up in a strong agreement, but nothing happens later on. An analysis of such a situation usually shows that no effective attempt was really made to put the solution into effect and follow it through to a successful conclusion.

After arriving at a solution to the problem, one should get the group to map out a program for effectively resolving it. If all persons have participated in the development of the solution, then they will recognize that it is their responsibility for making the solution work.

All that is needed is simply to go on record by either assigning or suggesting the "carry out" to people, based on their interests shown during the meeting and what may already have quite easily fallen into line with their normal responsibilities for which they are either suited or have prior experience. If, for example, a chef has been a major influence in arriving at a decision affecting the engineer, do not make the chef responsible, but leave the follow through to the engineer with the cooperation of the chef. This involves both parties and fixes authority as well as responsibility.

Follow through is always necessary. One should check up to see that each person is effectively carrying out what he should be doing and is handling his assignment in an efficient way. Such follow up is necessary at regular intervals.

The Close. Stick to the meeting schedule by closing on time. Arrange to stop a minute or two before the "deadline." Good meetings are not easy to close, because discussion, enthusiasm and interest may be lively. Nevertheless it is best to begin closing by summarizing and then closing the meeting. An alert, interested group will want to continue next time as actively as before. A cooling-off period with more time to think has the effect of settling people and may result in even more effective and decisive participation at the next meeting date.

Summary and Checklist for Conducting a Meeting

Those responsible for conducting meetings and organizing and leading conferences may find the following summary of seventeen helpful hints valuable as a guide and checklist:

1. Begin and end a meeting promptly and run it in a sincere, businesslike manner.
2. Should anyone arrive late at the meeting, take time out briefly to bring the latecomer up to date, thereby bringing him into the picture.
3. Avoid lecturing the group and remember that the objective of the meeting is to develop thinking and action.

4. Avoid getting the meeting stuck by sidetracking discussions.
5. When the discussion runs thin, summarize the points made and switch over or onto the next question.
6. Try to develop in each person in attendance the belief that he or she has been of genuine assistance in developing the discussion.
7. Quite often some participants say little during a meeting. Asking them questions or for opinions helps break the ice.
8. Receive every comment and suggestion as something worthy of consideration and avoid knocking down contrary opinions.
9. Praise publicly those participants who have done well.
10. Never ridicule or disagree with opponents. Rather continue the discussion in the hope of further enlightening contrary opinions.
11. Be tactful in bringing to order, participants who stray from the subject.
12. Assist participants in clarifying any points they may have difficulty in presenting.
13. Often it is helpful to re-state a participant's points that may not have been clearly expressed.
14. Because a successful meeting is usually a lively one with full discussion and divergent views, participants should be encouraged in their deliberations.
15. When disagreement develops, bring out the opposing views so that the entire group can assist in settling the difference. If this goes too far afield, return to the facts and present them objectively.
16. Skill, time and patience are to be employed in separating facts from opinions simply by saying, "Is that a fact, or personal opinion?"
17. If a meeting stalls, it is helpful to encourage participants who have considerable or even some prior experience, by asking for their opinions and views.

3

Publicity Guide for
Executives

If you have ever been interviewed by a reporter, you will know what can happen to your news. It may be written, phrased, interpreted and reported very differently from what you expected.

Here is a hypothetical but, nevertheless, realistic example of what can happen. Hotel X has a fire in its engine room. Smoke bellows out of the building, lights go out, and a fire alarm results in complete evacuation of the hotel. The hotel management makes no formal statement, but does not permit anyone to return to work or occupy the building until further notice. The hotel manager and his staff are busily engaged in investigating the cause of the fire, the damage to property, and the time required to return the hotel to operation.

A reporter from the City News telephones, "We hear that the hotel is on fire and that the employees have been temporarily laid off?"

The manager answers, "We do not know at the moment and cannot give any details."

The reporter feels he's noncommittal and is persistent. "Does the hotel intend to re-open soon? Will employees who are out of work be paid? How much? Will any lose their jobs? Is there a possibility of faulty maintenance?"

Avoiding answers could result in headlines such as this: "300 Hotel X Workers Jobless as Fire Closes Hotel."

But providing the reporter with answers might result in: "Hotel X Engine Room Fire Quickly Controlled; None Hurt . . ."

Incidents like this one have caused many hotels to engage professional counsel. Many others, however, have found it to their advantage to have the manager and his staff communicate with the press, and answer questions objectively. Public relations specialists may not be available at newsworthy events, necessitating other hotel representatives to be aware of the techniques of giving out information when the time arises.

Declaring Company Policy

One hotel company places responsibility for maintaining cordial press relations in the hands of its managers. It is the manager, or someone appointed by him, who acts as contact and liaison between management, the press and the public. As a general rule announcements should be signed by the representative, except when specific individuals are quoted.

Once the manager or his representative assumes the responsibility, his name, address, telephone number should be on file with every newspaper. He should not be annoyed at questions put to him at odd hours of the day or night. Newspapers have no hours.

Avoiding Bad Publicity

News media in every community look upon industries, hotels and other businesses for news. This occurs because every enterprise has an important bearing on the social, economic and, sometimes, political life of the community. Newspapers present to the readers news of public interest. Few desire to embarrass or pry into an organization's affairs unnecessarily.

Most bad publicity is the result of a lack of information and often an indifferent attitude toward the press. Newsworthy information should be made available to the press. It is to the organization's advantage to supply this information because it shows a willingness to cooperate, and a fairness in understanding the needs of the press. An indifferent attitude may result in damaging coverage resulting in, for example, a critical review or appraisal of a situation or condition, or an unfavorable report that will adversely affect the image of the hotel or motel. Confidences will be respected if they are requested. News of a confidential nature will be withheld if the request is made.

What Makes News?

In writing news releases, an objective as well as a subjective attitude is necessary. News material should take into consideration the tone of news and events at the time. For example, a national election, war,

PUBLIC RELATIONS

Public Relations: The recognition and cultivation within an organization of those virtues and values which become visible externally in the standing of the company with its workers and stockholders, its customers and prospects, the press and the public. It is neither a cover for shortcomings nor a substitute for good works. Public relations, in the corporate sense, begins with private relations: it is corporate character believably expressed.

HOTEL/MOTEL BACKGROUND

Past and present attitude of public toward hotel/motel, services, facilities, and operations.

Past and present policies of hotel/motel toward general public, guests, employees, labor, stockholders, press, and trade.

INTERNAL PUBLIC RELATIONS

Employee Welfare	*Employee Education*	*Employee Relations*
Safety program, medical department, family clinics, visiting nurses, recreational facilities, cafeteria and restaurant, mobile canteens, vitamin and salt tablets, picnics and company parties, day nursery, vacation services, and employee's clubs.	Job training, training for upgrading, employee meetings, special outside courses, scholarships, first aid classes, fire drills demonstrations, displays, posters, and guest contact training.	Bonus and retirement plan, insurance and hospitalization, emergency loans or credit union, management-labor groups, union representatives and shop stewards, grievance committee, employee publication, bulletin boards, trouble spots, outside field studies, shopping service and stores, music, and suggestion boxes.

EXTERNAL PUBLIC RELATIONS

Publicity	*Advertising*	*Direct Public Contacts*
Press releases, films, educators, and radio.	Newspaper, magazine, trade paper, films, radio, and direct mail.	Hotel/motel spokesman, sales and service staffs, receptionists, telephone operators, and elevator operators.

Business and Trade Contacts	*Organized Groups*	*Opinion Channels*
Trade associations, complaints and suggestions, fair practice codes, hotel training, service staffs, wholesalers and retailers, salesmen, and operators.	Fraternal organizations, women's clubs, consumer groups, parents-teacher's association, community clubs, boy scouts, boys' clubs.	Press, radio and movies, educators, national and local officials, labor unions and leaders, churches, county agents, and speakers and lecturers.

What **Public Relations** is in terms of a definition and a breakdown of internal and external phases.

explosion, flood, or other major event in the news will not aid a hotel or motel story in terms of getting favorable space. The individual needs of each of the papers must also be taken into consideration. Each paper has its own style and character, which should be observed in preparing any style of release.

As to news material itself, many news releases wind up in the waste basket simply because they do not really contain news. Or, they lose out in competition with more important or more interesting items.

You have the elements of a story whenever a thing, person, idea or event is new, novel, romantic and important to people. Or you can make news by connecting a person with important events, trends and plans that are of interest to people.

Sources of News

Assuming that proper consideration has been given to current news trends, making sure they favor your story and recognizing the individual tastes of various media, the next consideration pertains to the sources of news. Of a great many, an analysis revealed thirteen sources of business events in which newspapermen are generally interested:

1. The development of new services, particularly if they mean greater public use, development of new markets, or result in changes affecting the employees in a hotel, the decor, building structure, or mean expansion of some kind.
2. Expansion of facilities of any kind and how, when, where and why it will affect employees and the public, is news.
3. Changes in employee benefits, such as vacations, bonuses, awards or pension system, if new, are generally newsworthy.
4. Any promotions, demotions, transfers or changes in the organization of executives in a company makes news.
5. The development and installation of new safety techniques, are always of interest in terms of guests and employees, and particularly where preventive measures have been applied.
6. Anything to do with improving sales and the introduction of sales campaigns and specific methods, such as the Sheraton Sales Blitz, makes news.
7. Reports on earnings are interesting as are stock and bond issues, the sale and transfer of properties, or any figure information that has an effect on stockholders.
8. Installing new machinery, particularly when it improves service such as high speed elevators, escalators, production equipment,

Preparation

1. Outline individual project
2. Check outline with Publicity Department Head
3. Check with Account Executive
4. Prepare material
5. Review (together with illustrative material or ideas for same)
6. Get approvals where necessary (and indicate such approval on release)
7. Decide on release date, and mechanics of releasing—
      (a) Personal contact
      (b) Wire or cable
      (c) Messenger
      (d) Mail
8. Personally check copy in finished form before permitting its release
9. Notify clipping bureaus of release, giving all necessary particulars and providing copies of release for readers
10. Keep complete files on all stories, with date of release and other pertinent information

Sources

History of Hotel/Motel

1. Achievements.
2. People contributing to development.
3. Development of equipment, facilities.
4. Financial development.
5. Company's relation to community.

Production

1. Raw materials, origin.
2. Processes, techniques employed.
3. Plant facilities, equipment.
4. Economy and efficiency of operation.

Research

1. Laboratory and field facilities.
2. People employed in research.
3. Past achievements.
4. Current developments.
5. Future projects.
6. Work in cooperation with schools and universities, government, other industries.
7. Papers presented before learned bodies.
8. Economic and political aspects of research program.

Management

1. Hotel spokesman, for authoritative quotation.
2. Key people within the hotel who can speak with authority on matters under their jurisdiction—production, labor relations, research, sales, etc.

Workers

1. Number employed
2. Personalities: Workers interesting because of their background, personalities, accomplishments.

(Continued)

An analysis of sources, preparation and distribution of public relations material is clearly outlined in this comprehensive check list.

Workers (cont'd)

3. Provisions made for workers
    (1) Well-being, health
    (2) Recreation
    (3) Housing
    (4) Security
    (5) Safety
    (6) Training
5. Personal affairs of employees.

4. Provisions for the worker's families.

Product and Service

1. The need it fulfills.
2. How and why it was developed.
3. How it compares with other products.
4. How it is used.
5. Quality control methods used: company or outside laboratory.
6. Comparative economy and efficiency.

Merchandising

1. Merchandising methods employed.
2. Distribution of product.
3. Success stories.
4. Contests, premiums, deals, etc.

Hotel Policies

1. Government.
2. Labor.
3. Guests and consumer groups.
4. The community.
5. Stockholders.
6. Competitors.
7. Dealers and salesmen
8. Research.
9. Merchandising and promotion.
10. Maintenance of quality.
11. Price.

Services

1. Nature and extent.
2. How used?
3. How are they employed?
4. What do they accomplish?
5. Nature of in relation to:
    (1) Cost?
    (2) Convenience?
    (3) Superiority?
    (4) Availability?
    (5) Prestige?
6. Volume?
7. Has there been a rapid growth in popularity?
8. Can testimonials be obtained?

Publications

1. Technical bulletins.
2. House organs.
3. Inter-office correspondence.
4. Bulletin board information.

Distribution

Newspapers

1. City Desk, straight news.
2. Picture Editor.
3. Feature Editor.
4. Financial and or Business Editor.

(Continued)

Newspapers (cont'd)

5. Science Editor.
6. Travel Editor.
7. Women's Page Editor.
    (List can be extended indefinitely since large newspapers are highly departmentalized. Smaller newspapers have fewer departments, but in every case care should be taken to get material to the right editor.)

Wire Services

1. Associated Press.
2. United Press International.
3. Localized or specialized wire services, such as Dow Jones, City News.

    (In view of coverage of these services every effort should be made to give them what they want. Major wire services are departmental, so care should be taken to get material to proper person.)

Syndicates

1. Columnists.
2. Cartoons.
3. Feature articles and photographs.
    (Importance of distribution through most syndicates make special study of syndicate services well worthwhile. Get to writer or editor most likely to be interested in material.)

Magazines

1. General.
2. Fraternal.
3. Religious publications.
4. Trade, technical and Class publications.
5. House Organs.
    (Material for magazines, from large general publications to small trade journals, can in general be handled in two ways: either by direct placement with publications, or by giving writer or editor an idea or outline with all pertinent data.)

Photographic Services

1. Wire services.
2. News photo services.
3. Photo libraries such as Brown Bros., Galloway.

Literary Agents

It is sometimes worth while to outline idea and send it to literary agent of writer who might be qualified to do a story based on it. If this is done, do not send same idea to several agents unless they are so informed.

(Continued)

Distribution

Radio

1. Material sent direct to stations.

2. Material placed with such services as Transradio, AP or UPI, and relayed to stations by them.

3. Material sent to individuals on station staff, generally on an exclusive basis.

4. Presentation of message by means of guest appearance, tie-ins or interview over station or network facilities.

5. Utilization of station or network publicity departments for cooperative work.
(Material sent to stations or individuals on station may be in form of news release, script or transcription.)

Books

1. Direct placement of manuscript or idea with publisher.

2. Suggestion of idea to publisher, leaving him to assign writer.

3. Suggestion of idea to possible author.

4. Suggestion of idea to literary agent.

Motion Pictures

1. Suggestions to produers of entertainment films.

2. News and feature possibilities to producers of newsreels and short features, directed to editors.

3. Cooperative publicity with film company's publicity departments, tying in with personalities and productions.

4. Cooperative tie-ins to show merchandise in film.

Government Activities and Agencies

This field is so broad that a special study is necessary for each operation. News to Latin-America, for instance, may be channeled through Coordinator's office. Information touching upon a government bureau's operation may be received thankfully for release by that bureau's publicity people.

Cooperative Ventures

1. Other advertisers with whom tie-ins can be made.

2. Public Utilities, in home economics courses.

3. Stores, through training programs, displays, etc.

Others

Speakers and Speakers Bureaus.
Learned Bodies, Engineering and Professional Groups.
Fraternal Organizations and Service Clubs.
Schools and Colleges.
Contests.
Consumer Groups.

Displays and Exhibits.
Unions and Labor Leaders.
Direct Mail.
Clergymen.
Trade Associations.
Legislators, Federal, State, Municipal.

and also how it will affect employees, guests and earnings, is always interesting.

9. Layoffs of workers, how they may be absorbed into the economy elsewhere, special provisions to assist them in relocation and change, and anything to do with severance or accumulated pay is a good news item which helps to offset any unfavorable feelings.

10. Company parties, picnics and outings, complete with photographs and human interest subject material about executives, employees, wives and children, makes good copy.

11. News about accidents are always unpleasant; care should be taken to soften the release by showing what precautionary measures were taken or were in effect, indicating that the company did everything it could to prevent the accident. Company assistance to the injured should be included.

12. Veteran employees who retire, or who have anniversaries of long tenure should be publicized. It emphasizes to readers that the hotel values skilled service and respects seniority.

13. A great deal has been done about employee hobbies—those who paint, play a musical instrument or little known facts of historic value about the hotel, its guests, its employees, and the nature and extent of its services make for interesting reading.

Preparing a News Release

The first chapter may be helpful in offering suggestions on writing business communications, all of which apply to news releases. Avoiding writing errors, roundabout expressions, repetition, and unessential words are important primary considerations. Regarding news releases, here are some additional, rather specific and generally accepted rules to follow in preparing and sending out a news release to newspapers, magazines or wire services:

1. Include all essential elements in the first paragraph. Follow the rule of who, what, when, where, why and how.
2. Make sure all names and dates are accurate.
3. Check all figures for accuracy.
4. Make sentences short and objective; do not waste words.
5. Use adjectives very sparingly.
6. Type and double space all copy.
7. Type the name, address and telephone number of the representative in the upper left- or right-hand corner.

After a news release has been submitted, it will be used as is, edited, or discarded. When it is read on receipt, editorial policy will dictate whether the release is timely, will not be crowded off a page by other more pressing and immediately important news; interest, space and competition are the real controlling factors.

The Best Format

A survey conducted by Norman Odell Associates, Inc., a New York public relations firm, proved that editors are influenced by the appearance of a news release.

Questionnaires and sample news releases were received by 217 editors, representing newspapers, news syndicates, news magazines, consumer publications, business and financial media, medical journals and publications covering 32 industries. The editors were asked to submit their opinions on which release form they considered best. Replies were received from 113 editors, a 52% response, providing the following information:

Sample A, buff colored with the Odell name and trademark at the bottom of the release, was favored by 14% of those responding.

Sample B, a green tinted sheet with the firm's name at the top along with the trademark and bold lettering of "News Release", received 46% of the favored responses, a majority.

Sample C, on plain white paper with black lettering with all indentifying data at the top, was second best with a 40% vote.

Editors noted that the green tinted release made for easy reading, in addition to helping editors remember and later recognize releases from the same public relations firm.

Those editors who favored the plain white sample, liked its simplicity and readability.

Handling Bad Publicity

Bad publicity can harm not only the principals involved in a hotel or motel operation, but the very business itself. Unfortunately, bad publicity may not always be true to the action or event. It may be an interpretation by reporters, or rumors that make news; even later retractions never completely erase an emotion, a fixation, or just an impression. Naturally, efforts to avoid bad publicity and an awareness of pitfalls that can occur is essential. Here are some of the things that should be noted:

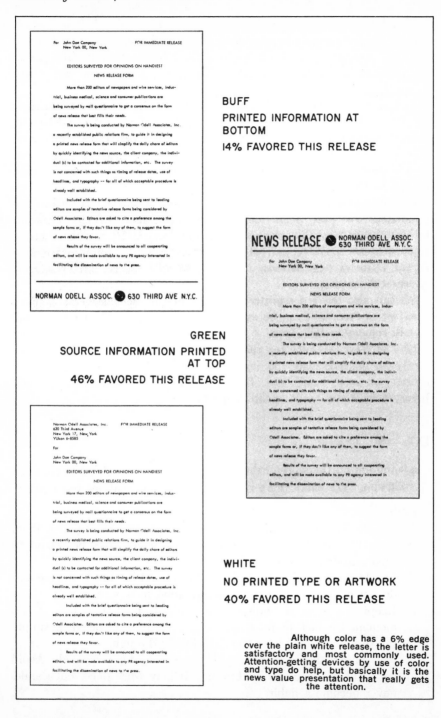

BUFF

PRINTED INFORMATION AT BOTTOM

14% FAVORED THIS RELEASE

GREEN

SOURCE INFORMATION PRINTED AT TOP

46% FAVORED THIS RELEASE

WHITE

NO PRINTED TYPE OR ARTWORK

40% FAVORED THIS RELEASE

Although color has a 6% edge over the plain white release, the letter is satisfactory and most commonly used. Attention-getting devices by use of color and type do help, but basically it is the news value presentation that really gets the attention.

How to Avoid Bad Publicity. Don't try to hide things! It is best to give all the facts simply because they cannot really be effectively hidden.

As an example, suppose an employee dies while at work. The police and coroner are notified at once. The press appears on the scene promptly.

Tell them exactly what happened. If more information is wanted, get it for the reporters. Explain too, what you have been doing to prevent accidents. Tell of the investigation that will follow, and how your safety program has effectively held accidents to a bare minimum. It is likely that you will get fair coverage, one which will not give your hotel a bad name.

When It's Confidential. There will be times when you are asked for information that you cannot, under any circumstance divulge. Explain to the reporter why the information is confidential. It may be that an announcement could reveal plans to competition; it might jeapordize current business negotiations; it might be of a secret and restricted government nature.

You can also tell the reporter that he will get the answer at a later date, just as soon as it can be safely released to him. Then notify him. He will remember the favor.

Off the Record. Don't as a rule, give any information "off the record." It may be misconstrued and used anyway, and you are the loser. A reporter can easily say, "Well I'll get it someplace else anyway, so don't be surprised if you see it in the paper!"

Do's and Don't's

In summing up the work of this chapter, it may be helpful to consider the following Do's and Don't's in handling public relations functions:

DO's.
1. Try to be as helpful with reporters as possible; giving them favorable attention shows consideration which may be repaid in their handling of your material.
2. Frankness is a valuable quality. One should be direct, sincere and do not mislead in giving any information to reporters.
3. Keeping cool is an indispensable aid. If unable to talk at the moment for lack of information or even poor disposition, simply say so; offer to talk later and then follow through.
4. Newspapers have deadlines. These should be respected. Avoid trying to get in under a deadline. It may work once, but should never become a habit.

5. Getting to know personally, local newspapermen and women helps in terms of maintaining a smooth-functioning relationship.
6. Keep an exclusive story exclusive, and a general news story should be made available to everyone.
7. Giving out news that is unfavorable is good policy; be sure to make it clear and factual; it usually will avoid a bad situation later on, such as a running story that for days remains unfavorable and verily feeds on itself.

DON'T'S.

1. Suppressing news is a cardinal sin in the business. Tone it down if you must, but don't suppress it entirely. If you do, it could leak out and backfire.
2. Never use the advertising door of the paper to get space. It breeds ill will and, except for some trade journals, does not really work.
3. Never ask to read copy in advance. This is an insult to the editor.
4. Arguing the presentation of a story is equally fatal. This is the newspaper's or magazine's own business.
5. One should avoid demanding corrections of a minor nature in a story. It is poor form to do so.
6. Talking "off the record" may get on the record eventually; so avoid it.
7. Never thank any reporter for "getting a story in the paper," but thank him for a well written piece, which will be appreciated by him.

4

Improving Verbal Communications

Communications has been a much bandied-about word in recent years. It has been used by practically everyone to prove a point, or cure an ill, and given as a reason for everything from business failure to divorce.

A basic definition of communications is simply the interchange of ideas and information among people. In communicating with people we try to inform, influence, and even control them.

The most commonly recognized and important form of communication, particularly for innkeepers, is public speaking. Here is a checklist of major considerations to observe in addressing any public (employees, stockholders, community groups, Lions, Rotarians, Kiwanis, etc.), which are basic essentials for any public speaker in business.

Preparing an Address

1. One should seek to communicate and not just to impress a public. The objective always is to transfer an idea to the communicant and have it understood.
2. Being completely prepared in thoroughly knowing subject material is a basic prerequisite.

34

3. Thorough preparation of the speech presentation, and organizing the material in logical sequence, is vitally important to the making of a successful address.
4. Rehearsing an address in advance, conquering the subject, feeling it and knowing it, will result in a confident delivery of the address by the speaker. If there should be some confusion during a speech and a line is forgotten, one should merely continue without a break, as only the speaker will be aware of any omission.
5. Preparation of one's own person as well as the speech is important to total effectiveness. An old adage has it that one spot, one error, no matter how neat one may be, can affect everything else.

Presentation

While preparation is the real secret which almost insures a successful presentation, concentrating on presentation will make an effectively prepared speech a polished, remembered and truly appreciated event by any audience. Here are some key points to remember:

1. "Keep it brief" is a good rule to follow. A long speech is neither necessary nor desirable. A short speech is better and more easily remembered, and it usually emphasizes the key points made! More important, it avoids the risk of boring an audience.
2. Diction is most important when it comes to maintaining clarity and understanding in the audience. Avoiding the slurring of words and phrases; speaking clearly, succinctly and in an even, controlled manner is necessary to insure rapport with the audience.
3. A good technique valuable and important to actors, is the use of pauses in the actual delivery. With poise and confidence, a silence after a point is made adds drama, emphasis, and importance to that point.
4. Speeding along in giving a speech, particularly if it is written and is being read to an audience, is, obviously, fatal to the speaker. Many public speakers, however, read, but the delivery is so well phrased that the reading is never really apparent.
5. Stage fright can be a problem. The best way to overcome it is to simply start speaking. Only a delay, throat clearing and fumbling can make it an apparent problem. There are some other, relaxing methods that may be successfully employed. These are:
   (a) Take a drink (one only).
   (b) Say a prayer in advance.

    (c) Take a walk in fresh air, if you can.

    (d) Have your wife in the audience.

    (e) Find a friendly face in the audience.

6. A wise public speaker will make his points twice and perhaps repeat them in summing up. Telling about your subject in advance, explaining what the topic is and why it is important, then developing it in the talk and summing it up at the close is good strategy.

7. Of great value is the use of visual aids and knowing how and when to employ them. While many good speakers do not need or depend on them, their use can add emphasis and sparkle to any presentation.

Building the Talk

It was Ralph Waldo Emerson who said, "Speech is power; speech is to persuade, to convert, to compel."

Public speaking is a combination of two basic and integral parts: What is said and how it is said. *What* is said is the sum total of the ideas, the order of their presentation and the words which are used. The *how* in saying it is the partnership of the physical delivery and the conviction of the message.

Whether one talks to an individual or to a large audience, he will find a common denominator which spells success. Both involve the effective application of the rules of personal selling. The only difference is in the size of the audience.

The first job in building a talk is choosing the subject. The first rule is to make the topic fit your audience in terms of their own interests. This approach, if carried out, will hold an audience's interest and attention. This offers some conflict which speakers often face. Just giving platitudes and meaningless, time-worn anecdotes will cause a speaker to flounder. It usually adds up to just another speech. The idea is to combine what is needed with what is wanted in terms of presentation. Listeners will appreciate getting a message in a skillful, pleasing presentation.

Be sure to tie in the topic in the title of the talk. A good test of a title covers three requirements—it should be brief, truthful and attractive. The title should capture the listener's interest immediately. Just compare "Life Begins at 40" with "Sane Attitudes on Working, Recreation and Dieting Are Important to Live Well at 40."

After selecting a title, select the topic and begin to gather the material. Here one can divide material into two major groups. The first includes the personal experiences of the speaker. The second consists of reference material which may be taken from other speeches, the trade press, books, articles, librarians and research organizations.

A plan on how best to organize the material follows. Even the colored preacher had a plan when he said, in response to a query on how to make a speech, "I tells 'em what Ise gonna tell 'em; den I tells 'em; den I tells 'em what I told 'em."

A well developed plan does four things for a speech:

1. It eliminates tiresome drifting.
2. It lends clarity to the talk.
3. It helps emphasize the main points—the "powder keg" ideas.
4. It endows the talk with brevity.

Just as in selling, a plan known as the pre-approach before making a sales call is vitally necessary. Therefore one should know something about the audience, its interests, the object of the meeeting, and other similar details.

After having appraised the audience, one is now ready to build the talk. Many say a talk should have an introduction, a body and a conclusion. But speaking in public is selling, therefore, sales terminology can easily be applied. The speech then should plan the *approach*, where you meet with your audience face to face and try to identify your ideas with those of the listeners. In the *presentation* let the audience feel that the ideas are logical, enjoyable and profitable. In the *close* one lifts the audience to emotional heights to where they will be willing to accept the ideas and act on them.

In the introduction one is the seeker of good will, saying in effect, "I am happy to meet and be with you," implying it without saying it. In the introduction make four important points:

1. A recognition of the chairman's introductory remarks.
2. A note of appreciation for the opportunity to speak.
3. Some reference to what has gone before.
4. A statement of the purpose of your talk.

Sometimes a formal introduction may be omitted and you drive directly into your subject with an interesting story, but it should be brief. A good rule of thumb is to spend no more than five or six sentences at the start on the introduction, and then be in the heart of your talk.

Keep your introduction to the very end of your preparation, subject to any last minute changes that may develop.

After this you get directly into the body of your talk where you present your main ideas. Experience has shown that the average audience has difficulty in remembering more than three or four ideas. Present them in a logical, interesting sequence so that the audience can easily carry from one idea to another.

Because one wants the audience to remember the ideas, be sure to make use of summarizing sentences and paragraphs. Do not fear repetition; audiences want views and ideas clearly expressed, and the use of illustration, comparisons, statistics or quotations are helpful. The ideas should be presented in language that narrates and not only explains.

Now having presented your ideas in a logical manner, you are ready to conclude. In your *close* restate your main ideas and then try to get your audience to approve them and act upon them. There are four ways to close your talk effectively. These are:

1. Make a brief restatement of your main point.
2. Raise a provocative question or a plea for action.
3. Tell an effective story emphasizing the idea you want the audience most to remember.
4. Recite an appropriate quotation.

That's about it. On ending your talk, smile and leave the lectern or platform. The applause will indicate whether or not it was a success.

The Use of an Outline

Preparing an outline forces thorough thinking of the subject. It also gives confidence as it almost eliminates forgetting and permits moving from one part to another. Your outline should look similar to this:

THE OUTLINE OF YOUR TALK

I.   INTRODUCTION (THE APPROACH)

    A. Recognition of chairman's introductory remarks.
    B. Note of appreciation for opportunity to speak.
    C. Reference to what has gone before.
    D. Statement of purpose of talk.

II. BODY (THE MAIN PRESENTATION)

    A. Idea 1.
        1. Given concreteness and emphasis by illustration, or comparison.
        2. Given authenticity through statistics or expert opinion.
        3. Summarizing statement.
    B. Idea 2. (Same treatment as Idea 1.)

III. CONCLUSION (CLOSE)

    A. Resume of main points.
    B. Motivation to action through:
        1. Plea.
        2. Appropriate story.
        3. Pertinent quotation.

Barriers to Good Communications

It is equally important to know and be able to recognize barriers in good verbal communications. Here are some principal areas to consider in speaking:

1. One should recognize that all people are different, and that there are no two persons who react the same to a stimulus. They listen differently and think differently, and one must try to find the simplest terminology as a common denominator in talking to them.

RECORD OF SPEAKING ENGAGEMENT

TO:_____(Public Relations Department, President, etc.)_____

FROM:___(Your name)_____

SUBJECT:_____

Date:_____
Time:_____
Place:_____
Event:_____
Sponsored by:_____
Topic:_____
Size of audience:_____
Attitude of audience:_____
Distance of travel:_____
Method of transportation:_____
Expenses:_____
Time consumed on speaking engagement:_____
Estimate of value to organization:_____
General comments:_____

---

2. The major point of the message may be garbled, which can happen for many reasons:
   (a) First, it may be that the major point cannot, for reasons of policy, be stated clearly and directly.
   (b) Second, one may not be permitted and therefore be unable to speak about any real issues involved.
3. A definite message may also be lacking. In such instances, if no message can be given, it is better to say nothing at all.

4. Being afraid of fear is a common barrier. The reasons usually can be traced to:
   (a) Fear of being misunderstood.
   (b) Fear of having a message distorted.
   (c) Fear of not being completely informed on the topic.
   (d) Fear of being exposed to criticism.
   (e) Lack of proper organization.
   (f) Lack of dedicated belief in the topic.

Record of Speaking Engagements

Making speeches to groups and various publics are valuable and important to the person making the speech as well as the organization being represented. An evaluation and record of speeches is useful in terms of showing the activity to principals and also is of real value to any public relations effort. An outline of such a report is found on page 39.

Summary

Our purpose in preparing this chapter has not been so much to cover the techniques of writing and giving a speech, but rather to define the major elements in good communications. It may be more helpful, as we have done, to define the major points in successful presentation, thereby avoiding the common pitfalls which all public speakers face.

5

Communicating with Employees

The most important public is the employee public in the hotel and motel. For more than 25 years business has been chiefly concerned with reaching the consumer, manufacturing and selling a product or services, and making a profit. Today we recognize that it is a fundamental necessity for business to make a profit, but it is not the major objective and purpose of a business.

The true function of business is to provide goods and services that are needed by consumers, and that also serve a useful purpose in our society. Profit is what is left over after expenses have been deducted. In addition to being necessary to the business for development, growth and to meet obligations to stockholders, profit is also an indicator of corporate efficiency.

The employee public is vitally important not only because it is found in large numbers, but because it is a part of many other publics such as owners, consumers, executives, workers, voters and the immediate community as well as the community at large. All of these various publics help to determine the acceptance of a hotel and motel operator's products and services, and their support is necessary to insure the success of the enterprise.

The Modern Corporate Viewpoint

Modern business no longer believes its employees should not be told things about management. Instead, it recognizes that employees want very much to know about the many things that make their company

different from another. Such knowledge fosters pride in the association
with the company, aids in developing teamwork, coordination, and
even mutual respect and understanding. Here are some of the areas
in which employees are interested:

The Employee Areas.

1. Knowledge of the company, its concept of organization and
   management, and what makes it distinctly different from other
   business organizations, is of major importance to current as well
   as prospective employees. A clear example is a comparison of the
   Hilton, Sheraton, Holiday Inn, and Hotel Corporation of America
   organizations. Here are four different corporate entities with
   separate identities and business philosophies, which attract and
   hold different types of employees.
2. Information on the makeup of the companies' services, how they
   were conceived, and how policies affect employees and guest.
   Making them known is of obvious importance and disseminating
   such information is a distinct advantage to the companies themselves.
3. General corporate policies on dividends, earnings, expansion,
   growth, promotions, retirement, new services development, are
   important to employees and make for a more wholesome environment.
4. Employees and staff appreciate any news or communication, preferably personal, on proposed layoffs, additions or changes in staff,
   the introduction of new equipment or anything that might affect
   their security and status.
5. The general business outlook, and how it specifically may affect
   the future of the company, is of keen interest to every employee.
6. Future income as a result of economic conditions which has an
   effect on business, as well as the prospects for future employment
   should be carefully made known throughout the organization. It
   is better to tackle the responsibility internally than to have the
   organization draw its own conclusions.

The Company Areas.

1. An organization does have an obligation to establish the relative
   and fair worth of jobs at all levels in an organization and the
   benefits of such a ladder of relative job money values is obvious.
   Employees and staff are aware of the possibilities for promotion,
   which in itself acts as a powerful incentive.

2. Advance notice on who might be affected by layoffs, and in what areas, in addition to what the organization might do on rehiring, is a company responsibility. The retention of good morale which is the result of such a policy, leaves the impression that fairness has been observed by the company, which is a real benefit and saving to it.

3. Clear, explicit instructions on what is to be done on the job by employees, and what the functional areas of duty, responsibility and performance are, is a company responsibility that can and always has paid dividends in performance results, quality and a minimum of friction.

4. The fact that a company is alert to the increasing needs and economic wants of its employees and incorporates this type of thinking into its internal communications program is a vital part of any employment stabilization policy.

5. Product planning and general improvement programs are news that is wanted by every level of employee and supervisor. That the future is sound and that corporate growth is being planned, let alone innovation in products and services, has a stabilizing as well as stimulating effect on the entire organization.

6. Many companies issue earnings reports or profit and loss statements to organizations for internal consumption. The effect is one of developing a sense of responsibility and interest in corporate economic affairs.

Most all of these major points were recently defined by the National Industrial Council, after holding 150 employee information clinics throughout the United States. The Council, and modern business today, knows well that providing such information is important to preserve the freedom of both individual as well as collective expression in our society.

A survey conducted by the General Electric Company a few years ago found that on an average, each employee in the company had outside contact with about 50 persons. These 50 represented all major skills, occupations, trades and walks of life. Obviously then, the average employee in a company can affect public opinion favorably or unfavorably, and influence the very success of a business.

Modern business today also recognizes that it is a part of the community; the two are inseparable, and the community is dependent on the successful functioning of that business.

As an example of what was not considered to be a community relations problem: almost anyone will recall the days when companies shut down

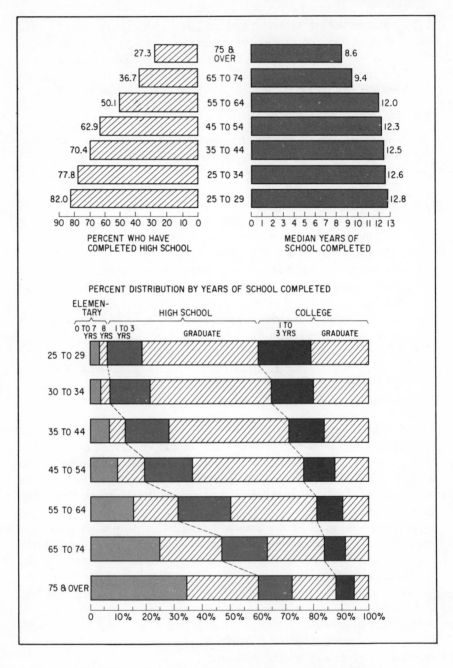

27.3

36.7

50.1

62.9

70.4

77.8

82.0

75 & OVER   8.6

65 TO 74   9.4

55 TO 64   12.0

45 TO 54   12.3

35 TO 44   12.5

25 TO 34   12.6

25 TO 29   12.8

90 80 70 60 50 40 30 20 10 0

0 1 2 3 4 5 6 7 8 9 10 11 12 13

PERCENT WHO HAVE
COMPLETED HIGH SCHOOL

MEDIAN YEARS OF
SCHOOL COMPLETED

PERCENT DISTRIBUTION BY YEARS OF SCHOOL COMPLETED

ELEMEN-
TARY   HIGH SCHOOL   COLLEGE

0 TO 7   8   1 TO 3   1 TO
YRS   YRS   YRS   GRADUATE   3 YRS   GRADUATE

25 TO 29

30 TO 34

35 TO 44

45 TO 54

55 TO 64

65 TO 74

75 & OVER

0   10%   20%   30%   40%   50%   60%   70%   80%   90%   100%

This chart, compiled and published by The Conference Board, is part
of a regular **Road Maps of Industry** service.

their plants without reprisal of any kind if labor conditions, rates of pay, union activity or other related causes were displeasing to the principals and owners of the business.

Because communities were directly affected and the businesses themselves suffered from a decline in public purchasing power, employers who once closed their places of business or threatened to do so when faced with union problems of organization or collective bargaining, are today by law unable to close or even temporarily shut down their operations. Even the mere threat of closing is now prohibited.

Recognizing Educational Levels

The Conference Board in its Road Maps of Industry service, Study #1690, published in May 1972, concerning the entire population of the United States, showed the following:

> For at least a half century, there has been a continual rise in the educational attainment of American workers. For example, median years of school completed by the U.S. labor force rose from 9.1 years in 1940 to 12.4 years in 1971, and had begun much earlier. During this period, the proportion of labor force participants with 12 years or more of formal education grew from 32% to 68%. The educational upgrading of the work force — necessitated by the increasingly complex nature of the economy and the concomitant growing demands for skilled workers — has played an integral role in boosting productivity.

These figures clearly show the very nature of the difficulty in reaching the majority of all the people in an organization with a message that they all can readily understand. The nature and make-up of the employee public within an organization must be understood, and the written, spoken and visual message must be styled and designed to fit them so that the resulting understanding will be clear and unmistakable.

The Values of Good Communications to Management

Now that management recognizes its inherent and basic responsibility to inform and keep informed all levels of its work force on its philosophy of business and plans for the future, the specific nature of the real objectives of such communications are defined in the following paragraphs:

1. Management must, in order to develop coordination, a unity of effort, sense of oneness, spread by word of mouth, by example and in written form, express its point of view.
2. All of management's communications efforts must be coordinated so as to arouse enthusiasm, and increase and maintain a high level of employee interest in the successful operation of the hotel or motel.
3. There should be a clear understanding on the part of management that good, sincere communications will and should serve to gain the favorable qualities of loyalty, resulting in better work quality and higher productivity among line and staff employees in the organization.
4. Not all the objectives are of the immediate and direct, upbuilding type inasmuch as they are also concerned with locating and correcting organization weaknesses such as absences, lateness, accidents, spoilage, grievances and insubordination, which require a medium and method of transferring information on the use of corrective action to the areas where it is needed.
5. Management must endeavor to get the employee's point of view through any number of well known and well established devices. Some of the most commonly used ones are running group meetings, dinner meetings with supervisors, suggestion systems, meetings with union representatives; others use the grapevine rumor factory and gripe boxes as a means of letting off steam and having them serve as a safety valve.
6. A most important area where management may effectively use communications, is in the warding off of doctrines that oppose the free enterprise system. Many companies have so-called political information programs which through any number of mediums and devices seek to educate and arouse employees to become aware of the injustices against business, be they political, social or economic.

Successful Communicating Methods

Here follows the most commonly used methods of communications in small and large organizations that have proved effective, reliable, and are respected by management as well as the rank-and-file employees in organizations.

Employee Attitude Surveys.   There are many varied and successful methods for making a survey of employee attitudes. Obviously an understanding of what attitudes are and what they can do or may fail to do in an organization is important.

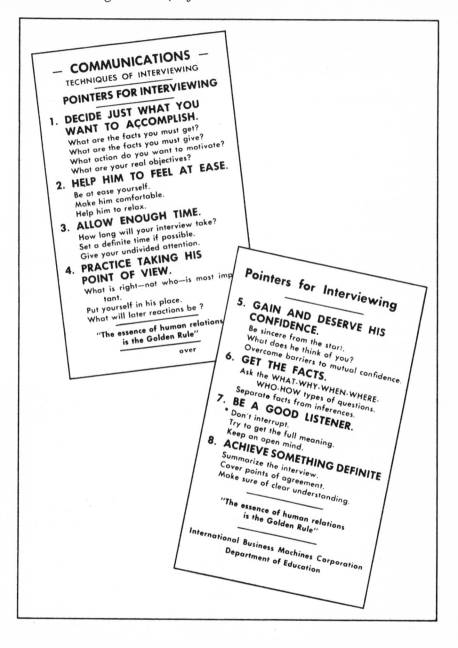

— COMMUNICATIONS —
TECHNIQUES OF INTERVIEWING

POINTERS FOR INTERVIEWING

1. **DECIDE JUST WHAT YOU WANT TO ACCOMPLISH.**
   What are the facts you must get?
   What are the facts you must give?
   What action do you want to motivate?
   What are your real objectives?

2. **HELP HIM TO FEEL AT EASE.**
   Be at ease yourself.
   Make him comfortable.
   Help him to relax.

3. **ALLOW ENOUGH TIME.**
   How long will your interview take?
   Set a definite time if possible.
   Give your undivided attention.

4. **PRACTICE TAKING HIS POINT OF VIEW.**
   What is right—not who—is most important.
   Put yourself in his place.
   What will later reactions be?

   "The essence of human relations
   is the Golden Rule"

   over

Pointers for Interviewing

5. **GAIN AND DESERVE HIS CONFIDENCE.**
   Be sincere from the start.
   What does he think of you?
   Overcome barriers to mutual confidence.

6. **GET THE FACTS.**
   Ask the WHAT-WHY-WHEN-WHERE-WHO-HOW types of questions.
   Separate facts from inferences.

7. **BE A GOOD LISTENER.**
   • Don't interrupt.
   Try to get the full meaning.
   Keep an open mind.

8. **ACHIEVE SOMETHING DEFINITE**
   Summarize the interview.
   Cover points of agreement.
   Make sure of clear understanding.

   "The essence of human relations
   is the Golden Rule"

   International Business Machines Corporation
   Department of Education

Wallet-sized cards such as the one above headed **Communications,** and which covers the techniques of interviewing, are helpful and effective. They can also be issued and used after a regular brainstorming or training session has been set up.

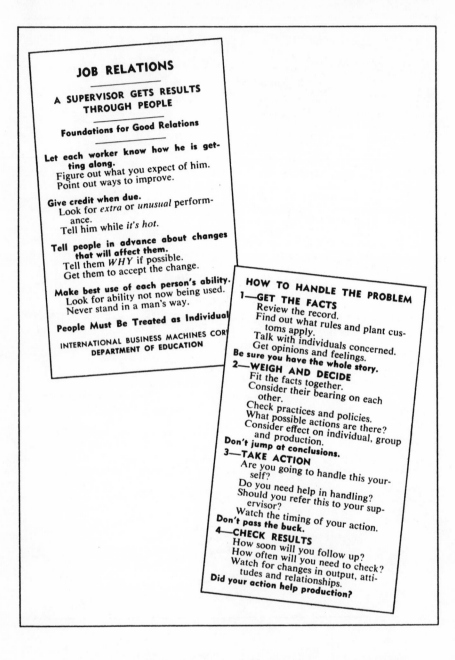

JOB RELATIONS

A SUPERVISOR GETS RESULTS THROUGH PEOPLE

Foundations for Good Relations

Let each worker know how he is getting along.
Figure out what you expect of him.
Point out ways to improve.

Give credit when due.
Look for *extra* or *unusual* performance.
Tell him while *it's hot.*

Tell people in advance about changes that will affect them.
Tell them *WHY* if possible.
Get them to accept the change.

Make best use of each person's ability.
Look for ability not now being used.
Never stand in a man's way.

People Must Be Treated as Individual

INTERNATIONAL BUSINESS MACHINES CORP
DEPARTMENT OF EDUCATION

HOW TO HANDLE THE PROBLEM

1—GET THE FACTS
Review the record.
Find out what rules and plant customs apply.
Talk with individuals concerned.
Get opinions and feelings.
Be sure you have the whole story.

2—WEIGH AND DECIDE
Fit the facts together.
Consider their bearing on each other.
Check practices and policies.
What possible actions are there?
Consider effect on individual, group and production.
Don't jump at conclusions.

3—TAKE ACTION
Are you going to handle this yourself?
Do you need help in handling?
Should you refer this to your supervisor?
Watch the timing of your action.
Don't pass the buck.

4—CHECK RESULTS
How soon will you follow up?
How often will you need to check?
Watch for changes in output, attitudes and relationships.
Did your action help production?

Because management's job is to get results through people, this wallet-sized card will be doubly helpful, not only as a convenient checklist on what the foundations of good job relations are, but also in the all important phases of handling problems in groups.

HUMAN ELEMENT LOSSES IN BUSINESS

Waste of material, energy, time due to aimlessness, lack of ambition, knocking - off, arguments, buck passing, loafing, ignorance of job, procrastination, absenteeism, ill health, loss motion, tardiness, etc.

Material Waste — avg. traceable waste/employee is 45¢ a day, $22.50 total daily waste — loss is $6,750.00.
Lost Motion — duplication of effort, disruption of schedules, lack of application — loss is 5% of payroll, $27,000.00.
Knocking-Off — 10 minutes before noon and quitting time — amounts to 16½ hours/day at $4.50/hour — loss $22,275.00.
Loafing — avg. 22 minutes/day/employee, 18⅓ hours daily at $4.50/hour — loss is $24,750.00.
Absenteeism — avg. loss is 3½ days/year/employee, 1400 hours at $4.50/hour — loss is $6,300.
Tardiness — avg. of four minutes/day/employee, 3⅓ hours a day at $4.50/hour — loss is $4,495.50.
Loss due to waste in one year is $91,570.50.

Mistakes due to carelessness, forgetfulness, guessing, disinterest, slighting details, lack of neatness, etc.

Mistakes — avg. traceable loss on 2127 mistakes was $846. Average/50 employees, 12 mistakes yearly at $846 — loss is $10,152.
Increased Supervision — due to mistakes, carelessness, etc. requiring one extra employee/50 employees at $216/week — loss is $10,800.00.
Loss due to mistakes in one year is $20,952.00.

Unsuggestiveness due to lack of initiative, disinterest, laziness, lack of purpose, etc.

Unsuggestiveness — 26% of employees gave avg. of 48 suggestions, three adopted at $6300 profit each. On this basis 74% could have given 137 suggestions, 4 adopted — loss is $25,200.

Rumors and Worry due to cliques, talkativeness, discontents, disloyalty, unfairness, etc.

Rumors — change in policies, shutdowns, decreased wages, etc. a 3½% of total payroll — loss is $18,900.
Worry — gossip, rumors, confusion, etc., at 2½% of payroll — loss is $13,500.
Loss due to rumors, worry in one year is $32,400.00.

Lack of Cooperation due to lack of teamwork, turnover, anger, favoritism, drifting, surliness, etc.

Labor Turnover — 10% or 5 employees, avg. cost of new employee is $477.00 for training, etc. — loss is $2,385.00.
Lack of Teamwork — due to friction, indifference, jealousy, etc., losses, though not accurate, are 2% of payroll — loss is $10,800.00.
Loss due to lack of cooperation in one year is $13,-185.00.

INVESTIGATIONS

14,500 questionnaires were sent to organizations located in every section of the country — in all lines of business and of all sizes. These figures were compiled from 10,463 replies in addition to personal investigations. These figures are as nearly authentic as it is humanly possible to make them. Fractions were disregarded in making final tabulations. Calculations were made on a basis of one year, consisting of 300 working days and 50 employees with an 8-hour day at an average wage of $4.50 per hour, making a total yearly payroll of $540,000.00.

LOSS
$180,307.50

TOTAL YEARLY
PAY ROLL
$540,000.00

The seriousness of losses in normal business operations, which may be traced to faulty and poor communications is shown. The material was compiled and published by the National Research Bureau, Inc., 415 North Dearborn Street, Chicago, Illinois.

Basically an attitude survey seeks to determine how employees, staff and even executives feel about anything internal or external as it may affect their company, its activities or its future.

There are various methods of making such a survey, all of which require skill, time and patience. Most important to the effort is the surveyor regardless of the technique employed, as he must be able to establish and maintain the confidence of the entire organization, which aids the survey's effectiveness and insures its success. Frankly, it is always the matter of confidence which either makes or breaks an effort, person, policy or any private or public matter.

One may use a well thought out questionnaire and issue it to an organization, either using personal mail, asking employees to complete the questions on and during work time, or by distributing the questionnaires in formal group gatherings which are called for this specific purpose. This latter method insures getting a better and more complete response, during a fixed period of time.

Another method requiring skill is the nondirective interview technique, wherein an apparently normal and pleasant conversation takes place between the interviewer and the organization staff member or employee. However, it is a conversation that has a purpose.

Information is developed and reviewed in the conversation pertaining to the company and the employee. Its source must remain confidential. When all the interviews are completed, the information is tabulated and may be paragraphed without revealing the identity of the sources. The obvious benefit of this type of method is that one may get a great amount of totally unexpected, even deeply revealing data, which provides even a deeper insight into the organization, than through the more limited, prepared-in-advance questionnaire method.

There are other variations of the above methods, but basically these are the most commonly used. While tabulation does appear to be a problem, it actually requires a great deal of interpretation and a weighing of information which calls for experience and judgment.

The results of the survey and the findings are used by management to correct unfavorable conditions, reshape policies wherever practicable, and bring about any changes that aid the general effectiveness and efficiency of the organization.

All those who take part in such a survey must be assured that the survey is being fairly and honestly conducted, and that the findings will always remain confidential as to the source, but that the results will be used to benefit them and the organization.

Individual Interviews. Keeping in touch with the organization by conducting individual interviews in an informal manner during the normal course of business often brings forth more information over periods of time than a more formal approach. Sometimes this means little more than informal visits with people while walking through a work area, stopping at a work station, talking with an elevator operator, desk clerk, doorman, or kitchen employee. Much can be detected by observing the mannerisms of employees as they handle their job assignments. Obviously, such things as interest or disinterest will be noted, and require interpretation. All of this serves to keep communications channels open, establishes rapport, and shows that management is interested in its people, the human resources of the organization.

Group Meetings. There are advantages and disadvantages to having group meetings held for the purpose of airing problems, getting opinions and reactions. It can be a strain on the principals as well as the participants who may or may not be willing to express themselves freely. Also, not all of those gathered may be willing or able to discuss a problem or a situation; some may fear embarrassment or may be unduly concerned in baring their true feelings.

But in looking at the positive side, meetings do serve the broad purpose of quickly getting at the problems at hand. A meeting has the added advantage of quickly providing on-the-floor explanations of any radically incorrect beliefs that may show themselves in the discussion. Furthermore an effectively organized and properly led meeting has objectives in mind which usually can be reached.

Company Films. Authorities estimate that there are some 50,000 films available today in the United States on a variety of educational and training objectives. Some deal with supervision, others with higher levels of management, and some even cover the policy making questions in business. Free films are available from major companies such as General Motors, General Electric, IBM, Metropolitan Life Insurance, and also from associations such as the Hotel, Motel and Restaurant Associations. Then there are excellent ones available from special service companies such as Jam Handy Associates in New York, the Bureau of National Affairs in Washington D. C., which have sound motion pictures, and sound slide films.

One can also easily make a film, either sound slide or motion picture in black and white or color, by writing a simple, purposeful script and using employees as models. Several hotelmen have either done this themselves or engaged professionals to do this for them. Employees enjoy seeing themselves on the screen, and it adds human interest and warmth to the entire procedure. If films are silent, narration can be given by a management representative, or a personnel or training director.

TELEPHONE POINTERS

ANSWERING

Be prompt – answer at the end of the first ring or as soon
as the light appears.
Be ready to talk as soon as you pick up your telephone,
being careful that the caller does not hear any side talk.
Speak clearly. Be sure the transmitter is 1/2" to 1" from
your lips.

IDENTIFICATION

Announce the name of your department and your name. When you
are called to a telephone which has already been answered,
announce your name. Do not say "Hello."

TRANSFERRING

You can transfer only incoming calls. Only transfer calls
when it is absolutely necessary.
Tell the caller where the call is to be transferred.
Transfer the call to the right department or person.
Calls should be transferred in the following way:
Move your plunger or receiver hook down and up slowly
to the count of 1-2 pause, 1-2 pause. Ask your operator
"Please transfer this call to _____

LEAVING THE LINE

If you can obtain the information quickly, ask the caller
"Will you hold on while I check that?"
Wait for the caller to acknowledge. Then lay the receiver
down gently, being careful the caller does not hear any
side talk.
If you cannot obtain the information quickly, explain and
offer to call back.

PLACING CALLS

Have the right number, and always identify yourself.

TERMINATING CALLS

Express appreciation or regret. Say "Goodbye." and wait
for the caller to hang up or say "Goodbye." Replace the
telephone gently.

A special chart placed next to each telephone extension greatly aids
the communications process. It tends to bring about succinct expression
and discussion.

Still pictures, namely slides, serve best in many cases because each slide or frame gives a total impression that registers and lasts longer in the mind of the viewer than motion pictures.

Public Address Systems. While very few hotels or motels use public address systems that are permanently installed in employee areas, there are more intercommunicating systems in use today than ever before. Unfortunately, few in the industry serve all employees except the larger organizations that see value in more extensive communicating devices. Managers can use such a system to make important announcements, and music can be piped over the system during working hours. It has safety features too, alerting employees of fire and other mishaps, either to warn them or give them instructions.

The Telephone. A personal call from the boss is a good, friendly way of reaching employees, getting answers on questions and giving instructions. Most important, it establishes rapport and develops *esprit de corps. corps.*

Suggestion Systems. This method of communication is a dangerous one to use if it fails to become a two-way medium of exchange. A good suggestion program cannot be accomplished cheaply; it needs the skills of professional design, color, artwork, good printing, a sound and convenient form of layout on paper that employees can fill out easily,

---

If You Have a Good Idea — Here's What to Do:

Just take a Suggestion Form from the Suggestion Box — write your suggestion on it and drop it in the Box.

Be sure to tear off your receipt before depositing the suggestion.

All suggestions will be judged by an impartial committee — solely on the basis of individual merit.

Awards for all accepted suggestions are from $10.00 to $50.00. You can make as many entries as you wish.

Special prizes will be issued every so often — and 3 grand prizes totalling $350.00 a piece, will be given to the 3 best suggestions each year. All employees are eligible for awards.

Be sure to have your entries in not later than the end of each month.

Winners will be announced 15 days after the closing of each months contest.

If you have any questions about the Suggestion Program — Ask any member of the Personnel Department.

Suggestion programs are a good way to develop enthusiasm and employee interest. Here is a good card advertising a simplified version of a Suggestion Program. It clarifies what has to be done by the participants as well as what the rewards may be.

and sufficient posters and payroll insert message forms to get a program going. But more than that, it needs fair rewards and a real series of incentives to get people interested. The biggest factor that really spells success for a program is publicity. Either a company newspaper, magazine or even a simple company mimeographed letter will serve to list suggestion winners. Photographs help very much, particularly if they show the suggestion winner identified with the suggestion and showing a management representative observing, praising, or congratulating the suggestion award recipient.

There are some problems, of course, in running such a program. For example, all suggestions, good or bad, must be reviewed and answered. Letters from management should be personally signed and issued promptly. The all important thing to remember is that the quality and number of suggestions may be directly related to the intellectual and educational level of the people in the organization.

Open House. This is a very successful medium and one that is particularly well suited to large organizations. For city hotels and motels, it is as good a medium as for organizations in a smaller community. The annual employee party is a good example of a form of the open house idea. It means bringing the family into the picture; workers are proud to show where they work, particularly in a hotel or motel.

Annual visits by families to the work areas where workers demonstrate their skills or at least show where they work, builds pride in not only the staff member or employee, but also in the families.

Participating in Union Affairs. Management should show itself in a representative number of union affairs by attending parties, dances, and other ceremonies. This is a very useful and important method of demonstrating good will and a fine way of maintaining good employee relations. It is often overlooked by hotels and motels simply because it may appear that such familiarity leads to a softening up of management. On the contrary, it greatly eases the attitudes of both labor and management, and make it even easier to negotiate simply because a common denominator has been reached.

Bulletin Boards. Here is a simple and effective way to maintain communications between employees and management. Pictures, memoranda, current events about the organization, laws and regulations, news of personnel and staff changes, suggestion program notes and winners, union activities, all have their place on the bulletin board.

Booklets. The Bureau of National Affairs and other organizations have developed excellent instructional and even simple informational type of booklets. For example, BNA has a whole range of booklets of the "How to" type that in simple cartoon and paragraph style, explain and cover

TO ALL OUR EMPLOYEES:

SOMETHING TO BE PROUD ABOUT!

There are many kinds of pride. But the greatest of all –
is the pride that grips all of you when you know you're
making good!

AND --- there's nothing like receiving compliments to prove
it!

Last week I received a letter I want to share with you. It's
from the President of the Rexall Drug Company. Here's what
he says:

> "Of all the hotels we have stopped at in America,
> I think we were more sorry to leave your lovely
> hotel than any other we have visited.

> "In the thirty-five years that we have been with
> the Company, we have visited almost every fine
> hotel in the United States and Europe. I think
> I can safely and truthfully say that the personnel
> at your hotel are more anxious to please the guests
> than any other hotel group with which we have come
> in contact.

> "I've been at your hotel before, but I just want
> to say that in the matter of food and beauty of
> your public rooms, there is nothing to surpass it.

> "With my very best wishes to you and all your very
> capable and courteous employees.

Yours very truly,

President

We can be justly proud. We've done our job well. It's
the spirit that makes us a great hotel -- a great organization.

Cordially yours,

Frank G. Wangeman
Executive Vice-President

Here is one of a series of successful bulletin board letters which is complimentary and particularly appreciated by the employees. Letters should also be placed near exits and entrances. Some hotels make them personal by sending them directly to employees homes, and the principal executive signs them personally. Another hotel uses a machine that types letters individually, making them even more personal.

Reading rack booklets are a big plus in any communications program. Better Business Bureau booklets, published by the Bureau of National Affairs, save headaches and dollars for employees. Subjects covered are of a practical nature and generally appreciated by employees. Many companies sandwich in booklets on economic subjects regularly, as part of an overall educational program.

How To booklets which cover all of the principal problem areas regularly faced by management and first line supervisors have proven very helpful. The booklets may be done in cartoon style, accompanied by easy-to-read, direct paragraphing, that makes for pleasant reading and boosts memory retention. They may be issued in connection with a meeting, conference series and formal program, thus laying the groundwork for further training efforts.

Featherbedding has always been a principal problem and one that may soon become chronic with the service industry. The General Electric Company, known for its highly resultful industrial relations policies, found the above ad against featherbedding, placed in the company magazine, of great value. The use of cartoons also aids in getting attention. (Courtesy of the Bureau of National Affairs)

HILTONitems

VOLUME 38, NUMBER 6   BEVERLY HILLS, CALIFORNIA   DECEMBER, 1974

Richard E. Smith Named Senior V. P.

President Barron Hilton has announced the election of four senior vice presidents following the recent Hilton Hotels Corporation Board of Directors meeting. Three Hilton vice presidents were elevated to senior vice president status; they are: Joseph W. E. Gardiner, senior vice president - food and beverage; Don Madsen, senior vice president - Hawaiian division; and Joseph Sivewright, senior vice president - rooms division. The fourth appointment is that of Richard E. Smith, senior vice president - employee relations and development.

Smith, 52, who was previously vice president - personnel with Holiday Inns, Inc. will assume his new position with Hilton immediately and make his office at the corporation's headquarters in Beverly Hills. While with his former employer he directed a program embracing personnel policy, human resource planning, training and development, compensation, benefits and administration and personnel statistics and records. He also developed a human resource computer system designed to accept input for the purpose of retrieving personnel information necessary in making management decisions and creating timely personnel records and reports.

He began his career in hotels in 1952

(continued on page 2)

Inflation Summit at the Washington Hilton

One of the most important conferences in recent history—President Ford's Summit Conference on Inflation—was held at the Washington Hilton with only two weeks' notice.

Other sites, including the State Department, Constitution Hall and the Kennedy Center for the Performing Arts, were all rejected by the White House as too small for the 800 national and international delegates and over 2000 observers.

The Washington Hilton, although honored to be chosen for the historic Conference, realized it would be no easy task. In fact, at times it seemed almost impossible because of the hotel's previous commitments during the busiest fall in its 10-year existence.

The biggest problem to be faced was the tight scheduling. The ballroom had to be turned over from the Conference ending at 5:30 the first day, to a dance for 2000 Shriners by 7 p.m. At 2 a.m. when the dance ended, the ballroom had to be turned back into the Summit site by 6 a.m. Saturday in time for the Secret Service clearance sweep.

When the Conference finished Saturday afternoon at 1:30, the ballroom again had to be set up immediately, this time for the Congressional Black Caucus's dinner dance for 3000 people in time for the 3 p.m. rehearsal.

To coordinate matters...

WITH ONLY TWO WEEKS' NOTICE, the Washington Hilton hosted President Ford's Summit Conference on Inflation for almost 3000 participants and observers. Seated at the presidential table are: Secretary of the Treasury William Simon; Senator Hubert Humphrey (D-Minn); Kenneth Rush, Counselor to the President for Economic Policy; Senator John Tower (R-Texas); President Gerald Ford; Speaker of the House Carl Albert (D-Okla); and Conference Executive Director L. William Seidman.

An employee house organ need not be expensive. Here is the Hiltonitems, published by the Hilton Corporation for its employees.

such subjects as "cutting costs," "cutting waste," "cutting absenteeism," "reducing employee turnover," "improving service quality," and many other subjects which are informative and useful to supervisors. Whole training programs can be built around these with ease.

Then there are simply reading rack types of booklets on government, business, hobbies and a fine *Better Business Bureau* series issued by BNA. This so-called "BBB" series covers many subjects such as "How to Stretch Your Paint Dollar," "Buying Storm Windows and Doors," "Dry Cleaning and Laundering Dollar Savers," "How to Choose Your Home Remodelling Contractor," "Stretching Your Used Car Dollar," and others. "Why use these?" the reader will ask. The answer is that the employees appreciate management's interest in their problems. Besides, reading racks are fun, and an instructional, educational book or two sandwiched in among others, is a good idea that gets the management message across.

	Agree	?	Disagree
My job is often dull and monotonous	☐	☐	☐
There is too much pressure on my job	☐	☐	☐
Some of the working conditions here are annoying	☐	☐	☐
I have the right equipment to do my work	☐	☐	☐
My pay is enough to live on comfortably	☐	☐	☐
I'm satisfied with the way employees benefits are handled here	☐	☐	☐
The company's employee benefit program is O.K.	☐	☐	☐
The people I work with are friendly	☐	☐	☐
My boss really tries to get our ideas about things	☐	☐	☐
My boss ought to be friendlier toward employees	☐	☐	☐
My boss lives up to his promises	☐	☐	☐
Management here has a very good personnel policy	☐	☐	☐
Management ignores our suggestions and complaints	☐	☐	☐
My boss knows very little about his job	☐	☐	☐
My boss has the work well organized	☐	☐	☐
This company operates efficiently and smoothly	☐	☐	☐
Management really knows its job	☐	☐	☐
They have a poor way of handling employee complaints here	☐	☐	☐
You can say what you think around here	☐	☐	☐
You always know where you stand with this company	☐	☐	☐
When layoffs are necessary, they are handled fairly	☐	☐	☐
I am very much underpaid for the work that I do	☐	☐	☐
I'm really doing something worthwhile in my job	☐	☐	☐
I'm proud to work for this company	☐	☐	☐
Filling in this Inventory is a good way to let management know what the employees think	☐	☐	☐
I think some good may come out of filling in an Inventory like this one	☐	☐	☐

Sample page from the SRA Employee Industry. (Courtesy of the Science Research Associates, Inc., Chicago, Illinois)

The good reading rack should be worker and staff oriented, as workers are primarily interested in themselves. Information about hobbies, recreation, health, safety, the family, children, sports, and self improvement are truly appreciated.

Annual Reports to Employees. This is a good practice, but care must be taken that nothing is left out of the report that goes to employees. It should be either the same as the stockholder's or a simplified version that is essentially the same. This gives employees a chance to see what and how the company is operating. As many employees are stockholders, such information is not confidential anyway. Furthermore, this device of issuing the annual report builds common understanding.

House Organs. So many company magazines and newspapers exist now that there is little argument against them. The idea of the house organ is to tie together the company as a body, giving it its own identity and image.

Many chains do this, with individual hotels and motels doing anything from a mimeographed sheet to a newspaper. Once begun, house organs generally remain.

Individual Letters. This is a helpful device, but one that should not be used too often or the personal touch may be lost. Personally signed letters dictated by the manager, sent directly to the homes of staff and employees, congratulating them on any accomplishment or sending greetings, condolences, and best wishes—whatever the occasion requires —are best. Official stationery should be used and the manager's signature should appear over his title.

The Grapevine. Use of the grapevine, or so-called rumor factory, is sticky unless skillfully employed. With this device, management lets it be known by word of mouth what it wants to have known. With a good, clear message, the problems of getting it garbled and misunderstood are minimal. But any misinterpretation down the line could be hazardous. Nevertheless, it is done and done often with good results.

Part II

Industrial Relations

6

The Labor-Management
Relations Act

With recent changes in the Federal Labor Law, and an increasing awareness on the part of hotel-motel managements, a number of pertinent questions regarding the application, nature and extent of the Labor-Management Relations Act are coming into focus, particularly because of the widening scope of national union activity. Because the subject is current and timely, the following basic tenets of this vitally important act, as it affects operations, has already proven of value to many operators.

The Broad Purpose of the Act

Simply stated, the Act was passed to guarantee the rights of workers in their relations with employers as well as unions, and to prohibit activities by either management or labor which are injurious to the general welfare.

Three major differences between the Wagner Labor Act and the present Act are:

1. Employers and labor unions are equal before the law by requiring both to assume definite responsibilities and obligations.
2. The rights of individuals and employees in their relations with labor unions are fully protected.
3. The rights of the general public, in connection with labor disputes affecting commerce, are now protected and recognized.

What the Act Does Not Cover

The Labor-Management Relations Act does not cover any business that does not affect commerce, employees subject to the Railway Labor Act, agricultural laborers, domestic servants, a person employed by his parents or spouse, government employees, employees of hospitals operated on a non-profit basis, independent contractors who depend upon profits rather than commissions or wages for their incomes, and supervisors.

The Employer's Rights

An employer or his representative is allowed to express any views, argument, or opinion about unions in oral, written, printed or graphic form, as long as he does not threaten or discipline, close his business or engage in other reprisal action for any choice employees make regarding whether or not they wish to unionize, or as long as he does not give or promise wage increases, improved working conditions or other benefits to influence their choice.

A supervisor has the same legal responsibility as an employer within the meaning of the Act. He is the employer's representative, speaks and acts for him, and, therefore, represents him in the eyes of the law.

Specifically a supervisor may:

1. Express his views regarding the union, openly and publicly but with fairness and tact.
2. He may also justify company actions, regarding policies and practices, and speak about them to others without danger of being in violation of the Federal Labor Law.
3. Any supervisor can answer union charges with facts, being certain to express himself clearly and objectively.
4. He may also explain that union membership is not a requirement of employment if this is in accord with the contract.
5. Discussing union dues and the checkoff with employees is also entirely permissible.
6. Such things as expressing a desire to talk directly with workers without the need of a shop steward being present, or making statements to workers on how unions operate are entirely permissible.
7. Any review with workers on the benefits they already have, can take place at any time and under any conditions.

8. Supervisors and management are also free to point out the disadvantages of belonging to a union without fear of any repercussion.
9. Acting in an advisory capacity in terms of countering or serving to clear up false or misleading information issued or coming from union spokesmen is also perfectly legal.

But in exercising all of these management rights, care must be taken in making statements that do not contain threats, or do not in any way indicate any form of reprisal. All conversation by supervisors to union members should be objective and not subjective.

Restrictions on Employers. There are also restrictions on employers with which every conscientious executive and representative of management should be familiar. These fall into five principal areas forbidden to employers.

1. An employer may not in any way obstruct or interfere with the wishes of any employees to join a union by threatening loss of a position, or indicating it may be necessary because of a desire to unionize, to close down a business. And questioning employees about union matters, spying on union meetings, or granting wage increases timed to defeat organizing efforts by unions, are also strictly forbidden.
2. Another serious fault is the danger of management's refusal to bargain collectively with any representatives chosen by the majority of employees. Such duly chosen representatives may have been selected informally and be without union affiliation, but the danger of a violation according to law is still present.
3. No employer or his representative may interfere with either the formation or operation of a union by helping to organize it, bringing pressure upon workers to join, playing favorites to any one or more unions, or in any way acting contrary to the independent and objective interests of any form of labor organization.
4. Discriminating against a worker in hiring or in setting the terms of employment as a result of or because of the worker's union activities is forbidden. Such actions by employers which take the form of discharging a worker because he took part in a lawful strike unless he has been permanently replaced, or refusing to hire a qualified worker and applicant for a job because he belongs to union and not another, all take the form of discrimination and are illegal.
5. Finally, no employer may discharge or in any way discriminate against any worker because he has either filed, brought charges, or testified against an employer, under the Act.

But the Act in no way restricts management in excercising normal management rights as to hiring, disciplining or firing any employees, which are in the normal course of business and which are in accord with established business procedure.

When it does become necessary to fire an employee and discharge him, the following test questions should be applied to any worker whom management and its duly appointed responsible representatives wish to discharge:

1. What was the reason for the action?
2. Was similar action taken against other employees for the same reason before?
3. Were written warnings or even verbal ones given?
4. Was the worker known to be active in union matters?
5. What has been the worker's record as to length of service, efficiency ratings, wage increases, promotions, or words of praise from the supervisor?

These are important test questions, for if an arbitrator or the Labor Relations Board finds that the employee has been, in its opinion, unjustly discharged, it can order the employee reinstated with full back pay.

The Employee's Rights

The rights of employees are clear and direct. The are three basic ones:

1. To present grievances to the employer or supervisor without a union representative, or his intervention, provided any adjustment is not out of line with the union contract, and provided that the agent has been given the opportunity to be present at such adjustments.
2. To form, join, or be of assistance in unions, to bargain collectively through representatives of their own choosing, or to refrain from any activities, except where a union shop contract is in effect.
3. To strike. However, there are some limitations such as "sitdown strikes," slowdowns, partial strikes, or strikes in violation of the no-strike clause in a contract.

Union Rights

There are major union limitations which will be of interest to both management and labor readers. Here are the principal ones which are prohibited under the Act:

1. No union may coerce, intimidate or use threats of force to get employees to join a union.
2. As to using coercion on an employer, no union may use it in an effort to force recognition and gain a signed contract from any employer.
3. A union may not cause or attempt to cause an employer to discriminate against any employees or to discourage membership in a union, and it may not seek pay for services not performed or promised to be performed.
4. Engaging in or instigating a strike aimed at forcing an employer to join a union or an employer group, or attempting to persuade an employer to recognize one union when another one has already been certified, is unlawful and in violation of the Act.
5. A union may not attempt to induce or seek to encourage employees of an employer to strike or to engage in an on-the-job boycott.
6. An employer cannot be forced or requested by a union to recognize an uncertified union.
7. Regarding work assignments: a union may not induce or encourge employees to strike in order to compel an employer to assign particular or special work to employees in a particular union, skill area, trade or craft.
8. Finally, the National Labor Relations Board can limit any union's attempt to pay fees to obtain membership in a union shop, if the Board judges the fees to be excessive.

It will be noted that these limitations are severe and serve to limit in balance the power of labor unions in their relations with management.

The National Labor Relations Board

Unquestionably the Board has some strong powers, which are designed to assist both management and labor in all just actions, and specifically to assist and endeavor to maintain a stability in establishing labor peace. Briefly the NLRB has authority in three major areas. These are:

1. To remedy, prevent wherever possible, and eliminate as best it can in an impartial manner under the law, any unfair labor practices of employers as well as of unions.
2. The NLRB is specifically empowered to conduct elections among qualified bargaining units to either certify them as official bargaining agents representing employees, or it may also decertify a bargaining unit, determining in effect that a union no longer represents the employees in the bargaining unit.

3. A large part of the work of the NLRB is to also conduct polls that determine whether or not employees in a specific union want to revoke their agreement and/or elect to be represented by another labor organization.

As to the rights of management, unions, and employees under the NLRB, either a company, union, or any employees may file a special form regarding a complaint of an unfair labor practice, directly with the NLRB, which then examines the complaint.

As to the actual steps: the first one is to dispatch a field examiner to the scene who personally investigates all charges and the conditions which brought them about.

After a reasonable time, the NLRB issues a formal complaint if the charges are found to be well grounded. This is followed by a public hearing and the issue of a report of findings to all parties concerned. The report is also publicly available. One organization, The Bureau of National Affairs, in Washington D.C., provides a complete weekly service that reports on all NLRB long and short form cases, thus providing 100% coverage. The NLRB offices throughout the United States use this valuable service as do many government, business, and labor organizations.

The NLRB, of course, reviews the case carefully and releases the reports described above, after it has rendered its decision.

In the event a company or union fails to comply, the NLRB then asks the United States Court of Appeals to enforce its orders, which is the final stage of enforcement and control.

Summary

The sincerest intentions of the Act, which are to maintain fair and equitable practices among all parties in the field of labor relations, are sometimes thwarted simply because some actions are difficult to prove.

For example, sickness in mass form is debated often enough as to whether it is a partial strike or not. To prove it to be otherwise is usually an impossibility.

Strikes and coercion on either labor or management's part are also difficult to prove, and sometimes an investigation of complaints is time consuming and made more difficult because the facts are not readily available.

But the fundamental principle of striving and working to achieve labor peace through mutual respect and understanding, long with a sincere appreciation for the rights of both parties, generally proves its worth, and the NLRB has proven itself to be an effective, objective agency.

7

Dealing with Labor Unions

Avoiding the Pitfalls of Management Interference

One of the biggest problems management all too often encounters is its own attitude toward unions. As a rule management does not welcome intervention of a third party in dealing with its employees. Once the union has established itself, it really means that management has failed in maintaining the confidence of its employees, and has been ineffective in communicating with and understanding the needs of the working force of its organization.

In attempts to ward off unionization, management must of necessity, avoid the pitfalls of illegal interference by any management member. The NLRB would naturally find that where union organizers were coerced, the company would be liable. But sometimes even such actions are difficult to prove, particularly when management has never expressed any anti-union sentiment. The NLRB can and has given companies the benefit of the doubt when company attitude was apparently sincere and showed no anti-union feeling.

What May Constitute Illegal Interference

Here are some of the major areas where difficulties, which often occur, may be avoided:

1. Avoid sponsoring and approving any anti-union petitions.
2. Never show favoritism for non-union members over those in the unions.

3. Neither give nor hold up any kind of benefits to influence employee attitudes against unions.
4. Under no circumstances may a department be closed down, a section or even the entire hotel-motel, so as to avoid meeting with or doing business with any union.
5. The hiring of a staff of guards, or even increasing a present complement, can easily be interpreted as intimidation, and a threat of strong-arm methods, both of which can be ruled illegal by the NLRB.
6. The ejection of union members, or pro-union factions from the employer's premises by non-union workers can result in the employer being found liable for not protecting workers during the time of their employment, even though the employer had no hand in such an action.
7. Should a friendly or rival union be found responsible for any coercive acts, it may be found guilty by the NLRB and forced to pay the costs of damages, even part of all back pay, which would be wages due those out of work temporarily. But such a liability is usually difficult to prove, and management often has to pay the bill.
8. Under no circumstances should management or supervisors have anything to do with anti-union petitions, leaflets or propaganda. Disapproval is as bad as approval. Only a *hands-off* policy by management will avoid violations of the labor laws.

Action Management May Take

Doing nothing, avoiding interference, showing neither approval nor disapproval are often the best means of discouraging interest in union representation. This often aids in showing that unions aren't necessary, and that management is really interested in fair treatment for all.

1. Management can enforce a no-trespassing rule on hotel-motel company property and prohibit anyone from entering onto or into the employer's property.
2. Management can refuse a union permission to hold meetings on or in the hotel-motel premises, but it must avoid refusing to rent to or provide space to a union purely because it is a union.
3. Management can request employees to work overtime and reschedule hours to fit business needs, but should avoid doing so with any objectives in mind as may be related to such things as preventing attendance at union meetings.

4. Management can prevent union organizers from entering the premises for the purpose of distributing union literature on the premises, provided that these rules apply to the general public as well. A simple sign saying that only employees may enter or be on the premises or grounds is sufficient to uphold the rule in the eyes of the law.

5. Management should make certain that there is no inequality in dealing with union and non-union employees. Granting or taking away privileges is a clear management right, but it must not in any way be retaliatory in nature. Management should never issue or make known warnings that privileges will be lost or withheld if employees organize.

6. Management's giving a raise or providing other benefits must not be connected with or in any way related to warding off or retarding union organizing.

7. Management may not threaten to close down or move elsewhere so as to discourage organizing, but is entirely correct in doing so for valid reasons, where business policy requires it. If, after nearing an agreement, it becomes obvious that management cannot continue to operate, it is free to take whatever steps may be necessary to enable it to continue in business.

8. Management is never required to bargain with any union unless the union or unions have a clear majority of employees in the bargaining unit. But management can ask the NLRB to settle the claim of a majority by holding an election among employees in the bargaining unit. This applies particularly where rival unions are involved.

The Right to Strike Is Not Absolute

The threat of a strike is something every innkeeper fears. Knowing exactly what to do, and what not to do under such circumstances is of primary importance. Even the mere threat of a strike presents enough of a problem. It can and often does affect the normal conduct and habit of business particularly when management does not take advantage of its rights, as allowed by law, and plans accordingly. Indecision or a wrong move often results in a public that is divided, consisting of those who support management, and those who fear either reprisals against them such as a last minute reversal affecting their position, or just plain being caught in the middle of the act of striking.

But the right to strike is not absolute. It is subject to both federal and state laws. The United States Supreme Court made this clear in a landmark decision quoting Justice Brandeis in Dorchy vs. Kansas, U.S. Supreme Court, No. 119 (1926), 272 U.S. 306 as follows: "Neither the common law, nor the Fourteenth Amendment confers the absolute right to strike."

And in another decision, UAW v. Wisconsin ERB — U.S. Supreme Court, Vo. 14, 15 (1959), the court stated:

> The right to strike, because of its more serious impact upon the public interest, is more vulnerable to regulation than the right to organize and select representatives for lawful purposes of collective bargaining which this Court has characterized as a fundamental right and which the Court has pointed out was recognized as such in its decisions long before it was given protection by the Labor Relations Act.

Recognizing a Strike

It is extremely important for management to know what a strike is and how it may be recognized. The reason simply is that strikers are normally protected by the labor laws, and management must consider all provisions of the law in dealing with them and the situation thus presented.

Generally, a strike may be recognized by employees stopping work, walking out, and setting up a picket line around the premises. But sometimes strikes are hard to identify, as unions may refrain, for example, from picketing, thereby seeking to avoid the penalties of an unlawful strike.

Types of Strikes

All strikes according to law fall into three categories:

Economic Strikes. This is a strike over wages, hours or working conditions. If any strikers are permanently replaced, management does not have to rehire them when the strike is over.

Unfair Practice Strikes. This is one that is judged to be caused or prolonged by unfair labor practices of management, and requires that all strikers must be re-employed if they desire to return when the strike ends.

Illegal and Unprotected Strikes. An illegal strike is obviously forbidden by the Labor Law. And unprotected strikes are those outside of the law, neither specifically banned nor protected by law. All employees who participate in illegal or unprotected strikes lose all rights under the law, and management can discharge or discipline them without any reprisal.

Essential Management Rights Defined

Regardless of what kind of strike is taking place, management is free to hire any replacements needed, provided that they were not brought in from another state, which would be in violation of the Byrnes Act, a federal law prohibiting interstate traffic of strike breakers. If a strike is judged unfair, most replacements can be permanent.

Management must be careful to avoid having an economic strike convert into an unfair practice strike while a strike is in progress. As long as management complies with the law, any form of strike will be judged economic. Economic strikers are entitled to reinstatement only if management has a place for them and replacement workers, hired during the strike, can be retained. No employees may be coerced into joining a strike against their wishes; they can choose to continue working as they please. Management can employ guards who must stay on duty during a strike and cannot join the strikers, or belong to their union.

Slowdowns by workers, when recognized by management, can result in discharge or discipline, for such acts are not protected by the law. The NLRB has ruled that workers cannot work on their own terms (slowdown) to force an agreement with management. Proof of a slowdown is often difficult; management must be certain of holding back by workers before taking action.

Refusal by employees to observe house rules or obey management orders is not a strike, but simple insubordination, allowing management to take appropriate disciplinary action.

A brief walkout by employees may be considered a strike, as is a failure to show up for work should a labor contract have expired.

Methods of Averting Strikes

Management faces a difficult job in trying to avert a strike. The best way to avoid it is to keep on talking, i.e., negotiating with the union principals. Appealing directly to employees, threatening a layoff or a discharge, or taking a poll of employee opinions, or asking to see the results of a poll conducted by an outsider, is a sure way of being found in violation of the Federal Labor Law by the National Labor Relations Board.

But there are several legal resources available to management to aid in averting a strike, that can be used without fear or concern.

Hiring Replacements. The most powerful technique is to announce that all strikers will be replaced when a strike actually takes place. But management must be sure that the strike is an economic one and that there is no danger of having the work stoppage judged to be an unfair labor practice strike.

The Strike Poll. A strike vote taken independently by employees of their own volition, or a poll without management's aid or influence, or an expressed desire by management to know or see the results, is not a violation of the law.

Keeping Open. The hotel-motel plant can and should be kept open during the period of a strike threat and while the strike is actually in effect.

A good, clear, simple, and direct story given to the public for general consumption, which avoids any direct or indirect references or threats by management which might influence the abandonment of the strike, is a highly effective, legal way to try to terminate a strike. And there is no danger, legal or otherwise, in employing this type of an approach.

Giving Protection. Management must take the means to protect all employees who wish to continue to work for the company that has been struck. In taking such action, the company will not be judged in violation of the law.

Using the NLRB. Normally management cannot ask the National Labor Relations Board to step into, conduct, or even monitor a strike vote, but it can insist on an NLRB investigation where it is believed that the union's methods or aims of conducting a strike may have been in violation of the Labor Law.

If enough facts indicate that a union is violating the Federal Labor Law, then the Board can and will seek an injunction in a federal court, against the union. This action is open to all management and at no expense.

Any such actions by unions as sympathy strikes, secondary boycotts, strikes against NLRB certifications, strikes to force management recognition of an uncertified union, make it mandatory for the NLRB to ask for an injunction against the union.

Using the Injunction

Management's going directly to a federal court for an injunction against a strike is risky, because the terms of the Norris LaGuardia Act (a law passed by Congress in 1932 making yellow dog contracts illegal, and which permits the issuing of injunctions against picketing under certain conditions), make such actions very difficult. Management, to get an injunction, must prove that:

1. All local legal means to protect company property have been exhausted.

2. Unlawful act, violence and/or fraud have been or will be committed.
3. Such violence, if continued or not prevented, will cause severe, if not irreparable damage.
4. All efforts to settle the dispute at all levels and through all channels have failed.
5. All proof must be given in open court subject to cross examination.

In handling any publicity efforts, management must avoid anything that will incite hatred or adverse feelings. Only facts should be presented. No individual, personal, direct appeals to strikers, workers or their families should ever be made.

However, newspaper advertisements and letters sent directly to strikers may be used and are considered best. A question-and-answer letter or advertisement which leaves it up to the reader to decide (a fill-in check-off type of form) has been used and is highly successful primarily to get people to think about the real issues involved. This is entirely within the law.

Public Opinion and Community Support

In many communities innkeepers are important enough centers of economic influence that the immediate community as well as the one at large is affected by any labor difficulty such as a strike or work stoppage. Hotels and motels often employ a considerable number of the community whose spending power is curtailed if they go on strike. Secondly, the hotels and motels attract many visitors and passers-by for food and lodging. If the hotel's-motel's services are curtailed by a strike, potential consumers are lost not only to the innkeepers but to the surrounding merchants. Third, these consumers may not frequent the hotel and motel when they return to the area even though it may not be on strike.

Sometimes entirely independent of innkeepers, committees composed of public spirited citizens are formed to try to bring the strike to an early end.

All such community efforts are usually of a self-generating nature, and management must avoid giving any apparent support or encouragement to such efforts. Under such circumstances management cannot be charged with the illegal strike breaking violation.

Management must not provide funds for such committees, and if, for example, the Chamber of Commerce is involved in leading, supporting or cooperating in any other drive or effort, the fact that the manage-

ment of the hotel or motel is a member of the Chamber of Commerce is
no problem as long as they do not participate in any Chamber activities
conducted on management's behalf.

Going Over the Union's Head

Dealing with individual strikers can be effective if the union has
no bargaining right. However, caution must be taken so that the NLRB
does not conclude that such an action is an attempt to break up the
union. If there is a no-strike agreement which the union has not observed,
management can safely appeal to individual workers to return to work.
A union, under such circumstances, loses its bargaining rights, which
are only restored after the strike is called off.

During an economic strike, management can appeal to strikers to return
to work, leaving out any threat or promises of special consideration and
benefits, as an inducement.

Voting on Management's Offer

Management cannot take a vote of individual employees' feelings
regarding its offer, unless the union agrees to it. Unions are generally
opposed to such a suggestion except when they feel that their viewpoint
will be supported by the persons who vote and who are union members.

But if the strike is a "wildcat" and the union says it has no control
over strikers in getting them back to work, the NLRB will permit management to write and appeal directly to strikers, and even hold a *by-mail*
election, provided that no threats or promises are used.*

Discharging Strikers

There are mixed court decisions regarding a company's right to
inform economic strikers that they will be discharged if they fail to
report to work by a certain time. Generally the NLRB will decide against
a company which attempts such a move, but in Kansas Milling Co.
vs. NLRB—CA 10-1950, an appeal court decided against the NLRB.

A company statement devoid of any threat or deadline to return to
work, which simply states that replacements are to be hired, is legal.
But such efforts at hiring, with actual employment following, must
actually take place, otherwise the NLRB can and will consider such
an action a threat. Economic strikers need not be rehired if their replacements remain.

---

*Fulton Bag and Cotton Mills, 74 NLRB No. 18 (1947).

Handling Violence — Using the Police

Hiring goons, arming non-strikers with black jacks and brass knuckles, or even having a supervisor present at a mob riot aimed against a union, are *sure fire* reasons for an NLRB ruling finding the company in violation of the Labor Law.

Management should issue instructions to all supervisors, telling them not to get involved in any way in any mob action or violence against strikers. Then if they do get involved, management is on record, can claim no responsibility, and is, therefore, not implicated.

If violence occurs or is threatened, the best procedure is to rely on the local police. Care must be taken that the police do not interfere with the legal activities of strikers, provided such activities are peaceful. The police are never accountable to the NLRB for any actions they deem proper and necessary. Under such circumstances, management is perfectly free to call in extra and private police forces without in any way violating the Labor Law. Management can offer to pay local police for their purely protective functions.

Employing Replacements for Strikers

Replacements are always labeled strike breakers and/or scabs by unions. This label often makes it difficult to recruit and employ replacements. But because the law permits the hiring of permanent replacements as needed, and because strikers have no guarantee of getting their jobs back, management has a good chance to fill its needs. The NLRB usually questions management's intentions because strikers who are replaced with permanent rehires lose their job rights and therefore cannot vote in any NLRB election held on management's premises. The NLRB, after an investigation, determines whether or not replacements were hired as permanent employees. If the following five questions are satisfactorily answered by the NLRB investigation, the NLRB will consider replacements to be permanent.

1. Management must have employed replacements before strikers make or have made any unconditional application for reinstatement.
2. Management must warn strikers in advance that they will be permanently replaced.
3. Replacements must have similar job experience before being employed.
4. Replacements must not be imported from the immediate geographical area; out-of-state replacements would find management in vio-

lation of the Byrnes Act, a federal law that prohibits out-of-state strike replacements.

5. Replacements must have been told that they were permanent and be aware of this fact on being employed.

Recognizing Objectives of Strikes

Not all strikes are protected by the Labor Law, and those that are illegal are sometimes not immediately identifiable. Unions, however, are expressly prohibited by law to foster or be party to strikes that support illegal secondary boycotts.

Should a union encourage and induce other firms to boycott the use of your premises or services, it will be doing so in clear violation of the Labor Law. Such instances are usually confined to cases where employees, who in the normal course of their work, refuse to work on certain items so as to stop the sale of such items to other parties, persons, and firms.

Only direct appeals to the public not to do business with you are legal. But if any employees condemn or talk down your services, facilities, and products, the NLRB would label them as disloyal. They are then not protected by the Labor Law, and management can discharge them.

Any union attempt to force management to recognize a union that has not been certified as the legal bargaining representative for the employees, permits management automatically to ask the NLRB to hold an election.

No union can force management to recognize it where another union has already been duly certified and recognized as the sole bargaining agent for the employees in an organization.

A union also may not force management to assign work and jobs to a particular union, except where management is refusing to observe the dictate of an NLRB order or certification of such a union.

Where certification of the current bargaining agent is "stale", more than a year old, an NLRB election is the best way out of the difficulty.

All strikes that force a management to act contrary to the law are illegal, but the NLRB and the courts have also decided on some forms of strikes which are not illegal and are not protected by the Labor Law. For example, a strike in violation of a union contract, or part thereof; one that is designed to force management to violate a contract; another which protests an action taken by a company regarding any management prerogative; and, finally, one that protests the employment of Negroes or any racial or religious groups, is outside the limits of the

Federal Law. (The latter is now also illegal in a growing number of states.)

Generally, every strike must have a valid reason and purpose. For example, if employees walk off their jobs and give no reason, or are unable to offer any legitimate excuse for such an action, they are not protected in any way by the Labor Law.

When Management Can Refuse to Bargain

If a union strikes management in order to force concessions from it which violate either the contract or the Labor Law, management can and should refuse to bargain. Management has the right to immediately appeal to the NLRB in all such instances. The NLRB then makes an investigation in order to determine whether or not an injunction may be obtained against the strikers.

Suits for Union Damage

If a strike is declared illegal, according to the four types previously described, then management can sue in a federal court for all damages incurred. They may also discharge all strikers, pick and choose from them as desired, cancel the labor contract, and refuse to deal with the union until all strikers return to work. However, if such strikers are reinstated, the right to punish the ringleaders may be lost.

Handling Non-Strikers

If it occurs, and it often does, that not all workers strike and some decide to remain at work, management cannot fire such non-strikers for refusing to take over strikers' jobs. But, management can give non-strikers the opportunity to obey the request to man *other jobs* or leave the plant and join the striking employees. Management can also pay non-strikers even though there is no work for them.

Sabotage

Sometimes non-strikers try to help strikers from the inside by such things as the breakage of china, glassware, flatware and supplies, and general damage to equipment and product. This is noted by an abrupt change in stock records or complaints, and is usually hard to prove as to the source. But such cases of proven sabotage can only result in discharge and discipline for illegal conduct without fear of reprisal by management.

Cooling Off Periods

Section 8d of the Federal Labor Law allows a 60-day cooling off period for all parties (employees and unions). During this time there can be no strike for modification or termination of the contract. Any employees who strikes during this time loses his rights under the law, unless he is rehired. Here is the procedure that must be followed under this provision in the law.

1. Parties to a contract desiring to modify or terminate it, must give the other party a written notice of proposed changes 60 days before the expiration date or before the proposed effective date of the modification or termination, should the contract have no termination date.
2. Each party must be willing to meet with the other and confer on the proposed changes during the 60-day period.
3. The party proposing the changes must notify the Federal Mediation and Conciliation Service within 30 days of the original notice to the other party of the existence of a dispute (if no agreement has been reached); if the company is located in a state that has a mediation agency, that agency must also be notified at the same time.
4. During the 60-day period, all terms of the existing contract must be continued in effect.

NOTE: If, as a result of an NLRB election during the 60-day cooling off period, the union loses its bargain rights, requirements 2, 3 and 4 above do not apply.

Management can refuse to reinstate all employees who engage in economic strikes during the 60-day cooling off period.

8

Negotiating a Labor Contract

When one considers that today's union business agents are professionals who consistently and objectively work at the business of managing a union, then hotel and motel managements, faced with negotiating a labor contract, as only an occasional task, face a real problem.

An active union has the benefit of labor counsel, research materials, reports, statistics, the advantage of the international union staff and counsel, plus its own well informed local union principals, and an alerted membership.

The average manager, with or without local, state and national trade association help, which at best is limited and exists primarily in the form of newsletters and information sheets, or a question-and-answer approach, is severely handicapped. He has a number of problems facing him daily, let alone labor relations which he may or may not be fully equipped to handle.

Some of the questions a manager will face as he nears a contract deadline, or even a first-time negotiation, are:

1. How to prepare for negotiations?
2. How to handle negotiations?
3. How to understand union strategy and deal with it fairly? (This is appreciated by union officials.)
4. What will union demands be and how to be ready for them?
5. What demands are to be made on the union in terms of corrective action?

6. What are management's rights, and union's rights?
7. How can management's rights be preserved, protected, and emphasized?
8. What errors must be guarded against in writing the contract so as to avoid later misunderstanding and grievances?

These are only some of principal questions that affect almost any hotel-motel operation concerned with negotiating with a union. Even if such negotiations are handled by an association, the individual interests of each individual operator must be considered, and therefore, it becomes a matter of personal and individual concern.

Preserving Management's Rights

The Bureau of National Affairs, the nation's premier research organization dispensing facts and information to management, labor, government and to the professions, published a landmark of information on the vital subject of *Management's Rights*. Written by George W. Torrence, a consultant to the General Electric Company, the study lists and clearly defines the traditional and normal management rights that management should exercise and protect.

Before entering into formal negotiations and discussions, an awareness of the following traditional management rights is important:

1. Right to require overtime.
2. Right to establish and enforce rules.
3. Right to discipline and discharge.
4. Right to establish and change work schedules.
5. Right to make changes in job duties.
6. Right to increase employees' work loads.
7. Right to have jobs performed by employees with less skill.
8. Right to determine ability, merit increases and promotions.
9. Right to use written tests.
10. Right to deviate from past practices.
11. Right to transfer work to a different seniority unit.
12. Right to assign bargaining unit work to a supervisor.
13. Right to set standards.
14. Right to allocate overtime.
15. Right to transfer work out of the bargaining unit.
16. Right to close down other departments or everything in case of a strike.

How Management's Rights Are Lost

Author George Torrence, in the Bureau of National Affairs treatise further points out that these basic rights are often lost because of eight basic mistakes. Four involve contract language and four are found in day-to-day bargaining while living under agreements. These are:

1. *Carless wording of contracts during negotiations and failure to see all of a provision's implications.* One example: an organization agreed to lay off senior employees last during reductions in force. Then a shortage in supplies stopped work. This called for a brief lay-off of several workers. But seniority was invoked and scores of changes were required to keep senior employees on the job.

2. *Surrendering a management right by spelling out only a part of it.* For example, an employee may be temporarily assigned to a different job when his regular work is not available. In an emergency, this meant a man's assignment could not be changed, as long as he had work of his own.

3. *Forgetting or withdrawing a proposal during negotiations.* One company requested a clause restricting stewards' grievance investigations to a reasonable time. But the provision was not included in the new contract. The union interpreted this as sanctioning unlimited steward activity and refused to check abuses.

4. *Poor language—"What does it mean?"—can tie management's hands badly.* One organization agreed to give senior employees preference in job openings—meaning preference in promotions. But senior employees claimed the easiest jobs as they came open within their classification; it required six or seven moves within a classification to promote a senior man.

5. *Loss of rights by default occurs when management does not use rights it should enforce. Past practice usually determines the deciding right with arbitrators.* One company had successfully resisted a demand for a paid-up uniform change period. But supervisors—to avoid controversy—let employees clean up on company time. An arbitrator ruled that the practice had become entrenched and should stand.

6. *Failure to explain contract provisions to supervisors and employees.* A contract provided time-and-a-half after eight hours, or an hourly bonus for evening or night work—but not both. Management did not make the alternatives clear to its accounting department. So one evening, a day man was granted both overtime and the night bonus. An arbitrator ruled that the accounting department was in the best position to interpret provisions—a costly precedent.

7. *Failure to back up supervisors on even minor policy can prove costly.* To avoid trouble, a company manager overruled a department head who had asked an experienced operator to switch elevators. The result: a new policy was set, providing choice of elevators according to seniority.

8. *Failure to prepare for grievance and arbitration hearings is a frequent cause for loss of management rights.* Two important rules apply in taking a case to arbitration—narrowing down the issue at stake, and preparing arguments thoroughly.

Nothing need be lost if management is alert to policy enforcement. And most union negotiators are reasonable to soundly presented arguments. Often informal talks with union officials between negotiating periods and during the year pay worthwhile dividends.

Preparing for Negotiations

The day to start preparing for a negotiation on your next contract is the day your present contract is signed. Bargaining is day to day, not annually.

Periodic meetings of department heads are required to keep up-to-date on possible new developments, within and without the organization, that may affect labor negotiations.

Record of Grievances. All grievances voiced by employees should be considered and constantly reviewed. They may indicate a clause or phrase that needs revision in the contract. Department heads are also the first to know of possible shortcomings of a contract clause, because they live directly with the contract each working day.

Outside Contracts. A record of the contracts of hotels and motels, bargaining session notes, demands and dates of re-openings, are among the items that should be at hand. Contracts of motels and hotels are readily available and will give you a better insight as to what the other hotels are doing. Union strategy, planning, tactics, organizing efforts, demands, and statistics will be helpful in shaping the thinking, actions, programs and objective policy of hotel and motel managements. Local wage patterns are also valuable in preparing for negotiation. Wages and benefits within and without the local hotel-motel industry will enable management to keep abreast of changes. Unions also supply information about the local and national rates paid. With this material at hand you can intelligently review your wage picture. As job classifications differ, a comparison of job descriptions is necessary to make certain that salaries and wages paid are being compared on an equitable basis.

Essentials for Negotiations

At the opening session with union representatives and with the management assistants, comptroller or chief accountant, analyst, or with a personnel and labor relations director (let him negotiate if he is mature and experienced), there should be a positive attitude that something good, fair, and mutually beneficial will result.

First Session. The first session's purpose should be to establish an atmosphere of sincerity, a willingness to cooperate and collaborate, and to attempt to reach an accord in terms of understanding.

It is important to set a timetable on the meeting, to prepare an agenda of what is to be discussed, or at least to have a simple introductory idea in mind, and keep a simple tally of what is accomplished. It is a good rule to listen rather than give many opinions on what is expected and wanted by management and principally the union.

Frankly, the major objective of the management team should be to get as much information as possible as to what union objectives, aims, and demands are, or hint at being. Getting the union's list of demands is usually no problem, but the meeting has another purpose, which is also to have the union receive a list or statement of demands from management.

The real purpose of this latter tactic is to try to have the union work the management list and to trade and bargain from it rather than from the union list of demands. The presentation of demands by both sides also settles the atmosphere and creates a spirit of mutual understanding regarding the nature of opposing demands. At the close of the first session, management should simply thank the union for fair presentation of demands and mutually agree on the date of the next session.

The Second Session. The purpose of the second, and strategically important, session should be to attempt to draw out the union on what it expects to accomplish, and what the union really believes to be of paramount importance in terms of gain as well as what is not.

In fact, management's opening remarks should be to say that its purpose is to fully comprehend the union's demands, and to aid it in developing a more objective and constructive attitude which will benefit both parties. The entire session should be one of clarification and definition and consist of an exchange of views.

The Third Session. Here the real purpose is to try to place management in the most favorable place in terms of further negotiations. At this point, management's draft of what is wanted, should be introduced and employed. This enables one to usually discard the union's proposals or at least those which are of the least interest.

The second session sets the stage for the third as to further exploring the merits of the union's proposals, and then following this up during the third session, and at the same time employing the tactic of using a management draft for discussions, bargaining and trading purposes.

Later Sessions. Naturally all of these sessions are developmental and are but the phases of a process that can be short or lengthy in terms of days and weeks of time.

But once the lines are drawn, later sessions can be tedious and very time consuming. A prepared agenda is a great time-saver in addition to keeping everyone objectively oriented and properly focused on the immediate nature of the issues at hand.

Management has the responsibility of bearing the suggestions and recommendations of department managers in mind. And the trends of the industry, particularly locally, are important. It is a wise procedure to let the union prove its points and refer back to the union any points for proof. Be sure to keep communication channels open by letting all management principals know how each of the sessions—and there may be many—are progressing. Any attempts at secrecy are harmful, place management principals in jeopardy because of contrary decisions they may make, unaware of a bargaining tactic or strategy by management, and it can and has placed management's immediate and long range objectives in danger.

The union keeps its membership continuously informed through bulletins, meetings, its own newspaper or letter, and through its shop stewards, thus attempting to establish unity in understanding and action.

The Final Closing Session. Assuming that agreement has been reached on all points, it is simply necessary to have the union and management principals appear at an appropriate, agreed-upon time for the signing of the agreement. Copies of the contract should be typed; if there are a few items still requiring last minute clarification, these few sections or clauses are to be left blank. Actually, as each point during negotiations is agreed upon, it should be initialed and dated by both parties. This generally eliminates any left-over items and avoids last minute delays.

Arranging for a group photograph of the signing, and a clear concise press announcement to go with it, covering essential details of the agreement, is good public relations, particularly if the tone of the group and the total picture reflects satisfaction, mutual understanding and agreement. Smiling faces help, too.

9

The Real Purpose of
Personnel Management

The strenuous nature of employer-employee relations in the past decade clearly indicates that the future will require even more effective management than before if the human relations problems peculiar to the hotel, motel and restaurant industries are to be successfully bridged.

In defining the objectives of personnel managment, it may be helpful for better understanding to first state precisely what these functions are.

Personnel Management's Basic Functions

All too often the mistake is made of centralizing human relations problems into one department with the belief that they should be handled by one source. In centralization, personnel departments are made even less effective.

The purpose of personnel management, however, is as a service function, assisting other departments in becoming as effective as possible in handling of personnel problems and situations as they develop.

Actually, good relations and the development of human resources can only be effectively carried forward at the point of contact between an employee and his immediate superior. The danger of centralizing is, therefore, readily apparent. Supervisory personnel will take the easy way out by avoiding or actually shunning the responsibility of maintaining good employee relations contacts, leaving this to the personnel department to accomplish. Obviously, this becomes a hopeless task and eventually fails, because when it reaches the hands of personnel people it is already far removed from the source and the time of need. With the personnel department coming between the employee and the supervisor, the opportunity for developing more effective human relationships and rapport between them is greatly impaired.

Most everyone knows that the function of personnel management is as a service function and not a line function. However, the temptation to take on or delegate line responsibility from the top down is so strong that it often achieves the opposite of what was intended.

Because of the necessity for continuous research and a constant awareness of ever-changing labor laws, regulations, ordinances, collective bargaining strategy and techniques, and because of the myriad of essential information that is available on other personnel functions pertaining to training, safety, wage administration, insurances and organization development, the job of the personnel specialists is unique in terms of service opportunities in an organization.

Obviously, any line executive is much too busy with his own particular area to worry about so specialized and complex a field. This then is a sufficient cause for personnel specialists to concentrate on assisting line executives, and seeing that good personnel practices are regularly administered by the line executives and supervisors in every part of the organization.

One of the most serious problem areas in large as well as small organizations, is that of maintaining effective communications. Effective communications consist of three-way communications, flowing from the top to the bottom, from the bottom to the top, and horizontally so that all people at all levels and in all ranks are constantly kept informed on the objectives, policies, and day-to-day matters of business which are of real concern and common interest to everyone in the organization. This means much more than merely issuing bulletins of information, publishing a newsletter, house organ, or even a judicious use of bulletin boards. Behind all of these mediums is the all-important question of understanding and being cognizant of organization relationships, and, as a result, communicating for the common good of the entire organization.

Have Personnel Specialists Improved Human Relations?

Without too much effort it is possible to prove that personnel people have done as much harm as good in establishing good human relations in organizations. It is not the result of a lack of sincere intentions by personnel specialists. Very often it is due to an imbalance and improper placement of functions in the organization. Adding to this the author has often found a basic misconception as to the real functions of the personnel department. In a great many instances the personnel manager or person carrying the function does not report to a major and principal executive in a hotel or restaurant organization. This limits the responsibility by denying it the necessary prestige to do an effective job. Then too, top management may have mistaken ideas as to the real purpose of the personnel management function. One can hardly expect miracles or even just ordinary results under such circumstances. No one can succeed in the face of constant adversity and overcome so serious a basic handicap at the start.

Another common failing to be avoided is the removal of functions from department heads and supervisors and centralizing these in the personnel department. The result of such a withdrawal is to destroy the prestige of department heads and supervisors in the eyes of their own immediate staffs.

For example, if the personnel department actually hires and has the final say on an employee, the new employee owes his employment to the personnel specialist and not the supervisor or department head. From a standpoint of executive control, the employee is less responsive, certainly at first, to a department head than if he had been formally hired by him.

While there are many examples that can be cited, the acid test is really to determine whether or not the personnel department is adding to or taking away from the prestige of department heads in their working relationships with employees. If every activity of a personnel department is examined in the light of this yardstick, then sound, effective and resultful organization relationships can be built.

Supervision and management in its broadest sense must, in order to be effective, get results through people. Unless the personnel function is so established as to aid line executives and supervisors in achieving management objectives, it is not performing a useful and much needed function.

Personnel people, much the same as public relations specialists, can aid their own objectives and add much to their own success by assuming a role of anonymity. By working through other operating executives and aiding them in their successes, they strengthen themselves. Very often the most successful ones are found in the background of an organization's image.

The Critical Area of Communications

This always has been and very probably will remain to be the major area of concern to personnel specialists and to organizations.

Good communications in any organization, large or small and just as needed in both, is simply a matter of getting full information through all ranks and levels in an organization.

The personnel specialist and his department must create, provide, and promote channels of communications that flow freely in every direction. Necessary steps must be taken for multiplying personal contacts in an organization. Communications must be both oral and written, for written statements are never enough. And most important is the need for checking the effectiveness of communications media.

It is a well known fact that where employees have become unionized, the third party element is the intervenor; the union does the communicating as the intermediary. Communications all too often breaks down completely under such conditions. As a result there is little or no communication between management and the worker. Further estrangement is evidenced by grievance settlements and contract negotiations, with the union in the middle as a clearance point between management and the worker. As a result, management all too often gives up and fails to try to maintain any line of communication for fear of being misunderstood.

This type of breakdown is totally unnecessary. With or without the aid of personnel specialists, management has the responsibility of communicating ideas to employees, whether or not the organization, large or small, is unionized.

Often too much reliance is placed on a house organ. In the innkeeping industry, particularly at worker levels, readership is low unless it is effectively geared to the reading level of the workers concerned. More effective communications, usually personal in approach, must be established if future conflicts are to be avoided. Management must, out of necessity, take the time to develop rapport through every means to gain understanding and acceptance of ideas and objectives.

How a Personnel Officer Can Cut Costs

Belt tightening in hotel and restaurant operations is not new to the industry. Tighter profit margins and competition usually bring about a cost awareness, with an emphasis on profit maximization — terms which incidentally are favored over the usage of "cost cutting."

Here are fifteen cost reduction ideas that are effectively in use:

1. Check all assignments to avoid overlapping and unnecessary duplication of effort.
2. Remove so-called deadwood personnel.
3. Eliminate all overtime.
4. Cut fringe extras such as excesses in meal privileges, travel and

entertainment, extra subscriptions, and memberships and parties.
5. If you have a house organ, keep it simple, publish fewer issues, cut down on the number of colors used, and have fewer pages.
6. Carefully investigate sick claims.
7. Contract out expensive screening and search investigations.
8. Have unofficial non-bargaining talks with unions to cut grievance time, avoiding interruptions and slowdowns.
9. Hire only the most productive, willing workers, and use physical examinations and reference investigations.
10. Make job induction and regular training a must.
11. Provide for rewarding selective merit increases.
12. Conduct and maintain an alert, vigorous cost reduction awareness campaign. Be sure to include meetings and brain storming sessions.
13. Wherever possible, use part time temporary help.
14. Toss out all unneeded files, copies, and correspondence to cut maintenance, and try to cut down the issues of memos that few people read.
15. Avoid unnecessary recruiting and shopping for recruits unless they are really needed.

The Challenge of Better Understanding

If the past and present serve as indicators for the future, then the coming years of incentive will provide even greater problems for management in developing and maintaining mutual respect and understanding with employees.

Unionization, which is still growing in the hotel and restaurant industries, will, as it has in the past, develop more class consciousness on the part of rank and file workers. This will add to the difficulties of management in developing and maintaining understanding as well as a point of view. Anything presented to employees will receive still greater scrutiny and be more critically appraised. It will be necessary, therefore, for management to develop and maintain a clear, direct, and sincere approach in presenting facts and opinions in order that they may be more readily accepted.

Inasmuch as hotel managements were not successful in earlier days in developing and cultivating full understanding before widespread unionization took place, much more effective means will need to be employed to achieve any degree of understanding in the future. And this includes greatly stepping up the communications techniques that have had any degree of success in the past.

Here lies the greatest challenge of all. All other areas of management must be carried forward on the mainstream of mutual understanding in order to succeed. There lies the opportunity for personnel management to contribute, develop, and build the bridge of cooperation to insure not only the maintenance of effective services, but a democratic way of life. If it can do this, personnel management will continue to justify its basic importance many times over. If it fails, then our opportunity system in the United States will not be able to continue to produce more for growing numbers of people as it has so bountifully done in the past.

Part III

Executive Methods and Controls

10

Sizing Up People Quickly

Much has been written about interviewing and selecting candidates for employment, selecting the most suitable, and upgrading them to positions of greater responsibility. It has always been an important subject. Today, however, smaller hotels as well as the large ones, have a greatly limited market from which to draw people particularly suited for hotel employment. This is particularly true of executives and those with executive potential.

As is the case with many companies, consultants are frequently called upon to appraise candidates in an organization for upgrading to key positions of responsibility, and also to recommend personnel for employment.

In doing so the use of tests is very helpful, but they have some limitations. Often a great many qualities that are extremely important in a hotel or motel executive cannot readily be tested by one test alone and given the proper rank of importance.

Clear judgment based on facts, impressions, prior performance, and characteristics is depended upon primarily. And one of the most helpful devices that has been employed is a Diagonostic Rating Form, simple and easy to use and which requires little time. The great value of it is that in talking with an executive or a candidate, one cannot readily conduct the type of question and answer interview commonly employed by personnel interviewers. This guide has the further advantage of use at any level, because the rating factors are based on the qualities that are important in any executive or employee who has any contact with the public.

HOTEL EXECUTIVE INTERVIEWING EVALUATION FORM

Name of Candidate_____

Position for which he is being appraised_____

1. **VOICE AND SPEECH.** Is the applicant's voice irritating, or pleasant? Can you easily hear what he says? Does he mumble, or talk with an accent which offends or baffles the listener? Or is his speech clear and distinct, his voice so rich, resonant and well-modulated that it would be a valuable asset in this position?

Irritating or indistinct	Understandable but rather unpleasant	Neither conspiciously pleasant nor unpleasant	Definitely pleasant and distinct	Exceptionally clear and pleasing

2. **APPEARANCE.** What sort of first impression does he make? Does he look like a well-set-up, healthy, energetic person? Has he bodily or facial characteristics which might seriously hamper him? Is he well-groomed or slovenly? Erect or slouchy? Attractive or unattractive in appearance?

Unprepossessing or unsuitable	Creates rather unfavorable impression	Suitable, acceptance	Creates distinctly favorable impression	Impressive, commands admiration

3. **ALERTNESS.** How readily does he grasp the meaning of a question? Is he slow to apprehend even the more obvious points, or does he understand quickly, even though the idea is new, involved or difficult?

Slow in grasping the obvious. Often misunderstands meaning of questions	Slow to understand subtle points. Requires explanation	Nearly always grasps intent of interviewer's questions	Rather quick in grasping questions and new ideas	Exceptionally keen and quick to understand

4. **ABILITY TO PRESENT IDEAS.** Does he speak logically and convincingly? Or does he tend to be vague, confused or illogical?

Confused and illogical	Tends to scatter or to become involved	Usually gets his ideas across well	Shows superior ability to express himself	Usually logical, clear and convincing

Although one can make marks during an interview, it is best to complete the form using the back blank page (which may be ruled with lines for additional comments) after a candidate has been interviewed and has left the office. Usually a check-off rating of characteristics in addition to a few paragraphs of comment will not only help in decision making for your immediate and future purposes, but will provide an adequate record for future reference.

HOTEL EXECUTIVE INTERVIEWING EVALUATION FORM
(Cont'd)

5. JUDGMENT. Does he impress you as a person whose judgment would be dependable even under stress? Or is he hasty, erratic, biased, swayed by his feelings?

Notably lacking in balance and restraint	Shows some tendency to react impulsively and without restraint	Acts judiciously in ordinary circumstances. Might be hasty in emergencies	Gives reassuring evidence of habit of considered judgment	Inspires unusual confidence in probable soundness of judgment

6. EMOTIONAL STABILITY. How well poised is he emotionally? Is he touchy, sensitive to criticism, easily upset? Is he irritated or impatient when things go wrong? Or does he keep an even keel?

Over-sensitive, easily disconcerted	Occasionally impatient or irritated	Well poised most of the time	Superior selfcommand	Shows exceptional poise, calmness and good humor under stress

7. SELF-CONFIDENCE. Does he seem to be uncertain of himself, hesitant, lacking in assurance, easily bluffed? Or is he wholesomely self-confident and assured?

Timid, hesitant, easily influenced	Appears to be over-selfconscious	Moderately confident of himself	Wholesomely selfconfident	Shows superb selfassurance

8. FRIENDLINESS. Is he a likeable person? Will his fellow-workers and subordinates be drawn to him, or kept at a distance? Does he command personal loyalty and devotion?

Keeps people at a distance	Does not easily attract friends	Approachable, likeable	Draws many friends to him	An inspirer of personal devotion and loyalty

9. PERSONAL FITNESS FOR THE POSITION. In the light of all the evidence regarding this person's characteristics (whether mentioned above or not) how do you rate his personal suitability for work such as he is considering? Recalling that it is not in his best interest to recommend him for such a position if he is better suited for something else, would you urge him to undertake this work? Do you endorse his application?

Unsuited for this work. Not endorsed	Might do well. Endorsed with hesitance	Endorsed	Endorsed with confidence	Endorsed with enthusiasm

SIGNATURE OF RATER

_____

Personnel Evaluation Form

Basic Instruction. Simply ask how the candidate compares with those who are successfully doing work of this kind. Consider whether his voice, appearance and manner would be a liability or an asset in such a position. Rate him or her by making a check ($\sqrt{}$) at that point in the scale where in your judgment, the candidate stands.

Keep in mind the kind of duties the candidate will be called upon to perform and consider whether his personal characteristics, as they reveal themselves during the interview, will be an asset or a liability in filling the position.

If his voice, for example, is so rasping or weak that it would give an unfavorable impression to those with whom he talks rate him low in this trait, toward the left end of the scale. If it is neither noticeably pleasant nor unpleasant, rate him at or near the middle of the scale. If his speech is free from disturbing peculiarities of accent and his voice so clear and resonant that it would be a distinct asset in the work he will do, rate him somewhere on the right half of the scale.

Similarly, rate the candidate on each of the other traits, keeping in mind the definitions of these traits as given on the Rating Form. If a candidate has made no impression whatsoever, either favorable or nufavorable, so far as one of these traits is concerned, rate him at the midpoint of that particular scale. Record the tentative ratings on each trait, by putting a check mark ($\sqrt{}$) on the proper scale at the point where in your judgment the candidate belongs.

When rating the last trait, "Personal Fitness", if—quite apart from any inexperience or lack of technical knowledge which he may have revealed—the applicant is definitely unsuited for the position, rate him far to the left. If he barely qualifies, that is, if he can be endorsed only with some hesitance, mark him midway between the lower end and the middle of the scale. If he can be endorsed with confidence, or with enthusiasm, place the check mark well to the right of the middle.

For additional comments and a word summary of your findings, use the back of the rating sheet.

11

Tips on Interviewing People

In their classic book *How to Interview*, Bingham and Moore state that the three main functions of an interview are:

1. To get information,
2. To give information,
3. To make a friend.

It is a good idea to follow these rules, no matter how brief an interview may be.

In interviewing, it is helpful to first establish a planned approach. While an application blank or the Executive Rating Form is of assistance in this process, these should be used only as guides. The application-blank type of interview, of repeating what has already been committed to writing on a blank, should be avoided.

One can begin an interview in this manner. First, establish rapport with the candidate by making some comment that shows you are interested in him. Offer a seat, smile and be cheerful; these things make a difference when you begin asking questions. Small talk about weather, travel, or a mutual acquaintance help.

Obtaining Information

Sometimes interviews fall flat simply because an executive fails to receive enough information and may find difficulty in encouraging people to talk. The technique of obtaining information during an interview is simple. Begin with a friendly approach. Remember that as an actor's or master of ceremonies' first job is to win over an audience, the interviewer's first job is to win over the person being interviewed.

Dividing the procedure of getting information into three main divisions is helpful. They are:

1. Work Experience
2. Education and Training
3. Personal Background

After you have established rapport and exchanged a few words, ask your lead question. This should be on work experience. Have the applicant begin talking about his last position, what he did there, how long he worked there, and why he left. Then continue on down the line. It will be observed that the applicant usually talks most easily about his past experience.

Next are Education and Training. Ask leading questions about each area. Allow the conversation to run so that you can make observations. Finally go into Personal Background: marriage, family, children, avocations and interests.

Often persons that approach your desk are quite nervous, even though they appear not to be. The sequence of information you ask and the procedure outlined here will relax him.

Three Helpful Rules

While the previous procedure may generally be followed, there are times when a more extensive interview is necessary. For example, a manager, engineer, accountant, stenographer, secretary or supervisor would require more time, whereas the porter, laundry worker or cleaner would in all probability require less. Both long and short interviews are based on similar principles. Both must fit the need of each situation. It is important to judge the applicant in keeping with your job requirements. Some good rules to observe are:

1. One should try to avoid hiring people who suddenly change occupations. For example, if a former secretary applies for a position as a clerk, emotional instability or an ulterior motive are often responsible. Hiring such a person might provide much in ability, but personality and the ability to get along with people may prove a difficulty in time.
2. Generally speaking, it is wise to hire people whose capacities, interests and abilities fit the job you have available. Exceptions should be carefully reviewed before making a final decision.

3. In interviewing, one eventually develops and follows a pattern of questions. After a time, this becomes a habit. While this varies where the job range is great, little difficulty is experienced in adjusting to each situation after a time.

Giving Information

Bingham's second rule suggests that information of some kind should be given. If for any reason the candidate's services are not suitable for employment, a courteous close, giving some information about the position in order to satisfy his curiosity, is helpful. If it is not confidential, give him an explanation what the job is about. Avoid too much detail, and do not say that you are unable to hire him, even if it is apparent he will probably not qualify. An example of one way to phrase it without offending the candidate is: "I certainly appreciate having had the opportunity of meeting and talking with you. Unfortunately I am not in a position to make a decision at the moment, as I have several other commitments. I will, however, be glad to get in touch with you later if the results of our search so indicate."

If the applicant becomes insistent, listen carefully, be attentive and again repeat what you have already told him. Make him realize that if he were in your position he would want to be just as fair in seeing to other commitments as well.

As to closing an interview, if you have been courteous and attentive, the close is easy. Simply smile, thank the candidate for visiting with you.

If, however, the candidate is worthy of further consideration, apply Bingham's second rule of giving information somewhat differently. This is largely a selling process. Begin by describing the position in some detail. Tell what is expected. Describe duties, responsibilities, conditions of work, salary and other benefits. Mention some of them, such as life, accident, health and hospital insurance, if they are available. Avoid going into detail, but later provide it in the form of booklets or other materials which describe what is available when the candidate is ready to be hired.

Then tell something of the organization, its operations and objectives. The executive should be proud to be a part of it, and the candidate will want to be, too. Let him know, by the conversation, that he is working for a worthy organization. He wants to feel that he has made a wise choice.

As to closing an interview, whether a person is hired or not, it is sometimes difficult to let people know that no further time is available. The problem really presents little difficulty for there are certain methods which will unconsciously move an interview to a close. For example, screwing on a pen cap and laying it down on the desk, placing one's hands on top of the desk, moving forward and shutting the desk drawer, placing the candidate's file into the file box on the desk, and finally getting up if necessary to show that the interview is over, are a few commonly used methods.

The Rating Scale

During the interview, or preferably immediately after it, rate the applicant by using the rating scale shown in Chapter 10. This form has descriptive scales to make it easy to rate various traits under consideration. Simply place a check mark on that portion of the scale that seems to best describe the candidate.

The rating scale is useful for two reasons. First it records first impressions to be referred to at a later date if necessary. Secondly, it acts as a yardstick in which to judge people more objectively.

The Application Blank

While this rating scale method is recommended for executive evaluations supported by a resumé submitted by the executive covering background, experience, education and personal qualifications, employee and supervisory levels require different handling.

For this purpose an application blank which also serves as a preliminary test, provides a sample of handwriting, and shows interest and effort in completing details, is very useful.

The application blank shown is easy to use, evaluate, and has many practical features. It contains a contract. It allows a candidate to check many of the jobs with which he is familiar, it may be crossfiled according to job classifications checked, and it has a quick rating at the top right hand corner in the form of a box, and a complete rating scale at the bottom.

After interviewing candidates, an applicant may be rated using this scale. Ratings are interpreted as follows:

App	Appearance	Eng	Energy
Ma	Mental alertness	Bkgnd	Background
Phys	Physique	Lsp	Leadership
Tho	Thorough	Pers	Personality
Man	Manner	Type A	Analytical
Exp	Experience	Type C	Conservative

FORM P 124

REFERRAL SOURCE: _____

PHONE (516) 825-8900

BROOKLYN • HUNTINGTON • HEMPSTEAD 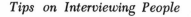 VALLEY STREAM • YONKERS • NEW ROCHELLE

COOKY's-Steak Pubs Inc.
RESTAURANTS

EXECUTIVE OFFICES/107 SOUTH CENTRAL AVENUE
VALLEY STREAM, NEW YORK 11580

APPLICATION FOR EMPLOYMENT

R	X
P	S

Social Security Number | | | | | | | | Telephone Number _____ Date _____

Name (Print) _____   Full Time ☐

Address _____ Position Desired _____ Part Time ☐
street

city   state   zip   Would you accept night work? Yes ☐ No ☐

Are you eligible to work in the United States? Yes ☐ No ☐   Would you accept temporary work? Yes ☐ No ☐

Are you employed now? Yes ☐ No ☐ If so, why do you wish to change? _____

Have you ever been employed by this Company? Yes ☐ No ☐ If "Yes," when? _____ Where? _____

Position? _____   Relative or friend employed by this Company _____

EDUCATIONAL INFORMATION
Draw Circle Around Highest Grade Completed

Grammer School: High School: College/University: Vocational/Technical/Professional School:
   5 6 7 8   1 2 3 4 Grad   1 2 3 4 Grad   1 2 3 4 Grad

Degree? _____ Major course of study _____   Name of College/University or Institution: _____

Are you now studying? _____ If so, what? _____

Where? _____

BUSINESS INFORMATION

In the space below, enter the positions you have held. Show last position first, and enter others in order backwards. Please give accurate date and addresses.___

Name and Address of Employer	Time Employed From	Time Employed To	Explain Your Duties	Position	Salary	Name of Supervisor	Reason for Leaving

Place a check √ to the left of positions with which you have specific or related-job experience

☐ Manager
☐ Ass't Manager
☐ Steward
☐ Secretary
☐ Typist Clerk
☐ Bookkeeper
☐ Cashier
☐ Telephone Oper.

☐ Bartender
☐ Waiter
☐ Bus Boy
☐ Kitchen Helper
☐ Utility Worker
☐ Porter
☐ Cleaner
☐

☐ Chef
☐ Cook
☐ Baker
☐ Broilerman
☐ Counterman
☐ Sandwichman
☐ Steamtable Man
☐

☐ Retail Bakery Clerk
☐ Driver

☐
☐
☐
☐
☐
☐

List any office machines you can operate:
_____
_____
_____

Remarks: _____

The layout of the blank is clear and easy to follow. It contains basic information with a breakdown of sections covering Personal, Physical, Education, and on the back, Business and Reference information. The blanks serve as a written test, and filling out of a form may be timed and also then examined as to its completeness in terms of detail and accuracy. Applications may be filed and cross-filed according to the job classifications checked off by the applicant. In keeping such a file up to date, most recent applications should be added to the front of the file holder.

Ini	Initiative	Type P	Persuasive
Temp	Temperment	Type M	Mechanical
		Type Ex	Executive

Rate each of these factors using either numbers, 1, 2, 3 or 4, which represent "excellent, good, fair and poor", respectively.

Under "Remarks" add any additional comments that are pertinent. As to "Type", simply place a check mark in the most appropriate space or spaces.

On the upper right-hand corner of the front of the application blank, there appears a box with the letters R, X, P, S, standing for "Rating, Experience, Position and Station." Rate the applicant 1, 2, 3 or 4; under "Experience" put the number of years of experience by just writing the number in the space provided; under "Position" write in the best qualifying position; and under "Station", where he is expected to be employed.

TELEPHONE REFERENCE INVESTIGATION

Applicant's Name .... Soc. Sec. No. ....
Person Contacted .... Date ....

....

Please Answer the Following Questions:

Approximately what dates was (he) (she) employed? From .... To ....
What were (his) (her) duties? ....

....

Was (his) (her) work satisfactory?   Yes .... No ....
If no, why not? ....
Why did (he) (she) leave your employ? ....

(He) (she) claims his earnings were $ .... Per ....
If false, how much did (he) (she) earn? $ .... Per ....
Was (he) (she) involved in any accident while at work? Yes .... No ....
If yes, please explain. ....
Have you ever known (him) (her) to drink to excess?   Yes .... No ....
Was (he) (she) cooperative with other employees?   Yes .... No...........
Did (he) (she) work hard and consistently?   Yes .... No ....
Was (his) (her) character: Favorable ...... Questionable ...... Unfavorable .....
Would you rehire (him) (her)?   Yes .... No ....
If no, why not? ....
Remarks: ....

....

....

Checked by ....

To check an employee's references it is best to use a telephone reference investigation form as shown. A telephone conversation, besides being quick and easy to perform, usually results in more facts about the applicant.

Reference Investigation

It is not necessary to check every applicant's references after he or she has been interviewed. Do this *only* if you expect to employ the person. Use the Telephone Reference Investigation Form, one for each of the jobs listed on the back of the application blank. Simply fill in the information at the top of the form, after contacting the supervisor or the name of the person given on the back of the application blank. A telephone check is usually much better than a written form to be filled out and sent in for reference. Much more facts are received by a telephone conversation, because few people wish to commit themselves to writing. A telephone check is also easier to make, as it requires less effort, with no troublesome forms to be filled in by a person giving information.

When a person is hired, the hiring date and other information should be filled in at the bottom of the application (Date employed, To start, Position, Department, Rate, Time, Full Time, Hours, etc.).

Be sure to have the application blank signed by the applicant in the space provided at the time he is being interviewed.

Attitude

Attitude is exceedingly important throughout the interview. It should be positive to insure getting essential information from an applicant. Become interested in the people you interview. A friendly and understanding attitude works wonders. Tact, consideration and courtesy are things everyone appreciates. Let the first contact with the applicant be a pleasant one. While interviewing, avoid interrupting an applicant's conversation, but be sure to maintain control at all times. Always be willing to listen to what an applicant has to say. It will permit pertinent information to be revealed which the applicant may be withholding.

12

Management Controls
for the Executive

Control means many things to many people. More than a question of semantics, control affects everyone in some form, and, at the same time, control is affected by everyone.

To the executive, control denotes the authority to govern and guide others in the performance of their work. Control is also discerning, in terms of perception, insight, and depth; for to be effective, control must of necessity measure, appraise, and evaluate processes, actions, and performance against established standards and goals. However, in the broadest sense, control is management—the art of achieving results through people.

We can divide management's function into planning, organizing, directing and controlling. The success of both direction and finally control, is dependent on how well one has planned and organized. The most effective form of control results in the smooth functioning of the organization, with only an occasional suggestion and follow up from the executive.

Control is an art and a skill that is learned and developed. Leadership requires the ability to think deeply and to search within one's self. It is a process of self-examination to appraise one's own thoughts, feelings, and intuition. While management cannot create leaders, it can assist in providing conditions under which leadership qualities can be recognized and developed. With time and experience in making decisions, one's decisions become programmed results. This is where one sees the apparently decisive leader making and giving immediate decisions. Closer examination would reveal, however, that the responses were the result of patterned behavior, for the normal mind is but a computer with the experience of prior similar situations serving as a base. It is entirely true, however, that intuition, powers of observation, and creative imagination offer a basis for true leadership. It was Dr. Alexis Carrel, who in his memorable classic book, *Man, The Unknown*, said:

> Men of genius, in addition to powers of observation and comprehension, possess other qualities, such as intuition and creative imagination. Through intuition they learn things ignored by other men. A true leader of men does not need psychological tests when choosing subordinates. He appraises in a flash a man's value, senses his virtues and vices. A great scientist instinctively takes a path leading to a discovery. The knowledge that great physicians sometimes possess concerning their patients is of such a nature. This phenomenon was formerly called inspiration.

Management Control

In business, where leadership and control is of a specific nature, and with which we are concerned here, we may consider control to fall into three areas:

1. The nature of the control process in management,
2. The objectives of effective control and how to achieve them.
3. The special objectives of executive control

Nature of Management Control

In the business society, and it is a social order unto itself, control is a process that enables an executive to seek results which come as closely as possible to the objective. Such control then, consists of directing, disciplining and supervising people to get them to assist in reaching desired standards of performance results, and intermediate and long-term goals. Control also seeks to minimize any errors and to prevent discrepancies from arising between plans and results. And finally, control must by its very nature, be continuous; there can be no periods of omission or failure to maintain adequate lines of control.

Measurement enters into control when standards of performance and product are set, and an evaluation is made regarding results. Planning in its broadest sense must of necessity precede standards as well as measurement. The noted Frederick W. Taylor, more than 40 years ago did just that. He set standards through time study and then checked performance, resulting in rather frequent changes in standards by reason of improving the sequence of motions and the methods of doing work.

Naturally, not all can be measured for there are many factors in control that make for difficulty in measurement. Some of these, although there have been many attempts made to measure them which to a degree are successful for a period of time, are attitudes. The beliefs people have, human capacities, thought processes, personalities and prejudices are frankly difficult to interpret and to turn into positive advantage to the executive. If they are negative, then the objectives of management can suffer seriously. Attitude surveys are often useful and helpful, but are limited because of their being dated the moment they are completed. And then, management may not be able to make proper or effective use of survey findings.

One well-known hotel corporation is very strong on management controls of a financial and cost-finding nature, but it is woefully lacking in communications and most important, coordination. The corporation has bulletin boards, a house organ, and conducts staff meetings, but all this is far from reality. Middle management is very poorly informed on many matters, the lack of which has lowered their morale and that of the employees. The company does turn in profits, but not as a result of rendering superior services supported by strong internal and external public relations. Here, is this particular corporation, most all of the mechanical aids of control are either in use, expected to be used, or have been in effect at one time or another.

Some aids to control and measurement in use in industry today are mathematical, particularly statistics, which is the application of the probability theory to problems where exact measurement would be impossible. An example of this is the opinion polls used by market research and product-planning organizations.

Electronic devices are also useful, such as data processing equipment and automated equipment for correlating data for control and decision-making purposes.

Nature of Executive Control

Up to now we have briefly covered the bases for control in general, and some of the tools used to achieve control. The most important area, of course, is that with which the executive and administrator is concerned.

In establishing and exercising executive control, we first depend upon and must test the climate, tempo and attitudes in an organization, for as we have already stated, it is the human element that really contributes or detracts from successful control. Control is always to be aimed at achieving results, and not at people or things. Therefore, selling control and maintaining it is a matter of persuasion.

In terms of control procedures, there is a variety to choose from, but here are the major areas:

Positive:
1. Observation — audit and review
2. By example
3. Through the use of records and reports
5. By standing rules
6. By budgets

Negative:
7. By Censure
8. By disciplinary actions

Techniques of Executive Control

One of the major contributions in management has been the work of Professor Erwin Schell of the Massachusetts Institute of Technology, whose noted work, "The Technique of Executive Control," and whose teachings have woven themselves into the foundations and framework of modern business.

He sets forth that there are psychological tools of conduct and disposition which an executive may use to produce positive and proper responses in an organization. These, if properly used, provide the proper atmosphere and background for executive action.

Executive Tools of Conduct

Stimulating Tools. There are two. The first is enthusiasm, which is contagious and emotional in nature. Enthusiasm, to be effective, must be sincere at all times and not simulated.

The other is cheerfulness, a basic quality that shows confidence and conveys strength of purpose. One can be cheerful and still serious, for cheerfulness is an attitude that is in itself optimistic.

Stabilizing Tools. The first of two tools is calmness. Nothing tones down a difficult situation more than apparent self control, especially in a leader. Calmness, a product of experience, strength and true thoughtfulness, is the result of sincere self discipline.

Perhaps even more important as to the aspect of calmness, is consistency. But this does not mean that a person should be placid. Emotions are rarely constant, and one cannot be stimulatingly enthusiastic and also calm. It is in a crisis where calmness is of greatest value, and this is what we stress in the use of this tool of stabilization.

Time-Saving Tools. There are four of these. The first is to be receptive, which makes employees come to an executive willingly without being apprehensive about it. Putting anyone at ease so of his own free will he will come forward with an idea or a complaint, creates an atmosphere of unrestraint essential to understanding.

Next is simplicity achieved through the use of clear, simple expressions, and speaking and writing in a language this is easily understood.

Frankness is a never-failing quality that is encouraging. It results in facts being openly understood. This saves time in permitting prompt consideration of the problems and the issues.

Expression and impression—used together here—save time by driving home ideas, statements, and thoughts without repetition. A tone of voice, the use of well chosen words, saying exactly what is meant, and avoiding unnecessary conversation, make for progress.

Conforming Tools. The first of these is firmness, which again brings up confidence and secures an atmosphere of conformance to the will of the executive. One can be mild but firm, gentle but sincere, thereby showing careful forethought. But such a quality should be flexible in that it must not convey obstinancy or irresolution.

The second is tact, a quality and approach that is basically necessary in any position or station in life. Briefly, it is recognized as the ability to appeal to the positive moods of the individual, such as loyalty, duty and justice. It seeks to remove negative factors such as hatred, resentment, suspicion and anger. The net desired result and effect is to achieve mutual understanding and cooperation.

Then there is tolerance and patience, which are extremely important and desirable, but often the most trying. So much organized ignorance exists, confounded by impatience, so as to create almost intolerable atmospheres in organizations. Hurry is waste and worry, encouraging fear, and suspicion, and resulting in the dangers and consequences of dissatisfaction.

Restraining Tools. Natural dignity denotes authority, commands respect, and conveys the confidence of knowledge. It also shows a sincere regard for responsibilities not only to the company, but to others. Never must dignity be simulated.

Courtesy is the great defensive tool of the executive, and a great time saver. Courtesy begets courtesy, if by example alone. The business of business can be conducted more easily and quickly with courtesy. It was Richter who said, "Men like bullets, go farthest when they are smoothest."

Tools of Loyalty. The basic tools of kindliness and friendliness alone are not enough to fashion complete loyalty, as a sincere basis for developing understanding. What is perhaps more important is justice and the observance of the Golden Rule: "Do unto others as you would have them do unto you."

How to Fire Tactfully

Firing someone is always an unpleasant task. But there are human aspects which should be considered that can greatly minimize the ill effects of such an act.

Managers and lower echelon employees differ in their handling. This is because an executive is usually thought of as a member of the immediate family. While the employee is considered a family member, too, his lower status often makes it easier to assist him in any relocation effort, than the executive.

Here are some management methods that are successfully used to separate supervisors, middle management, and executives.

1. The Sahara assignment. This is where a person is given a low-level, come-down task, or is sent to conduct a survey which no one reads or uses.
2. The move upstairs. This means a promotion with little or no authority to do anything.
3. The bypass technique. This is used when no one really wants to do the actual firing. It begins by excluding the person from conferences, meetings, and memoranda.

All of these methods result in a separation sooner or later. The person simply gets the hint and begins searching on his own with the approval of management. Usually there is no time limit, but pressure builds up as time passes, and gentle suggestions are followed by direct offers to assist in job placement.

In rank and file level cases, fair and human treatment is essential to minimize harmful effects. In such situations it is wise to simply use existing procedures. Usually the process begins with a verbal warning, followed by a written one if the condition continues, always being sure to spell out the consequences. It usually ends with a final warning which simply says that if the condition or rule infraction does not cease by a specific time, dismissal will follow.

In all cases, a written record of what transpires should be kept and maintained by the immediate superior to the individual. If a personnel department exists, it should also be copied.

Never fire spontaneously. Constructive discussion pointing up the favorable as well as the unfavorable aspects of performance is necessary and human. Help and never hinder a person. There is simply no such thing as a bad person. Everyone has a right to live and to work.

Also avoid firing anyone in an offhanded manner. Privacy is a must. Analyze the dismissal, discover if you will that the employer may well be a root cause. No one is 100% wrong or right. Callous firing and dismissals for any reason, usually strike back at the employer. It destroys morale, lowers production and service, and sets up chain reactions of dismissals and resignations that give the employer a bad name.

The employer's role through management representatives, must help in every possible way to help the about-to-be-fired person to keep his self-respect and his standing with colleagues.

Never attack character, integrity, or personal aspects of a person's behavior. The situation can and sometimes may be reversed. Many a fired person somewhere moves elsewhere and up the line, remembers his experience, and metes out the same type of treatment to the very individual who offended him unjustly before, and who now may be a subordinate.

13

Organization, Management, and Control of Records

In planning about installing, designing, organizing or streamlining a records system, one should ask the following questions:

Why are certain records necessary?

How many should there be?

What should they consist of?

How can I design them easily?

How can I use them effectively?

What will they cost?

These basic considerations show the importance of carefully evaluating your records' function in relation to your overall program. In thinking about the problem, it is wise to keep the objectives of the program, its size and scope, and special plans and budget limitations clearly in view. They guide one's judgments as to how to proceed.

Today more and more importance is being placed on the development and care of accurate, and up-to-date records. The increasing responsibility and widening scope of operations, what with more government regulation of business, calls for prompt and sound decisions, based on facts.

Only records can provide this information. Such a "silent organization" generally has three major purposes:

1. To provide a running account of essential information on every function, before, during and after an action takes place.

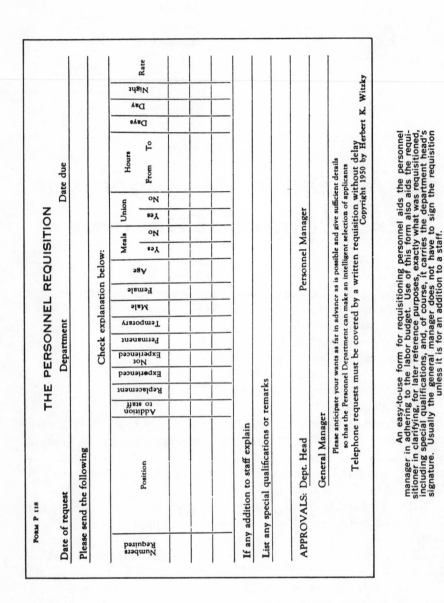

FORM P 118

THE PERSONNEL REQUISITION

Date of request　　　Department　　　Date due

Please send the following

Check explanation below:

Numbers Required	Position	Addition to staff	Replacement	Experienced	Not Experienced	Permanent	Temporary	Male	Female	Age	Meals Yes	Meals No	Union Yes	Union No	Hours From	Hours To	Days	Day	Night	Rate

If any addition to staff explain

List any special qualifications or remarks

APPROVALS: Dept. Head　　　Personnel Manager

General Manager

Please anticipate your wants as far in advance as is possible and give sufficient details
so that the Personnel Department can make an intelligent selection of applicants
Telephone requests must be covered by a written requisition without delay

Copyright 1950 by Herbert K. Witzky

An easy-to-use form for requisitioning personnel aids the personnel manager in adhering to the labor budget. Use of this form also aids the requisitioner in clarifying, for later reference purposes, exactly what was requisitioned, including special qualifications, and, of course, it carries the department head's signature. Usually the general manager does not have to sign the requisition unless it is for an addition to a staff.

2. To reflect conditioning factors and the course of a function during operations.
3. To study the facts obtainable from records and help determine future policy.

Records as Control Instruments

Records, obviously, should also be considered as control instruments. Not only do they serve as indicators on the course and behavior of operations, but as study and research will show, they also provide useful information for statistical comparisons, reports and memoranda which has a direct bearing on operating costs. The effective utilization of the research element in records should be carefully considered; it pays dividends in time.

Let us first consider the definition of a *form,* which might prove interesting and helpful: A form is a blank arrangement of copy and lines on some material, usually paper or cardboard, that is made up for the purpose of recording information.* A moments reflection will show that this apparently simple definition is really all inclusive showing the true basis of any form.

The Number Required

As to the number of records required in a hotel, a four-year review of record systems in 127 hotel companies shows an average of 102 basic records. Smaller hotels with less than 500 employees showed proportionately less. No steadfast rule can be devised as to how many are required; it depends solely on the organizational problem.

The following list however, can be used as a guide from which to select those which are necessary and apply to a hotel.

Those That May Be Printed	Those That May Be Mimeographed
Front Office:	*Accounting Department:*
Passengers' Bills (Rack Slips)	Payment Voucher
Agreement on Pets	Discount Voucher
Patron's History Cards	Waiters' Orders
Rack Slip Envelopes	Room Service Maitre's Order
Luggage Custody Form	Sales Resume
Advance Payment Receipt	Check Cashing List
Certified Mail & Cable Receipt	(Restaurant)
Label for Mail Forwarding	

*Coleman Lloyd Maze, former chairman of the Management Department of the School of Commerce, New York University.

Those That May Be Printed	Those That May Be Mimeographed

Front Office (cont'd):
Registration Card
Debit Order
Hotel Stickers
Good Morning Labels
Equipment Rental
Rack Cards
Mail Delivered By Hand
  (Book)

Telephones:
Telephone Messages
Envelope Messages
Local Calls Vouchers

Laundry:
Price List
Laundry Bill with Rates

Accounting Department:
City Account Bills
Permit to Withdraw Goods
Accounting Sheets (large)
Accounting Sheets (small)
Kardex Sheets
Daily Reports
13-Column Paper
Payment Voucher (card)
City Account
Checks — Dining Rooms
Checks — Room Service
Room Service Order
Kardex Cards
Passenger Bills (copies)
4 Column Book
2 Column Book
Quadrille Booklets
Accounts Receivable (sheets)
Equipment Inventory Cards
Cover for Accounting Books

Cashiers:
Foreign Currency Exchange
Debit Voucher
Credit Voucher
Cashiers' Envelopes
Adding Machine Paper

Storeroom:
Food Order to Storeroom
Beverage Order to Storeroom
Food Order to Ice Boxes
Fresh Food Order
Fresh Food Inventory
Plaque and Cutlery
  (Delivery)
Report on Merchandise
  Received

Cashiers:
Report on Foreign Currency
Cashier's Report
Check Cashing Form
Bill Transfer

Front Office:
Departure Cards
Payment Order on Agency
  Commissions
Room and Rate Change
  Voucher
Mail Forwarding Cards
Reservation Form
Daily Report (Rooms)
Night Clerk's Report
Arrival and Departure Cards
  (Bell Boys)
American Plan Notification
Control Sheet (Bell Captain)
Log Book

Telephones:
Long Distance Calls Report
Long Distance Calls Voucher
Early Call Sheet

Laundry:
Housekeeper's Wash Order
Waiter's Wash Order
Laundry Note Book

Those That May Be Printed	Those That May Be Mimeographed
Cashiers (cont'd):	*Personnel Office:*
Check Cashing Form	Application Form
Banquet Quota Receipt	Uniform Delivery Order
	Advance on Pay Sheet
Personnel Office:	Overtime Vouchers
Payroll Sheet (Employees)	Application for Vacation
Payroll Sheet (Workmen)	Hours Leave Permit
Social Security Envelopes	
Discharge Form	*Housekeeping:*
Registration Book for	Lost and Found Voucher
Workmen under Age	Maid's Occupancy Report
Workmen's Contracts	Housekeeper's Room Count
Kardex Cards	
	Miscellaneous:
Storerooms:	Daily Time Sheet
Order for Banquets	Key Control Sheet
Bin Cards	Key Replacement Slip

Total forms to be printed: 56
Total forms to be mimeographed: 46

The Scientific Approach

On being confronted with the problem of developing, installing, and operating records, it is best to begin by measuring your operation. Then study and evaluate the practicability of other known systems; finally one should adopt proven methods and tools to fit the specific needs, whatever they may be.

Define the Objective. To simplify the technique, the following approach may be used as a guide:

1. Define the objective. What is expected and wanted?
2. Observe, collect and study data.
3. Interpret data.
4. Evaluate, weigh and decide.
5. Apply; go ahead with the forms; use them.
6. Check them in use. Evaluate their efficiency, make changes as required.

Consider System and Procedure. In designing forms, it is well to know how they fit into a regular work routine. System is the operating and connecting element in designing forms. Each one should dovetail into another, affecting a smooth pattern and guaranteeing a minimum of effort and time in operation.

System, nothing more than an orderly method of doing work, should be simple, direct, cover the objective, and be flexible, modern and practical.

In drawing up forms, be sure to chart the flow of each operation into which your form fits. For example, in handling a new employee, follow the applicant through the entire employment procedure, from application blank to employment and follow up.

If one wishes to revamp an old system, first survey the scope of the entire operation. Do this by studying operational steps, and know the role each form plays in the system.

Arrangement is important. The lines drawn and space allocated must fit actual needs. If a typist has to copy information, be sure she does not have to jump all over the form. Try to have similar information appear on the same area and space on all forms. That's known as zoning and dovetailing. If information is to be copied from a registration blank onto a history card, be sure to check for zoning.

Everyone knows forms are expensive. Once printed they represent a considerable investment. Errors discovered later are often too costly to correct. Therefore, it is well to keep in mind whether your forms are machine or hand-written, the number required, how many are handled in one operation, the size of the filing equipment, and the life expectancy of the form.

Proper Equipment

Putting Color to Work. Use color. It is helpful in locating information easily and quickly. In handling or dispatching, it saves time, eliminates errors and speeds up routine up and down the line. Then, too, color has a strange psychological appeal, a factor in reducing boredom. It gets attention, holds interest, and is easier to see than size, print, or a symbol. Its slight additional cost is secondary to the greater efficiency obtained. Visible record control systems use color effectively to keep an accurate control on merit ratings, grievances, warnings, accidents, absences, lateness, and other information.

Buying Equipment. Buying proper equipment can save money as well as adding to the efficiency of your system. Cabinets and drawers that take up little space but are easy and fast to operate, are generally best. It is wise to consider the long-range view. If the initial cost seems high, considerable clerical savings over a period of time are often possible when using the correct equipment.

Designing the Record Form. Simply take a sheet of paper and list

PERSONNEL AUTHORIZATION CARD

Name_____ Date_____

Address_____ Tel. No._____

Address_____ Tel. No._____

Date of Birth_____ Soc. Sec. No._____

Locker Number_____ Time No._____

Approved by Personnel Department for Employment_____

DEPARTMENT RECORD

Personnel Department

Plaza Employment Date_____ Job Approved For_____

PAYROLL CHANGES AND TRANSFERS

Date	Position	Rate	Date	Position	Rate

HOW TO USE THIS FORM

This is your personnel authorization record for this employee. Use it to record transfers or changes in job classification, payroll and address. When an employee is transferred you should return this card to the Personnel Department.

When an employee is terminated, use the back of this card. All you have to do is check the reason for leaving, rate the employee, and then put this card in a sealed envelope and give it to the employee to take to the Personnel Department. If the employee has already left—just send the card in a sealed envelope to the Personnel Department.

P-162

(vertical text, right margin): THE BEARER — Name_____ Department_____ Time No._____ Has been interviewed and all accounts cleared. He should be paid all wages due to ____, 19____, including ____ except ____. Name_____ Personnel Manager — No employee will be paid unless he presents this slip signed and approved by the Personnel Department.

TERMINATION REPORT

REASON FOR LEAVING—CHECKED BY DEPARTMENT HEAD

Reduction in Force		Drinking		Poor Attendance	
Leave of Absence		Gambling		Better Job	
Retirement		Insubordination		Not Enough Pay	
Sickness		Dishonesty		Work too Difficult	
Unknown		Poor Work			

RATING TO BE CHECKED BY DEPARTMENT HEAD

	Excellent	Good	Fair	Poor
Quality of Work				
Dependability				
Cooperativeness				
Job Knowledge				
Conduct				

Would you RE-EMPLOY? Yes_____ No_____ EXPLAIN_____

Last Day Worked_____ Dept. Head Signature_____

EMPLOYEE'S STATEMENT (To Be Filled in by Personnel Department)

_____

_____

Signed_____ Signed_____
Employee   Personnel Department

(vertical text, left margin): If any items are lost, amount charged should be written into the space provided. This will be deducted from the final pay. — Personnel_____ Laundry_____ Housekeeping_____ — Each Department should sign for all items returned: Linen Room_____ Valet_____

Often department heads have no individual records of employees, and must rely in too many cases on the personnel department for contacting an employee. This authorization card, kept by department heads or the manager, is useful as it contains a complete record of the employee, including termination information as well as a rating by the department head, and also has space for an exit interview which may be signed by the employee, and which adds to the effectiveness of total reference information available after an employee has left an organization. When an employee leaves, the form is returned to the personnel department; if there is none, the card may be returned by the department head to the comptroller or manager. It also provides a check on valet, laundry, and locker key items which may be outstanding.

the items that should be located on the form. Then consider system and procedure. Next, on another sheet, roughly sketch in lines, considering form specification and layout. Finally, fill in the information from the first sheet, completing the form.

Then check the work, making sure it dovetails into the system. After testing it in actual practice, it is ready to put into effect.

The success of your operation depends on the time spent in preparation. If governing principles have been correctly applied, the result should be a smooth, easy application. It is directly related to the success of the operating part of the hotel or motel program.

Management and Control of Records

Managing records simply requires supervision "from the cradle to the grave," and this applies to large operations as well as small ones.

It is best to appoint one person in the organization to be responsible for forms control. In most hotels and motor hotels the comptroller's office, chief accountant, or analyst are the best ones to handle the function. In smaller operations the owner or manager should do this.

Ideally, whoever supervises forms control must be well grounded in office work simplification, systems, procedures, accounting, and statistics. He should know basic form design and requirements of all types of printing and reproduction. He should be well versed in developments of office machines and filing methods, and be creative in nature with an open mind for new ideas. He must be able to deal tactfully with all types of employees in every department.

A centralized control of forms should be established for the definite purpose of reducing expenses, eliminating duplication and waste of time and material, and assuring standardized practices, thus maintaining uniform setup, proper coordination, and proper identification of the forms themselves.

Some of the suggested major duties of the established supervisor for forms control are:

1. Authorizing new forms, including design. Checking needs, quantities, functional requirements, and usage. Assigning and registering form numbers, and furnishing specifications.
2. Revising forms including the obtaining and adopting of suggestions covering improvement of forms and their handling.
3. Canceling forms because of combinations, changes in procedures, and discontinuance of certain functions.
4. Maintaining a stationery stock catalog showing form numbers,

form names, and suppliers. A logical and satisfactory method of assignment of form numbers consists of a series of numbers for departmental grouping plus groups for letterheads and envelopes, followed by individual form numbers, followed by letters as follows:

B representing book
C representing card
E representing envelope
P representing pad
S representing single sheet
T representing tag
X representing continuous and snap-out

In some instances the above letters would then be followed by:

A representing 25 sheets or sets
B representing 50 sheets or sets
C representing 100 sheets or sets

"X" snap-out forms may also have a suffix number to represent the number of parts in a snap-out set. Thus F 12-125 PB would indicate form number 125 under department number 12 and would be furnished in pads of 50 sheets or sets. F 8-67X8 would indicate form number 67 under department number 8 and would be furnished in snap-out sets of 8 sheets each.

5. Maintaining a form file which would include copies of specification sheets on all new, revised, and cancelled forms as well as printers' samples of each form. This file would also include samples of certain forms that do not bear form numbers such as special trial forms in the experimental stage and certain work sheets and form letters produced by outlying offices. This latter classification would include some forms for temporary or out-of-the-ordinary use where registration would be impracticable.

6. Planning and conducting surveys pointing toward improvements in forms, systems, and procedures.

7. Preparing information for necessary bulletins and instructions regarding use of forms.

8. Investigating the application of new office equipment and systems to current work.

9. Approving or reviewing for approval the purchase of office machinery and equipment.

10. Maintaining report registers covering essential details regarding all authorized reports. Report register sheets should be arranged by departments, and space should be provided for report number, report name, preparing office, frequency, when and where due, form in which presented, number of copies, description of contents,

and dates of approval of original preparation and subsequent revisions.

11. Maintaining a manual for retention and destruction of records, showing form numbers, form names, and retention periods in the various offices. This manual would also include provisions for retention and destruction of records other than those on numbered forms.

Forms Control Checklist

Managers of records should exercise continuous follow up and approval to insure efficiency and economy. Here is a list of essential details to follow up on any forms program:

1. Can any unnecessary forms or reports be eliminated?
2. Can any unnecessary columns of lines or forms or reports be eliminated?
3. Can the number of copies be reduced?
4. Can two or more forms be combined into one to advantage?
5. Can any reports be issued less frequently?
6. Can some reports be completed in pencil instead of being typed?
7. Can last digits on some statistical reports be eliminated?
8. Are there duplications that can be eliminated?
9. Is any unessential information shown?
10. Are any details carried without a useful purpose?
11. Would an existing report or tabulation serve the purpose for which another report is being prepared?
12. Are there advantages that can be obtained by standardization?
13. Does each report do the job for which it was designed and stop there?
14. Can handling be reduced?
15. Can any waiting or traveling time of papers be eliminated?
16. Can the series of movements of people, equipment, and papers be reduced?
17. Can peak periods be minimized?
18. Are machines being utilized to the greatest extent that is practicable?
19. Are forms functionally correct?
20. Do the forms, as prepared and distributed, adequately check, regulate, and control the operations for which they were designed? Are the purposes accomplished in end results?

How Long to Keep Records

A supervised records management program can save thousands of dollars. Records which legally are no longer required, can be burned or destroyed, releasing valuable filing and floor space. Naturally, there are also savings in upkeep, cleaning, clerical checking and general maintenance and handling. Records in hotels generally divide themselves into nine groups. Here is a listing, also showing retention time.

I. Books of Original Entry

1. General Journal
2. Cash Receipts Journal
3. Cash Disbursements Journal
4. Sales Journal
5. Allowance Journal
6. Purchase Journal

Permanent records. Should be kept in auditor's office five years, and then placed in permanent storage.

II. Books of Secondary Entry

1. General Ledger
2. Operating Ledger

Same as I.

III. Subsidiary Ledgers

1. Accounts Receivable Ledger:
   (a) Transient Ledger
   (b) Lease Ledger
   (c) City Ledger
   (d) Delinquent Ledger
   (e) All other trade accounts
   (f) Receivable Ledger

May be destroyed three years after the accounts are closed or become inactive. These records should be kept in auditor's office one year, placed in storage for two more years.

2. Subscribers to capital stock

Permanent records. Should be kept in auditor's office until all balances are closed and all stock issued, and then placed in permanent storage.

3. Equipment Ledger:
   (a) Furniture and equipment
   (b) Tableware and linen

Should be kept in auditor's office permanently.

4. Accounts Payable Ledgers:
   (a) Trade
   (b) Contractors

Same as III-1.

III. Subsidiary Ledgers (cont'd)

5. Notes Payable Register   Same as III-1.

6. Capital Stock Records   Same as III-2.

7. Minute Books   Permanent record. Should always be accessible.

IV. Vouchers and Invoices

1. Purchase vouchers: Permanent record. Should be
    (a) Fixed asset additions   filed separately from other
        and replacements   vouchers and kept in auditor's office for at least two years and then placed in permanent storage.

    (b) Other purchase   May be destroyed after six years,
        vouchers   being retained in auditor's office two years and then placed in storage.

2. Petty cash vouchers   Same as IV-2a.

3. Restaurant checks (cash)   Retain until regular audit is completed, but at least six months.

4. Charge vouchers including   Retain until account has been
    restaurant checks   paid, but at least one year.

5. Allowance vouchers   Same as IV-4.

V. Departmental Sales Records

1. Room Count   May be destroyed after six years.
2. Restaurant Cashier's Sheets   Should be kept in auditor's office
3. Telephone Traffic Sheets   until audit is made, and then
4. All Other Departmental   placed in storage.
    Sales Journals

VI. Reports

1. Controller's Daily Reports   Permanent records.

2. Housekeeper's Reports   May be destroyed after one year,
    (including Maid's Reports)   or after regular audit.

VI. Reports (cont'd)

3. Report of Night Clerk	Should be preserved as part of controller's report if the latter does not contain the same information, otherwise may be destroyed after one year.
4. Report of General Cashier	Permanent records.
5. Daily Food Cost Reports	May be destroyed after one year.
6. Monthly Food Cost Reports	Permanent records.
7. Monthly Audit Reports	Permanent records.
8. Transcript of Guest Ledger or machine summary	Retain as long as guest account cards—one year in the auditor's office and two years in storage.

VII. Front Office Records

1. Register Registration Cards	May be destroyed after three years.
2. Room Rack Slips	Should be destroyed as soon as guest departs.
3. Information Rack Slips	Same as VII-2.
4. Departure Books	Same as VII-1.
5. Mail Forwarding Cards	May be destroyed after three months.
6. Receipts for Safety Envelopes	May be destroyed after one year.
7. Receipts for Valuable Packages	May be destroyed after one year.
8. Record of Mail Returned to Post Office	May be destroyed after three months.
9. Rooming Slip	May be destroyed after one year or after regular audit.

VII. Front Office Records (cont'd)

10. Record of Bell Service	May be destroyed after three months.
11. Credit Cards	Guests should be requested to renew annually and cards not renewed after two years may be destroyed.
12. Front Office Cash Sheets or Machine Cash Vouchers	Same as VII-4.

VIII. Payroll Records

1. Applications	May be destroyed after employee leaves.
2. Employment Contracts	Permanent records.
3. Time Cards and Time Books	May be destroyed after one year or after regular audit.
4. Payroll Sheets	May be destroyed after six years.
5. Employee Earning Records	Same as VIII-4.
6. Payroll Checks or Receipts	Same as VIII-4.
7. Extra Wage Vouchers	May be destroyed after one year, or after regular audit if listed on payroll sheets.

IX. Personnel Records

1. Personnel Requisition	One year.
2. Labor Journal or Employment Journal	One year.
3. Preliminary Application Blank	Three months.
4. Regular Application Blank	Six months, or longer if desired; permanent for employee.
5. Regular Reference Investigation Form	Six years.

6. Telephone Reference   Six years.
Investigation Form

7. Request for Physical   May be destroyed immediately.
Examination

8. Introductory slip or pass   May be destroyed immediately.

9. Dept. Personnel Record/   Returned to Personnel if/when
History   employee leaves.

10. Regular Personnel Dept.   Indefinitely.
History Card

11. Weekly Personnel Activities   One year.
Record

12. Multiple Change Notice   Six years.
(used for change of rate,
classification, status,
address, leave of absence,
termination)

13. Leave of Absence   At end of leave of absence.
Agreement

14. Change of Address Notice   Indefinitely.

15. Absence Notice   Indefinitely.

16. Merit Rating Report   Indefinitely.

17. Medical Pass   May be destroyed immediately.

18. Medical Release for Work   Indefinitely.

19. Dept. Accident Report   Indefinitely.

20. Accident Inspection Report   Indefinitely.

21. Monthly Accident Record   Three years.

22. Monthly Labor Turnover   Indefinitely.
and Employment Analysis

23. Personnel Journal (usually   Indefinitely.
    monthly classifying all
    activities)

24. Transfer Journal   Indefinitely.

25. Wage Adjustment and   Indefinitely.
    Increase Journal

26. Termination Journal   Indefinitely.

X. Miscellaneous

1. Cancelled Bank Checks   May be destroyed after six years.

2. Cancelled Notes Payable   May be destroyed after six years.

3. Requisitions   May be destroyed after one year.

14

Managerial and Cost Control

It was approximately ten years ago that progressive leaders in the hotel industry began emphasizing the need for scientific management and bringing it to the attention of hotel men everywhere. During this period, significant changes and techniques in organization, planning, personnel administration, finance and the analysis, interpretation and control of business costs have been introduced and applied.

However, due to the unprecedented rise in operating costs, the problem of their control has received major attention. The increasing complexities of operating hotels profitably in the face of rising competition, increasing taxation, more government controls and rising costs, call for prompt consideration as to the use and adaptation of new methods and techniques to maintain adequate profit-to-cost ratios.

Other major industries have served the hotel industry well by providing a useable source of readily adaptable, pre-tested techniques. They are the result of over forty years of experience, largely due to these industries having the need for effective solutions to problems at a much earlier period in our industrial history. The effective implementation of cost control depends on five major factors:

1. Organization of the function.
2. Basis for cost control.
3. The tools of cost control.
4. The divisions of cost control.
5. A practical approach to control.

Organization of the Function

Cost control is a tool of management and, therefore, someone in an organization must be responsible for it. In modern industrial organizations this person is usually the cost accountant or comptroller. This also holds true for many hotels. In some instances, a special analyst or analysis department is set up for this purpose. In all instances, however, the functions should have top level reporting responsibility so that they become an effective executive working tool.

Basis for Cost Control

The basis for control is standardization. A standard is a recognized, acceptable, and carefully determined measure. It relates to all the components of cost. Thus we have standards for labor, materials, supplies, direct and indirect expenses, each of which has definite measurable characteristics which can be precisely determined. Without this no accurate degree of control can be effective.

Tools of Cost Control

Standards are divided into two general classifications:

1. "Current" Standards
2. Basis or "measured" standards

"Current" standards are often referred to as "guesstimates". They have a place in control but are usually used for lack of a more precise measure and are often better than no standards at all.

Positive control, however, is best established with measured standards. These represent the real tools of control. Based on a solid foundation of facts and analysis they are determined from carefully measured basic factors such as time, size and quantity, which are further subdivided. For example, a standard material cost for food is determined by measuring the cost of all the elements in a portion served a guest. To this is added a standard labor cost which should be determined by time and motion study, and job analysis, and then priced at the wage rate for the occupations handling the item. Then a standard overhead cost is added which consists of expenses inherent in the total operation, reduced to a unit charge under conditions of normal operation. These are obtained by analyzing total expense charges in relation to the activity that produced them.

All of this serves as a basis for the next area of control, namely managerial control, otherwise known as budgetary control which is a separate function.

Divisions of Cost Control

Cost control consists of three divisions:

1. Material cost control
2. Labor cost control
3. Overhead cost control

Each requires separate handling. We have current examples—a food and beverage control function, and payroll analysis function, both of which were originally operated as separate departments or functions. The last is not as well known or often found as a separate function, but it is usually a responsibility of the comptroller in the hotel, or the accountant in the motel.

Material control deals with physical and material things. It is quantitative and qualitative in approach. Thus we have portion control and standard specifications as examples which are part of food control systems today.

Labor cost control is based on labor standards set after careful study of work time (man-hours) required to perform functions according to an established routine based on a study of layout, floor work and function, etc., to determine the most economical procedure and method.

Overhead cost control always contains a proportion of fixed expenses such as heat, light, power, taxes, insurance, and is made up of direct and indirect expenses which do not include materials or labor.

Practical Approach to Control

Many control systems fail to accomplish what they set out to do. They accurately gather, clarify and interpret data, but often overlook people who should be taken along every step of the way. Fear of the unknown is worse than fear of a specific thing. Staff resistance can effectively block sincere, worthwhile management objectives.

A psychological approach, taking into consideration the best elements of the accounting and industrial engineering techniques, seldom fails to produce desired results. Communications concerning a general project or work in process should be open and above board. It was Glenn Gardner who said that there should be three-way communications—from the to top the bottom, from the bottom to the top and horizontally.

Tapping staff thinking releases the will to work, provides mutual interest and points the way to improvements, changes and savings that are more definite and lasting.

Measuring an Operation's Profitability

Nothing has served industry better in recent years than visual aids. In control and financial management, break-even charts effectively used in other industries make it easy to see the condition of an organization at a glance. Du Pont's amazing progress in control is directly related to their chart room in Wilmington, Delaware where well over 300 charts are maintained and regularly reviewed by top management. These measure every phase of management. Believing in Confucius who said, "A picture is worth a thousand words", Du Pont executives in a few hours of time at periodical meetings are able to appraise the organization's profitability.

Balanced Management

While the very first thing that concerns a manager or operator is the profit and cost relationship of his hotel or motel, important consideration given to balanced management is even more essential. No matter the size, whether it be a large or small organization the elements of sound management must be present.

Experience in many situations in evaluating the practical application of management programs in companies and hotels reveals eleven major areas in question form, the answers to which will reveal the soundness and balance of an operation.

Determining an Operation's Effectiveness

1. What are the profit volume relationships for food, rooms, beverage, and other services? Are they in keeping with standards? Have these standards been evaluated?
2. Are the products sold—rooms, food, beverages, public spaces, and other facilities and services satisfactory, pleasing, and in keeping with public demand?
3. What is the sales volume, and the potential?
4. Are the duties, responsibilities, and functions for departments, clearly established, understood, and organized for maximum efficiency, flexibility, and control?
5. Are controls over budgets, inventories, and payrolls in line with standards set? With the industry? Can they be improved through study and re-evaluations?
6. Are sales methods, channels of coverage, policies, and techniques adequate, convenient, and resultful?

7. Are services, facilities, layout and methods, best utilized? Is labor most completely utilized?
8. Are new methods sought, installed, developed, and analyzed?
9. Are cost ratios and structures in line with competition higher or lower in relation to services?
10. Are industrial relations, personnel and human relations policies up to date? Is there harmony, teamwork, and efficiency so as to provide the maximum for payroll dollars?
11. Are wages correctly established? Too low or too high? What is the wage plan and basis for pay and increases?

Techniques for Managing Change

Managing change is a technical consideration that requires knowledgeable care. Changes must always be introduced so as to minimize losses in productivity. And they must maximize the duration of the benefits of change, making certain that the change in method, concept, and procedure is really a suitable solution to the problem which caused planning the change in the first place.

Change in our society is faster than ever before, speeded up by higher educational levels in society, faster communications and transportation, and aided by radio, television, and greater human expectations in life.

In the hotel and food service industry, change is just really beginning to take place on a broad scale. This is due to obsolescence in methods, procedures, construction spurred by competition, new technologies, systems, equal opportunity, more leisure time, and new products.

Admittedly conflict is found in the human reaction to change, and in the increasing need for change itself. And it is clearly affecting the performance objectives of managers and their function.

Progressive organizations look at managers as change specialists and expect them to be able to diagnose, define, understand, and work effectively in the management of change itself.

There are really only five basic steps in the effective management of change. They should be thought of as consecutive links in a chain-like procedure. They are:

1. *Association.* This is the first step. It means the interaction of everyone involved in the change. All persons who work in the group, and who are related in any way to the effort, must of necessity have the opportunity to work and deal with each other on the very nature and extent of the change itself.
2. *Involvement.* There must be time allowed through which all per-

sons affected by the change are able to understand it through dialogue, discussion, and review.

3. *Relationship.* This is a rather positive emotional attachment among all those who are associated with and who are taking part in the change.
4. *Commitment.* This is the vital link which assures active participation in all the processes of change.
5. *Action.* This is the final step, which simply means putting the change into effect.

In and during the entire process, feedback, through association and contact, is essential. Discussion — the employment of all related data, facts, and understanding thereof — are the key elements that make change truly resultful and effective.

The Future

Greater refinements in the application of management controls and simplified systems with less paper work, fewer reports and less detail which provides more freedom to management, and a realistic application of all the elements in scientific management, will at least insure the operator and manager that he is doing all he possibly can to maintain a profitable operation that stays ahead of costs rather than behind them.

15

Conducting a
Profit Improvement Program

The scientific management of a business today depends on many factors. A principal one is that the products and services it produces must meet the demands and requirements of the public. But management must be able to supply goods and services at prices which the various publics it serves will pay.

In the innkeeping industry, rising costs have largely been met by increasing room rates and food and beverages charges. The danger of this procedure is readily apparent. It has already pointed up a marked decrease in unit sales by pricing services and facilities out of the reach of present as well as potential new markets.

One answer to meet this problem successfully has been to apply a planned cost reduction program that measures, simplifies, combines and utilizes new methods. Truly we say, "You may know what your costs are, but do you know what they should and could be?"

The techniques that were employed have paid for themselves out of savings, and economies and even resulted in improved services and new standards of performance.

A Typical Case History

After 20 years of management under one of the largest and best-known hotel companies in the United States, a major hotel located in a principal city was acquired by another well-known chain. The hotel had been successful, was well located, benefited from a national reservation referral system, and had been operating under a standard cost system under which daily reports were issued comparing performance against standards and budgets. For about three years prior to the acquisition, the hotel was experiencing difficulty in meeting management objectives and in lowering its operating costs. With the change in ownership, the condition became worse, and, naturally, feelings of apprehension and insecurity on the part of the staff and the employees were prevalent.

After five months under new and experienced management, internal resistance and the state of morale was strong enough that it began to place not only the earnings position but the public relations image of the hotel, in terms of the immediate community and the public at large, in serious jeopardy.

Plan of Action

After meeting with principals and talking with some of the department heads, which actually took the form of a preliminary survey, a complete outline of a profit improvement program to be followed by a direct, on-the-job application and installation of solutions to problems, was developed for the hotel. Objectives and a timetable were established which projected how and at about what time improvements and changes were expected to be put into effect. An estimate was also prepared to show how rapidly the costs of the profit improvement program and the survey would pay for itself out of savings, economies and recommendations on increasing sales volume.

Once the work was begun, every phase of the operation in the management of the property including each division, department, functional area including procedures, methods, standards and overall policies, were evaluated and changed as required after conferring and obtaining the approval of the new owner and his Operating Board of Directors.

Conditions Necessary to Success

Every organization has its own self-generating image replete with a built-in body politic, peculiarities, structural and personal differences, attitudes, and various sociological backgrounds. Under strong, able leadership all of these factors can be successfully coordinated in order to achieve desired goals with a minimum of friction and resistance.

In conducting the preliminary survey, it was necessary to perceive, recognize and appraise these conditions. Experience, time and an aptitude are essential at this critical opening phase of any similar survey and program. In this particular situation it resulted in creating an awareness of three important conditions:

1. Management was completely aware of the seriousness of the problem.
2. Management had confidence in the counselor's experience to help.
3. Management was ready to act.

As a result there developed mutual responsibility, maximum interest and cooperation by meeting with the staff and principals to explain the approach and methods leading to change. This was a continuous process, a constant meeting of minds in order to develop solutions to problems and obtain the necessary cooperation to put them to work.

Typical Problems and Results

In beginning a program of this kind, it is usually wise to tackle a problem area which lends itself to direct and easily recognizable solutions, and where a majority of agreement pertaining to recommendations and changes will be found. This builds confidence and assists in obtaining cooperation, and establishing mutual respect. Sometimes the major problem area requiring immediate solutions must be studied first. Usually, this falls in the aforementioned category, and a few points of agreement on recommendations, resulting in immediate successes, will be established.

In this particular hotel study, sales and promotion was not only an immediate project, but the major and most serious concern of the new owners. It was therefore, necessary to begin the study in this functional area.

Sales and Promotion. A major problem area of primary concern to management was the Sales and Promotion Department. Analysis and study resulted in a complete realignment of staff functions, duties, and responsibilities.

Procedures were changed, quotas were established, staff duties were simplified, all sales and follow-up letters were revised, the operation and use of guest history systems was revived, promotional plans were developed, mailing lists and tests were established, a sales kit, more effective tie-ins, improved contact utilization, and closer cooperation with the Front Office Department was also established.

Management. Following the analysis, the duties, functions and responsibilities of management were reorganized covering such classifications as General Manager, Resident Manager, Executive Assistant Manager, Assistant Managers, and other principal department heads.

This resulted in greater efficiency, tighter control and better co-ordination, through proper alignment of functions and responsibilities.

It also provided a direct saving of more than $50,000 per annum in management payroll alone.

Payroll. Prior to the survey a payroll control system had been installed to control payroll and effect reductions in staff.

After six months, union and employee resistance to the payroll reduction suggestions ended in slow-downs, breakage and widespread absenteeism.

For example, in one month alone 2243 absentee days were recorded.

The analysis revealed that primarily records rather than people had been studied with the result that many suggestions had not been co-operatively developed and were found unworkable. Little time had been spent studying and analyzing functions so as to combine, simplify, and thereby bring about logical savings.

The importance of working with people had been largely overlooked. Poor morale had affected services and this was noted in the community relations survey which was also conducted.

Working closely with employees, and the staff, operating factors to common denominators were reduced. Functions were simplified and combined, eliminating overlapping and duplication wherever possible, and introducing many time and labor saving methods.

The staff put recommendations in operation. A simplified "one man" payroll control was followed. While the original installation was very thorough, it was unnecessarily complicated and too detailed to be really effective.

Again forms and procedures were cut down to "basic essentials." The result was a simplified plan, easily understood, that produced a cost conscious group of department heads and provided them with the simplest tools to plan and maintain proper staff requirements.

Department head morale improved too!

Food Costs and Control. The effectiveness of the food control system was evaluated. It was found that negligible savings had been effected in the six months take-over period. Food costs hovered between 46.06% and 46.08% for the six-month period and were the same for the same period of the previous year.

Simplified procedures, reduction of the staff, and decentralized food control responsibilities were recommended. The food cost dropped to 41.02%. Actually some of the responsibility was returned to the staff; better morale resulted and the staff appreciated management's confidence.

These are only a few of many examples, each in a major problem area.

Results. After completing the installation, a complete report of accomplishments was submitted, which served as a record and future guide, showing savings and economies which had been effected. Also the record of progress to a forecast of about double the profit over the previous year was charted.

The work was the result of a team approach which insured follow-through and a sincere continuation of the program.

The Audit Guide

Working rapidly and objectively depends largely upon the extent to which a survey and program is organized in advance. Here follows a survey outline in five parts, which has been effective over the years:

1. *Policy Evaluation.* Since policies are the foundations of any operation which governs procedures and the organization, a study of various written and unwritten policies is necessary. Instructions, rules and regulations, bulletins, statements, minutes of meetings, and memorandums should be carefully reviewed. The purpose is to determine whether the objectives of the organization, no matter how large or small they are, are being achieved, and whether or not such objectives and policies are in balance with the hotel's requirements.

   These usually cover all operating functions, and may be classified as follows: Basic policies give a broad picture of long range objectives and show which way the organization is heading. General policies are within the framework of basic policies and are usually of a short range nature. Their authorization lies with general management as compared to basic policies, which lie with top management. Departmental policies stem from basic and general policies, and are for the guidance of operating departments within the organization. They are usually determined by department heads and approved by management.

   A review of all policy is basic to a completely objective study. It alone points the way to improvements in procedure and changes in management thinking which guide the organization. Policies must be flexible; they must be in keeping with operational trends and the times. Here the experience of specialists who are constantly in touch with many different organizations is valuable as it provides the latest thinking as well as practical tested experience.

2. *Organized Structural Analysis.* This analysis determines the existing arrangement between the various activities and functions of

the organization. It ascertains whether the objectives of the organization are being harmoniously obtained.

It determines the correct relationship, proper linkage and coordination between cooperating units, and makes sure that they are correctly and carefully defined.

Line and staff functions are defined and separated into the most economical, smooth functioning organizational structure.

Techniques Employed

(a) Study and review of manuals, charts, and graphic materials.

(b) Use of job analysis forms, work schedule sheets for payroll, records of seniority, and job classification.

(c) With the above techniques, the following can be determined:
   (1) units of work and their functions,
   (2) problems under each unit and their function,
   (3) supervision or committees served,
   (4) future plans for expansions and retractions,
   (5) operating problems,
   (6) future operating trends.

(d) Preparation of an organization chart with brief job descriptions, listing operating problems for each department.

3. *Department Analysis.* In addition to the above analysis an individual study of each department or organization unit is necessary. This analysis includes:

(a) Working conditions

(b) Condition of equipment

(c) Layout

(d) Work schedules

(e) Payroll analysis

(f) Production analysis (statistics, with a write-up of procedures and systems)

(g) Product analysis

(h) Employee and guest relations evaluation

4. *The Areas of Profit Volume Relationship.* This final stage in a profit improvement survey covers the most important area of volume and profits and of all related factors.

Here a clear, easy-to-understand picture of the organization presents its futures earnings position. It also shows where expenses are out of line, and where profit and revenues must be increased. It indicates exactly what has to be done and where, in the organization.

5. *Technique Employed.* The organization's standards are established and appraised, not only for what they are, but for what they should be and could be. This can be done in either of two ways:

(a) A comparison and evaluation of the overall figures.

(b) A detailed analysis of all income and expense accounts.

The latter method is so superior to the attainment of real control, that no other method is necessary nor should be attempted.

The analysis begins with a review of all income and expense items in the general books of account. Each account requires an examination to see how it has been influenced by the activity of business during the periods under consideration.

It will be evident that some accounts are not greatly affected by the degree of business activity. To determine which expenses are fixed and which vary, and which can be regulated, a series of "break-even charts" should be made for different time periods. First, a breakdown of fixed, variable and constant or regulated expenses, against gross income must be made as shown in the table. Then industry comparisons can be made and analyzed. Such cost comparisons are helpful, and the organizations with lower costs are the real moneymakers in the industry today.

Charts and Graphs

In the analysis it was found that charts and graphs, whose scope depends on the hotel's size, are extremely helpful in keeping the organization moving forward. A list of some of the charts and graphs which may be developed are:

1. Percentage of payroll against revenue for various operating departments (see Table on page 140).
2. Covers compared to man hours for food service operations (merely to show trends).
3. Sales charts on rooms, foods, beverages and other services.
4. Rates of absenteeism and employee turnover.
5. Inventory control records.
6. Repair and maintenance costs.
7. Food, beverage, and other service costs.
8. Occupancy charts on rooms and banquet areas.
9. Breakeven charts for various departments.

Nothing has served industry better today than visual aids for control and interpretive purposes. Even the smallest operation can benefit by a few simple charts requiring only a few hours a month to keep up to date. These, in addition to the financial report, help to oversee the operation, charts its progress, as well as guide the future of the business. That is why more and more hotels and motels are using such control methods today.

The advantage is obvious. The operator or manager is given free time

19— Average Occupancy 61% January to June		19— Average Occupancy 80% January to June	
Fixed Costs		**Fixed Costs**	
Insurance	$ 5,987	Insurance	$ 20,529
Taxes	————	Taxes	————
Interest	350,922	Interest	344,282
Depreciation	199,016	Depreciation	208,578
Amortization	255,204	Amortization	255,268
Management Fee	33,260	Management Fee	33,006
TOTAL	$ 844,389	TOTAL	$ 861,663
Constant Costs		**Constant Costs**	
Departmental Expenses (Includes Social Security and Employee Relations)	$ 741,704	Departmental Expenses (Includes Social Security and Employee Relations)	$ 783,841
Administration & General	234,212	Administrative & General	212,279
Promotion & Publicity	103,730	Promotion & Publicity	93,600
Heat, Light & Power	148,743	Heat, Light & Power	135,703
Repairs & Maintenance	66,006	Repairs & Maintenance	125,786
Salaries & Wages	1,451,177	Salaries & Wages	1,503,973
TOTAL	$2,745,572	TOTAL	$2,855,182
Variable Costs		**Variable Costs**	
Food	$ 616,351	Food	$ 663,446
Beverage	333,680	Beverage	316,788
Telephone	53,547	Telephone	64,670
Valet	19,114	Valet	25,170
Laundry	18,149	Laundry	19,101
TOTAL	$1,040,841	TOTAL	$1,089,175
FIXED COSTS	$ 844,839	FIXED COSTS	$ 861,663
CONSTANT COSTS	2,745,572	CONSTANT COSTS	2,855,182
VARIABLE COSTS	1,040,841	VARIABLE COSTS	1,089,175
TOTAL COSTS	$4,631,252	TOTAL COSTS	$4,806,020
TOTAL SALES	$4,722,241	TOTAL SALES	$5,450,011
TOTAL COSTS	4,631,252	TOTAL COSTS	4,806,020
SIX MONTHS AVERAGE PROFIT	$ 90,989	SIX MONTHS AVERAGE PROFIT	$ 443,991

to objectively manage and develop his operation, even though his normal working day is a long one.

This thorough approach takes into consideration all the elements that make up a business. And it is the surest way of getting at fundamentals. As in a medical examination, only the thoroughness of the diagnosis will point the way to improvements that are positive and lasting.

Cost Objectives. The opportunity for cost reduction is widespread today. It is important for each hotel and motel to establish an aggressive program defining costs as to what they could and should be, and thereby effectively reducing them.

FORECAST ON OBJECTIVES FOR 19__ AND 19__				
SALES		19__		19__
Rooms	83%	$ 4,870,000	85%	$ 5,220,000
Food	80%	3,900,000	85%	4,430,000
Beverages	66%	2,570,000	70%	3,100,000
Other Sales		595,000		655,000
Total Sales		$11,935,000		$13,405,000
COSTS				
Food	38%	$ 1,482,000	37%	$ 1,640,000
Beverages	28%	719,600		
Departmental Expenses		1,340,000		1,410,000
Administration & General		833,700		860,000
Payroll, Taxes, Employee Relations		189,000		180,000
Advertising & Promotion		170,500		210,000
Heat, Light, Power		402,600		450,000
Repairs and Maintenance		195,200		200,000
Salaries and Wages		3,040,000		3,000,000
Fixed Expenses		1,650,000		1,600,000
Other Sales		220,000		245,000
Total Costs		$10,242,600		$10,663,000
Net Profit		$ 1,692,400		$ 2,742,000

The above forecast shows what changes in the profit volume relationships are possible after adjusting various costs and putting new pricing policies into effect.

The results shown on the graphs were affected with basic economies in payrolls, constant and even fixed costs, and new, planned-for-business — the result of market research and resulting objective merchandising, promotion, sales and basic changes in services and products, in keeping with determined present and future public preferences.

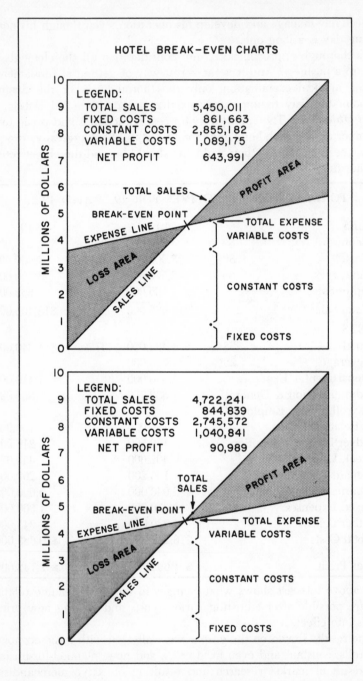

Hotel break-even charts.

The Basic Chart

This is a square with a 45° line on which the hotel's sales are plotted, reading from the bottom left-hand to upper right-hand corners. The scale in dollars is located on the vertical axis, the range suited to the organization's present and potential sales volumes, was set up at $10,000,000.

In setting up the basic chart, total sales appear on the sales line, total expense on the expense line below the amount of sales. Where the expense line and the sales line cross is the break-even point. The area between the two lines below the beak-even point is the loss area, and above, the profit area.

This chart is the basic work sheet on which future changes in volume, in policy, or economic conditions are quickly drawn or visualized.

The value of the chart rests on these obvious, but, too often, neglected important facts:

1. For a business at a given time, the relationship between sales and profits is easily predictable.
2. This relationship is not a constant ratio of expense to sales since only variable costs vary directly with the volume of business, while constant and fixed costs usually do not change without study and evaluation.
3. Changes in the size of the business or in the expense ratios are immediately reflected in the chart.
4. After changes occur in policy, economic trends, or revised operating standards and costs, a new relationship between sales and profits results, which is reflected in the chart.

16

Cutting Telephone Costs

Long distance calls as well as regular calls are considerable problems for management. Here is a procedure ·based on a study of 10 hotel companies where telephone expenses were well controlled. Regardless of the size and value of any operation, the cost reduction methods which follow can result in successfully slicing considerable dollars from telephone costs.

Cut Conversation Costs

Keeping Staff Informed. Let your staff know what costs are and how they compare with other operations. First figure out the average cost per message. Dò this for long distance as well as local calls. Include federal taxes on telephone, telegraph and other mediums. Then make this information available to the staff. It will usually show that the less expensive letter or telegram can save money.

Proper Telephone Service. Use a station-to-station rate wherever possible, particularly if a message can be answered by a. secretary or a staff member. But if the person to be called is an executive or manager traveling about, the person-to-person rate is a valuable service.

Note the extra charges for person-to-person calls; these do not increase with the length of the call. If the call is important, the fee is an excellent investment.

Organizing the Conversation. By eliminating the personal talk about weather and other items, many five-minute calls can be cut to three.

Preparing a simple outline organizing your thoughts in advance is the answer. A three-minute hour glass will be a great help in holding calls to a minimum.

Information on Costs. If the calls are charged to departments, review all the tickets prepared by operators and analyze them. Time and charges should be discussed with persons running up long bills. Sending tickets to departments monthly for review and approval is helpful, too.

Encourage Switching. On calling other hotels and home offices, it is easy for people, on completing their calls, to be asked that the calls be switched. In this way even the remote caller talks to many people, with the cost of this time on the telephone being absorbed with another call and charged to other departments and offices.

Some study is needed to point up any inequities.

The Conference Circuit. Most switchboards provide special circuits which permit two or more people to talk together. The use of such circuits saves time, resulting from expensive repetition and switching time. Conference appointments can be set up by mail.

The Communication Cost Chart. A basic chart, see illustration, gives communication costs from your office to points throughout the United States. It can be very effective in reducing communication costs. A typical chart shows circles radiating from the central point with costs for various types of messages shown at each zone. A telephone company representative will be glad to provide one locally. Usually, most companies have these available.

A staff informed of the importance of cost reduction will find such information helpful, particularly when it is on desks, and in convenient, easy-to-see-at-a-glance locations.

Convert Calls to Letters. Speedy air mail service, with added special delivery, is helpful in savings. A telegram is better than air mail special delivery (and is usually less expensive than a long distance telephone call), and a night letter rate may well serve your purpose.

Many companies use distinctively printed forms and envelopes which indicate the urgency of the message and the need for a printed reply. The first copy is white, the file yellow, receiver's reply copy blue, and the receiver's copy is orange.

The post office will be glad to examine a list of frequently called points, advising whether air mail, special delivery will reach those points by 9 A.M. of the following business day. Making comparisons of such costs points the way to postal service bargains.

Convert Calls to Telegrams. Check the communication cost chart and note whether or not costs differ. Often the telegram is equally effective. It narrows down to the speed required. If a message needs a prompt

150   EXECUTIVE METHODS AND CONTROLS

NEW RATES FOR COAST-TO-COAST INTERSTATE CALLS

DIAL-AND-SAVE ONE MINUTE RATES

FULL RATE	35% DISCOUNT	60% DISCOUNT
WEEKDAYS	**EVENINGS**	**NIGHTS & WEEKENDS**
Monday-Friday 8 a.m.-5 p.m.	Sunday-Friday 5 p.m.-11 p.m.	Every night 11 p.m.-8 a.m. Saturday— day and night Sunday— day and night except 5 p.m. to 11 p.m.
First Minute **56¢**	First Minute **36¢**	First Minute **22¢**

Additional minutes cost less than the first minute.

Dial-direct rates apply on all interstate calls (excluding Alaska) completed from a residence or business phone without operator assistance. They also apply on calls placed with an operator from a residence or business phone where dial-direct facilities are not available. For dial-direct rates to Hawaii, check your operator. Dial-direct rates do not apply to person-to-person, coin, hotel-guest, credit card or collect calls, or to calls charged to another number, because an operator must assist on such calls. Rates quoted do not include tax.

OPERATOR-ASSISTED THREE MINUTE RATES

STATION-TO-STATION
Full rates apply at all times
First 3 minutes
$1.95

PERSON-TO-PERSON
Full rates apply at all times
First 3 minutes
$3.55

Additional minutes same as dial rate. Applicable discounts apply to additional minutes during "Evening" and "Night & Weekend" periods.

This handy communications cost chart can be duplicated and pasted in telephone books or next to telephones, or under the glass-topped desks. When used together with a timing device to hold calls down to a minimum, substantial savings can result.

reply and may require another telegram, then a telephone call may still be less costly.

An added value of the telegram is that it provides a written record of what has transpired. This is important for reservations, purchasing, and other similar purposes where the written record is important.

About TWX

The Bell System publishes a TWX directory which gives identification numbers of TWX locations throughout the country. Direct connections are easy to make and you get a written record with immediate replies. Normal typing speed is slower than actual typing, about 45 words a minute, which is 1/3 of normal talking speed. These rates are lower than station-to-station long distance, but the verbal exchanges helpful in a telephone conversation are not, of course, available.

TWX is generally an expensive investment, particularly with limited use. Monthly lease rates should be reviewed, and the ability of an operator to write low-cost, minimum TWX rates should be analyzed.

Savings in Fixed Equipment Charges

Here is an important area where savings are possible. Requested changes in equipment, additions, etc., are costly. The analyzing of every change will pay for itself. Here are major areas where savings are possible:

Check Hold Relays. Many offices have hold buttons for answering several calls and holding them. This is an expensive "hold relay" device. A review of these systems often shows that the holding device is not used sufficiently to warrant its cost.

Check Unused Buttons. Many telephones have more buttons than they sometimes need. A check on the use of buttons will show whether or not and to what extent buttons are used. Persons having buttons must immediately talk on telephone calls received by others.

Discourage Personal Calls. Here, if an internal dial-out system responding to the out dial digit ("9") is used, many telephone calls can be restricted simply by cutting off the number "9" response.

Have the operator take a record of names of persons who ask for outside wires. Install pay stations around the work areas and halls.

Eliminate Intercom Lines. "Intercom" is a costly feature making it possible for a man, for example, to talk directly with his secretary without dialing an extension or asking the operator for it. A PBX Bell System dial telephone exchange (rented) brings the same results by a dialing of one digit after pressing your secretary's button. This clears the dial tone from the line and gives private conversation when she presses her button connecting with your line. This requires rental of the button and buzzer unit used by executives anyway.

Eliminate Lighted Buttons. The lighted telephone button helps in large offices, such as the Sales Department, but it is expensive. If one person can see or hear another person talking, within a small office, it is not necessary to have a lighted button.

Helpful Operating Suggestions

The time consumed in using telephones is an important item in telephone expense. Here are some helpful suggestions to speed up your business:

The Buzz System. If an executive normally calls his secretary for instructions, he should try these time-saving code calls:

One buzz: "Take incoming call on my line."

Two buzzes: "Pick up your 'phone. I want to talk to you."

Three buzzes: "Please come to my office."

Four buzzes: "The man in my office is staying too long. Come in and remind me of an appointment."

Making Outside Calls. Use your secretary's or other line when making outside calls. Keep the line free for incoming calls. If the line gets a call, it can still be answered, or a buzz to the secretary will have her answering.

Transferring Calls. Transfer calls by flashing the operator. Avoid dialing "O" for operator. Simply depress the cradle button slowly to get your operator.

Long Distance Calls. Stay on the line for long distance calls. Avoid leaving the line and being called. Today's direct-dial long distance operations are very prompt. Incidentally, telephone charges increase if one is not on the line, and being available when the call comes through is good manners.

Improving Services

Service Survey. The biggest help to a hotel or motel can be the telephone service survey which the telephone company makes, telling one exactly how calls are answered by your staff. Simply call the telephone supervisor and arrange for a survey.

The Trunk Line. The telephone company will gladly make a "busy study" to see how many times callers have received busy signals. Surveys such as these are extremely helpful to measure the adequacy of service in a hotel or motel.

17

Management Consultants

At one time or another the question has arisen whether or not to engage a consultant and the following questions have probably been raised:

What are consultants, and how do they operate?
How do consultants get business?
What do they charge?
How the need for a consultant may be determined.
In what areas can a consultant be of assistance?
How consultants are chosen.
How can a client insure getting a good job done?

Professional Advisor

The consulting profession has grown in 40 years from the old well-worn term "efficiency expert" to today's professional advisor. International acceptance has shown that managements and governments, too, obtain valuable aid from consultants.

As an industry, with approximately 1,915 firms in the United States receiving annual fees of over $406 million, consulting firms range from individuals to those with personnel numbering a hundred or more. Most firms average less than 10 people; some are key man operations; others form partnerships or incorporate. The personnel consists of educators, from schools and universities; specialists; manufacturers and suppliers with special technical and product knowledge; and public accounting firms.

Promoting Business

All consultants engage in some kind of sales solicitation. This may consist of sales letters, sales literature, business salesmen, and publicity. Some firms rely largely on direct mail; others publish reports and low cost services to get interest and attention; others write articles and speak before business groups. Word-of-mouth advertising and repeat business also play important roles. Public accounting firms rely largely on writing articles, making speeches, and word-of-mouth publicity.

Earnings and Fees

Current rates paid consultants range from $75 a day for a junior, to $150–$250 a day for a senior, and up to $350 a day for a partner.

It is a good idea for a client to ask for a cost estimate, and a range, such as from $10,000 to $12,000, for a job plus expenses. If costs run over the estimate, a responsible firm or person normally will absorb the difference.

Management consultants say little about their earnings and clients are often suspicious of the fees they earn.

Fees are generally very close to costs, as the figures below show. It is actually not a lucrative business, but one where hard work and concentration is clearly evident.

Here is a typical firm's earnings' picture. It has offices in Connecticut and New York, has a total staff of nineteen people, and charges an average of $200 a day with more for top partner participation.

Consultants' Salaries (20 people)	$220,500	49.0%
Office Salaries	40,950	9.1
Bonuses	18,000	4.0
Travel and Entertainment	29,250	6.5
Rent and Maintenance	11,250	2.5
Training Material, Textbooks, etc.	17,100	3.8
Insurance for Employees	9,000	2.0
Depreciation and Equipment	4,950	1.1
Taxes, Payroll, and General	5,400	1.2
Income Taxes	40,950	9.1
Net Profit (reserved for contingencies)	52,650	11.7
Total Billings	$450,000	100.0%

Determining the Need for a Consultant

The president who says, "I think we need a going over", or a manager who feels outside help—impartial and objective—will be the best way of getting answers and insuring results, determines the need for a consultant. He may justly feel that an insider would cause friction and internal problems, that may bring on more problems.

Companies generally use consultants when:

1. Management does not have the time or staff to do the job.
2. Management tried to do the job and failed.
3. Management needs outside help for internal reasons.
4. Management wants a "fresh" approach.
5. Management wants information not normally available.

There are more direct "tell tale" signs and "symptoms" such as the following, which can help to decide whether a consultant is needed:

1. High turnover of personnel with too many saying "I quit".
2. Declining business in relation to market potential.
3. Increases in operating costs.
4. Drastic and unaccountable shifts in business.
5. Excessive reliance on opinions of committees or executives with the result that ideas are lost.
6. Loss of repeat business.
7. Complaints.
8. Loss of big accounts to competitive companies.

Basically, a consultant can help because he is an experienced outsider who should be able to give facts honestly and objectively. He applies his broad knowledge and stays with a problem until it is solved.

Areas of Assistance

There are a great many areas where consultants can be helpful. The following are some of the services generally used by companies:

1. Conducting a survey to study public reaction to services.
2. Establishing a personnel program.
3. Finding key people.
4. Assisting in formulating compensation plans for executive and regular personnel.
5. Conducting special studies of individual departments and individual problems.
6. Conducting a sales method analysis.

7. Setting up or reorganizing a sales department.
8. Conducting a payroll analysis.
9. Reorganizing the company.
10. Purchasing services and analysis.
11. Establishing training and staff development programs.
12. Determining whether or not to expand.
13. Planning facilities; estimating costs.
14. Determining costs of material and equipment and supplies for a new project.
15. Handling purchasing from the lowest factory source.
16. Reducing operating expenses through planned cost reduction programs.
17. Preparing job analysis and specifications.
18. Conducting studies determining the nature and cost of new products and services and predicting their successful marketing and acceptance by the public.

There are many more, of course. These, however, are the ones most generally provided.

Choosing a Consultant

There are many kinds of consultants, and generally a specific one for each job.

The Controllership Foundation of the Controller's Institute in a special study on consultants has defined various yardsticks for selecting a consultant. Here are some of them:

General Reputation. Does the consultant have a reputation for getting the job done well and quickly? Will he be courageous enough to speak his mind? Does he express himself effectively?

Consultant and Staff. Does the consultant have an adequate staff to handle the assignment? Is the consultant going to maintain constant interest in the problem? How does he rate?

Whether or not a consultant should have direct experience related to a problem or not, is a question. The conclusion drawn by the Controller's Institute is that objectivity and the proven ability to successfully solve problems are essential.

A number of other significant factors require management's attention and consideration in arriving at a decision.

1. The organization that considers engaging a consultant should clearly have in mind what it expects him to do.

2. As a first assignment, it is a good idea to first suggest a limited assignment to the consultant.
3. Talk to several consultants and then decide on the one that suits you and your company best.
4. Remember that the size of the consulting organization is no guarantee of a successful job. Small groups, or an individual, may be better suited for reasons of interest, specialization or concentration of effort.
5. Be prepared to ask for references and check them personally.
6. Get a written proposal that spells out what the work is to cover, how it will be done, whether a written report is to be submitted, how long it will take and what it will cost, and how much time the "key" man will spend on the job.

"Consider this", says Robert F. Dick in a paper for the American Management Association on the subject of consultants. "He should be a man with who you can get into a verbal scrap, but whom you will still almire and respect."[*]

Guidelines

A good beginning usually paves the way for a good job. Here are some guides to help a consultant, and the client, to see that this is done.

1. The organization should be briefed in advance and be familiar with the purpose of the work and the scope of the assignment.
2. The personnel within the organization should be told to give the consultant full and complete information.
3. Data should be gathered in advance for the consultant, so that he can save you time and money by avoiding delay.
4. A liaison man should be appointed to help and work with the consultant when and as needed, and who will follow his work.
5. The consultant should meet the key people in the company, so that there is sufficient rapport between him and top management.
6. Management and the consultant should review periodically the original proposal to make sure that the work being done is according to the agreement.

When management and the consultant both carry out their obligations properly, a good job is almost sure to result. Maximum benefit depends on effective follow up, allowing enough time to review recommendations, and then putting them into effect with the consultant's assistance.

---

[*]We as a consulting group do not particularly agree with Mr. Dick's opinion, but include it for the reader's consideration.

A consultant should avoid tackling additional problems as he proceeds with an assignment. He should also avoid giving, or being asked to give, recommendations before a pre-established time.

He should discuss, at any opportunity, with management preliminary finding and conclusions. And he should not offer agreement on things he honestly disagrees with.

Finally, a consultant's work should not be expected to automatically continue. People in any organization will resist change, and a periodic follow up by the consultant is advisable. A recheck for which there is a charge, or placing the consultant on a retaining basis, is the best way to insure follow through by an organization.

18

Profitable Purchasing

Purchasing is a basic function in business simply because the costs of the product, namely the goods and services rendered by the hotel, the motel, and institutional organizations to various publics, depend almost entirely upon the efficiency and economy with which raw materials and supplies are purchased. But this does not mean that price alone is a major factor, for quality and the proper product purchased according to specifications, is the prime consideration. Then there are other bases to be considered, such as quantity, the reliability of the supplier and/or manufacturer, and most important, service. Very often service proves the most important determining factor, where public satisfaction is important.

One hears of "Scientific Purchasing," and it is well to consider the definition of *scientific*. It is a branch of study concerned with the observation and classification of facts, resulting with the establishment of verifiable laws. Applied to purchasing, one might say that the organized nature of a purchasing approach, based on objective and well-defined methods, might permit the word *scientific* to rightfully apply.

Purchasing that is scientific involves a knowledgeable use of material requirements: the present, immediate and even long-term future of markets, new products, manufacture and their availability. The organization's financial position and policy need also be observed by the by the objective purchaser. Market conditions may, for example, indicate that a large quantity of an item could be bought to good price advantage, but a further look at the company's financial record may show that a tight money policy may be necessary, which along with a slow rate of usage and used .storage space, would preclude a large purchase.

Other factors such as changes in style, possible deterioration, tie-up of needed capital, insurance and labor cost, weigh heavily in any final decision. Credit and the cost of time payments are other considerations.

Really intelligent purchasing must of necessity, strike a balance and point the way to an objective decision.

The Development and Use of Specifications

Specifications are complete, detailed statements in writing, which describe exactly what is to be bought. Sometimes this is a purchasing responsibility, but more often it is an engineering or planning function. In smaller organizations, it is a department head's function, sometimes subject to the considerations of other departments and principals who may have related responsibility, and also the overall executive who may be concerned for reasons of quality, appearance, or other policy considerations.

At Pan American World Airways' Intercontinental Hotels Corporation, it was first the responsibility of the Director of the Planning Department, and later the responsibility of the Planning and Administrative Department. The functional analysis of the Director of the Planning Department, taken from the Corporate Organization Manual pertaining to the Planning and Purchasing Department, was as follows:

General Functions. The Director is responsible for the planning, specifying, requisitioning, scheduling, purchasing, shipping, budgeting, control and expediting of all materials, equipment and supplies for all new projects, and for hotels in operation; accountable for purchasing expenditures of up to $10,000,000 on new projects and at the rate of $1,000,000 a year on hotels in operation.

The Director is responsible for research and operations analysis on hotel management and operating problems; issues management information to hotels; prepares and conducts surveys and reports; does organization planning, executive placement and personnel administration for hotels; office management and services (New York Office); approval of invoices, maintenance of general files and communications.

Detailed Functions.
1. The Director analyzes prospective purchases of materials, equipment and supplies for all hotels.
2. Develops specifications through analysis, appraisal and selection of items based on utility, economy and availability.

3. Supervises and checks the preparation of requisitions.
4. Sets up appropriations, budgets proposed expenditures, classifies completed requisitions into normal or other expense, and approves them.
5. Obtains the necessary funds from hotel companies to cover expenditures by check, cash deposit or letter of credit.
6. Obtains necessary documentation to clear purchases such as pro-forma invoices, import licenses and consular declarations.
7. Schedules and follows up purchasing and shipping items to insure prompt and safe delivery of merchandise and supervises the maintenance of schedule and control charts depicting the progress of movement of materials, from the date of planning, specification and purchase to the time of actual arrival at the point of destination.
8. Receives, reviews, handles and distributes, and is responsible for the collation, recording and filing of all material concerning planned, proposed and completed purchases.
9. Makes recommendations to the president, and vice presidents in charge of operations and finance, and to IHC hotels on new commodities, equipment and supplies.
10. Studies, analyzes and assists top management and IHC hotels with certain layout and installations; obtains cost data and helps determine the advisability of proceeding with such work.
11. Observes and interprets market conditions in order to take advantage of the most advantageous procurement conditions.
12. Approves, records, and forwards to the PAA Accounting Department all invoices for IHC and hotel purchases.
13. Conducts research and operations analysis on hotel management and operating problems, and issues information to management on such subjects as systems, methods, procedures, design of forms, new products and their uses, sanitation methods, and control, recipes, foods, laundry formulas, etc.
14. Administers personnel of IHC hotels, covering selection, placement, safety, executive, staff and supervisory training, wage and salary administration and employee services.
15. Recruiting, selection, psychological testing, administers and placement of executives and department heads into IHC hotels.
16. Responsible for certain office management services (IHC New York Office) covering communications, maintenance of office supplies, general and central files, approval of IHC invoices, cash vouchers, government tax and insurance reports, and maintaining employee wage and hour records.
17. Handles correspondence and maintains personal and other contact

with international and domestic hotels in English, Spanish, French and German with IHC, other hotels, manufacturers, suppliers, PAA offices, trade associations, professional organizations, and government agencies.

18. Maintains over 3,000 hotel contacts, research and catalogue files, executive personnel applications, active hotel personnel, hotel correspondence and subject files.

Occasional Functions.

1. Issues monthly status reports on the progress of purchases and accumulated costs.
2. Conducts management surveys, prepares reports and confidential studies, and assists in organization planning and development.

This is a major corporate approach, quite common to regular industry, where planning departments exist, as in the case of Koppers Coke, Burroughs, Carrier, Thompson Products, and the Ford Motor Company. Credit must be given to Pan American World Airways, Intercontinental Hotels Corporation's founding first president, a former General Motors vice president, Wallace S. Whittaker, whose vision and objectivity resulted in establishing the basis for the company's growth and, incidentally, its first period of record expansion.

Specifications drawn up by the Director were completely detailed master lists for all new hotel properties and other hotels in the chain. They were of the performance type, covering not only specifications, but also results expected in terms of performance expectancy.

All specifications were filed and found available in five forms:

1. By specification named for each hotel.
2. By requisition and attached purchase order.
3. By monthly log.
4. By card index.
5. By manufacturer's file.

The most important record was the specifications manual, which contained every detail, but the most recent purchase was always consulted for added information.

The Place for Purchasing

As can be seen from the above, purchasing's place depends upon the size of the organization. In hotels and motels, purchasing, quite naturally, is of major importance. Here are four forms of common arrangement of the place in the organization for the purchasing function:

TO:

HERBERT K. WITZKY & ASSOCIATES
342 MADISON AVENUE · NEW YORK 17, N. Y.
Specialists in Planning.

You are hereby authorized to purchase, as our agent
and for our account, the material listed below:

REQUISITION   DATE:_____ NUMBER:_____   PUR. 107

(ORDER NUMBER) ➤

THIS SPACE FOR PURCHASING USE ONLY

Check To Show "BILLING INSTRUCTIONS"   WEIGHT IN LBS.
( ) DOMESTIC   _____ TO _____ P.P. INS.
( ) EXPORT   _____ TO _____ RAIL EX.
_____ TO _____

SHIPPING DESTINATION

ESTIMATED WEIGHT _____ POUNDS

| REQN. NO. | | CHARGE | | POINT OF ORIGIN | | F.O.B. POINT | | TERMS |

ITEM NO.	QUANTITY	UNIT		DESCRIPTION Where known, enter Manufacturer's Name	PRICE
				(EACH REQUISITION IS TO BE LIMITED TO ITEMS OF LIKE NATURE)	

☐ CONFIRMATION OF _____ DATE:_____
APPROX. DATE GOODS NEEDED AT DESTN._____
FORWARD STATUS INFORMATION TO:_____

Special Instructions

Consular Declaration:

APPROVAL SIGNATURE

_____

Title

Company Name

Address

Method of Payment

☐ Check Attached

☐ Letter of Credit

This form is needed in purchasing for individually owned units as well as units in chains. It gives all the essential information such as shipping destination, quantity, description and price, if known, as well as the date the goods are needed at the destination. It is up to the purchasing function to promptly provide products including lower priced substitutes, forwarding such information in the form of a status report to the purchaser, who then confirms it or otherwise advises as to the disposition of the order.

1. Purchasing as a department in a chain, serving more than one unit.
2. Purchasing combined with control or under administration in a chain.
3. Purchasing in a single unit, often combined with storekeeping.
4. Purchasing decentralized, with each department preparing its own specifications and doing its own purchasing, subject to executive approval.

The fourth method should be avoided wherever possible, simply because the knowledges of markets, products and ability to buy wisely and well is not everyone's forte. As a skill, buying requires a special appreciation and patience.

Under decentralized purchasing, obviously not every department head treats the function as a primary one, and any secondary consideration of it can easily prove costly, not only in actual cost, but also in errors of shipment, quantity, and control.

The advantages of centralization are obvious, and the department heads true to their own particular function will favor delegating and centralizing of the purchasing function. But the departments can contribute very greatly to the success of any central effort by providing advice and direction on material purchases and supplies. The specialized knowledge and abilities of the Executive Housekeeper or Housekeeping Manager are particularly important. An appreciation for decoration and maintenance finds the housekeeping executive invaluable, with experience and knowledge not available anywhere else in the organization.

In terms of financial responsibility, the Housekeeping Manager has practically the entire physical plant under his immediate direction. The same also applies to the Food and Beverage Manager in operations having extensive food and beverage purchasing requirements.

Functions of the Purchasing Executive

Among the many functions of the executive responsible for purchasing, regardless of whether it be centralized or decentralized, may be defined the following:

1. Prepare performance specifications based on necessary research, analysis and review in cooperation with other principal operating executives who may be concerned, or whose advice and experience, whether of an operating or a policy nature, may be helpful.
2. Make purchases of necessary materials, equipment, and supplies according to duly authorized and budgeted-approved requisitions. These may be new purchases, or as dictated by stock, and inventory records.

3. Obtain the lowest possible prices, but not at the sacrifice of quality and service.
4. Watch over and secure delivery as promised.
5. Attend to all the elements essential to sound purchasing. This includes securing at least three quotations from reliable sources, preparing necessary purchase order forms, checking invoices, and other details.
6. Keep all necessary records, receipts, reports, manufacturer's files and other data.
7. Maintain a follow up of orders placed for the safety of the organization and as a protection of the services and the upkeep of its facilities.

Qualifications of the Purchasing Director

The person selected or responsible for purchasing, whether for his own department or for the organization, should first of all be honest, turning down anything at any time for personal gain to avoid influencing his buying decisions.

Broadmindness, tact, consideration for others, sincerity, an open mind, and a willingness to listen to salesmen who bring valuable product information to the fore, are other major qualifying factors.

The Six Major Knowledges Required

1. *Economics.* A fundamental appreciation of the economic structure of business and an appreciation of credit.
2. *Sources of Supply.*° This should include immediate, new and even foreign sources of supply in different parts of the world. Reliability of sources, names of principals in organizations, credit and experience ratings and supplier reputations should also be known by the responsible purchasing principals in an organization.
3. *General Business Conditions.* Efficient purchasing requires a keen knowledge of business conditions, and maintaining a constant alert for news that may affect prices. Detecting price trends, either up or down, is also necessary.

°The Director's responsibility at PAA's Intercontinental Hotels Corporation, covered sources of materials and equipment in every major field, and major country in the world. Catalogs and specifications, with buyers' guides, and issued by foreign governments and their agencies, were effectively maintained by the director and his department.

4. *The Organization's Service and Facility Requirements.* Just purchasing from specifications alone is not enough. Buying should be objective, backed by a secure working knowledge of how items purchased are used. Often such a knowledge, plus an understanding of the manufacturing processes and peculiarities, enable the person charged with the purchasing responsibility to suggest modifications in specifications, to either buy more economically or to suggest a substitute. The technical knowledge of a skilled purchaser often proves valuable to the efficiency of an organization.

5. *Office Procedure.* An understanding of clerical procedures will assist the function in rendering efficient services, and this is particularly true where purchasing is decentralized.

6. *Commercial Law.* Because legal questions may arise over contracts, warranty, liability, and passing of title, much trouble can be avoided by having a good working knowledge of commercial law.

Organizing the Purchasing Functions

If there is a centralized purchasing function in a chain or a single unit of an organization, the responsible person need also be concerned with such things as the preparation of a budget, matters of discounting for prompt payment according to agreed-upon terms, and the organization of work as well as supporting records and accompanying equipment.

In a large organization such as PAA's Intercontinental Hotels, a staff of from 5 to 8 persons handled all the functions of buying, ordering, invoicing, controlling, shipping, and filing. Such a unit handled over thirty million dollars of complicated foreign purchasing.

A later re-organization and combining of functions, as noted earlier under Planning and Administrative Department Functions, carried a smaller load with added planning and staff functions.

If only one person were concerned with purchasing, these essential functions would be necessary:

1. Analyzing requirements.
2. Ordering and buying.
3. Controlling and follow up.
4. Handling invoicing and payment.
5. Inspecting.

Matters of policy concerning standardization of materials and supplies, long range or hand-to-mouth buying, quality and quantity need also be given consideration. In making decisions, immediate and long-term considerations on such things as space, spoilage, style and money should be taken into account.

A common sense policy is a safe policy. This rule may be followed in many situations when extremes challenge a responsible person. Speculation on a good "cheap" buy may turn out to be expensive, a demonstration of an advanced model may fail without adequate testing. The middle-of-the-road policy is safer, particularly when experience is still being added. Anxiety is thereby avoided and stability is assured—a worthwhile consideration in any sized function, whether decentralized or not.

PURCHASE REQUISITION FORM

TO:								PUR. 107

HERBERT K. WITZKY & ASSOCIATES REQUISITION DATE:_____ NUMBER:_____
342 MADISON AVENUE · NEW YORK 17, N. Y.
Specialists in Planning.

You are hereby authorized to purchase, as our agent and for our account, the material listed below:

(ORDER NUMBER) ➤ [   ]

THIS SPACE FOR PURCHASING USE ONLY

SHIPPING DESTINATION

Check To Show "BILLING INSTRUCTIONS"
( ) DOMESTIC
( ) EXPORT

WEIGHT IN LBS.
_____TO_____P.P. INS.
_____TO_____RAIL EX.
_____TO_____

ESTIMATED WEIGHT _____POUNDS

REQN. NO.		CHARGE		POINT OF ORIGIN		F.O.B. POINT	TERMS

ITEM NO.	QUANTITY	UNIT		DESCRIPTION	Where known, enter Manufacturer's Name	PRICE

(EACH REQUISITION IS TO BE LIMITED TO ITEMS OF LIKE NATURE)

☐ CONFIRMATION OF _____ DATE:_____
APPROX. DATE GOODS NEEDED AT DESTN_____
FORWARD STATUS INFORMATION TO:_____

Special instructions

Consular Declaration:

APPROVAL SIGNATURE

Method of Payment
☐ Check Attached
☐ Letter of Credit

Title

Company Name

Address

The requisition form is very useful for budgeting control purposes and formalizing requests. It is initiated by the person making the request.

Part IV

Executive Compensation

19

Executive Compensation Problems, Policies, Procedures

If the present is any indication of the future, then the currently pressing problem of how to adequately compensate executives in proportion to their risks and responsibilities in decision making is destined to bring about major conceptual changes in compensating tomorrow's executives.

"The seriousness of the problems dates back to 1939 when taxes and living costs began rising sharply. Between 1939 and 1950 industry increased the number of its employees 50% and its profits increased almost 300%. During the same period, however, the average gross compensation of the top policy group of policy making managers increased only 35%. Middle management compensation went up 45%, that of supervisors and foremen rose 83%, and white color and hourly employee's compensation more than doubled. When tax and cost of living increases were adjusted for, top management's purchasing power had been cut 59% in eleven years and middle management's 40%. Only white collar and hourly employees maintained or improved their purchasing power".*

Just how far the erosion of tax rates has affected purchasing power may be seen in the following example.

---

*Fortune Magazine.

WHAT TAXES TAKE OUT OF PEOPLE'S INCOMES

Income Group	Average Income	Average Tax Federal	Average Left After Tax
Under $3,000	$ 1,934	$ 166	$ 1,768
$3,000 to $5,000	3,945	393	3,552
$5,000 to $10,000	6,481	833	5,648
$10,000 to $15,000	11,879	2,059	9,820
$15,000 to $20,000	17,160	3,574	13,586
$20,000 to $30,000	24,111	6,025	18,086
$30,000 to $50,000	37,653	11,970	25,683
$50,000 to $100,000	66,368	27,694	38,674

The above applies only to Federal taxes, to which must be added State and Local taxes. The following table shows the added tax burdens that must be carried by taxpapers in various areas in the United States.

Northeast	37.9	
Pacific	35.4	*Includes* taxes of all
Mountain	33.8	kinds as a percent of
North Central	33.6	income payments to
South Atlantic	33.4	individuals
South Central	30.7	
U. S. Average	34.1	

Also to be considered are the ever increasing forms of taxation. There are now sales taxes in existence in thirty-two states, which incidentally amount to one dollar out of every four collected by these states.

Inflation Makes It Worse

Inflation alone, as already pointed out, has more than halved the average executive's salary. Take a married executive with 2 children, earning $30,000 a year in 1939. He would have to earn $124,000 a year today to have the same disposable income as in 1939. But based on statistics, this executive in all probability is not earning much more than $50,000 a year today. Thus, there is a $74,000 a year deficit to be made up for a period of years in the past, and until retirement in the future.

However, the problem is just as severe for the corporation—how to hold talented executives, and what can be done to maintain their interest and incentive or dedication to corporate objectives, if one can refer to them as that. The executive obviously is in the proverbial middle, in a squeeze, without the benefit of any collective agency or effort to help him. He depends on salaries, bonuses and secondary benefits, such as deferred pay, to survive, and the sum of all compensation he receives is valuable only in terms of purchasing power, which as we already know is growing smaller each year.

The Executive Philosophy

There has been a growing tendency among executives to believe that they have a right to share in the earnings and profit of an enterprise, which they are helping or have helped to create, maintain and develop, whatever the case may be.

This belief was formerly held sacred by the very top executive echelons of corporations. George Washington Hill, of American Tobacco fame, and five others with him in 1912, were getting 10% of net profits, or $8,222,245.

In 1929, this arrangement resulted in only $360,000, but produced $2,670,000 over and above stock rights and salaries valued at more than one million dollars.

Of course, such fantastic examples are now almost obsolete, having been curtailed by the U. S. Supreme Court in 1933—the first time a suggestion had been made by any court of law to question the amounts paid by corporations to its executives, as a danger to spoilation or waste of corporate property.*

This curtailment did change and start a trend in profit sharing, with percentages of profits being paid. It resulted in corporate directors since then insisting on other restrictions on such pay arrangements to protect stockholder interests. An apparently recent and sound trend has been the deducting of non-recurring capital gains, since it confines the executive's share to operating incomes he has helped to produce. Du Pont's Merit Bonus Plan, for example, excludes participation in income from investment capital, including General Motors stockholdings.

Not desiring at this time to discuss the question of techniques and methods of compensation (with a discussion of refinements, such as restricted options), the point is made that the whole question of how much to pay and by what method, has now reached corporate as well as middle management executive levels, where incentives and currently effective compensation policies and methods must of necessity be applied.

The Corporate Viewpoint

The real question of course, is what is reasonable compensation? And most important, how far can a corporation go without seriously endanger-

*Rogers vs. Hill, U.S.S.C., 1933

ing the financial structure of a corporation and even affect its growth or
its freedom in a competitive society?

There are dangers in such tightly operated industries such as meat
packing, retailing, warehousing, foods, with profit ratios ranging from
4, 3, 2, and 1%, with some dropping below even that.

There is not one agreeable formula, and the question in even secondary
management levels is often subject to negotiation and individual bargaining. But, it is raising and has constantly raised the question on a variety
of types of compensation, direct and indirect.

Basic Concepts of Executive Compensation

Of primary consideration in evolving a plan of compensation is to first
define executive and middle management and classify it into three
generally accepted compensation concepts. These are:

1. To consider executive and middle management equal in value to
   that of which persons of approximately the same ability and
   experience can be obtained in the open market.
2. To consider that time and experience values developed in a specific
   situation by executive and middle management should be compensated for by proportional increases and benefits within the course
   of time.
3. To consider the contributions of executive and middle management
   comparable to that of stockholders. The greater this investment,
   the greater the return to both parties. Therefore, there should
   be no more reason to impose a limitation upon compensation paid
   than there is in the case of dividends.

The first of these concepts applies to money agreements, both verbal
and written, having fixed salary arrangements. The second is common to
large companies that recognize the increasing value of the trained,
experienced executive. The last, a comparatively new concept, is relative
to our changing economy. It is largely the addition of direct participation
in earnings, recognized as a clearly stipulated condition of employment.

Considering the problem of diminished purchasing power, the second
and third concepts are more realistic in satisfying management's desire
for adequate compensation; also satisfying the corporate interest's desire
to preserve initiative and insure satisfactory earnings.

Elements of Sound Compensation Planning

In planning for adequate compensation, both corporate and executive
needs should be considered. Any plan which seeks to compensate fairly,

may have these elements in common:

1. It must be satisfactory to both the corporation and the parties concerned.
2. It must provide security to the executive and middle management during employment and retirement.
3. The compensation structure must be comparable to that of other competitive industry levels.
4. It should be balanced so that only a portion of total compensation is directly affected by taxation.
5. It should be fair to all who are covered, and also act as an incentive to junior management levels, to insure progression.
6. It must of course, comply with various government and Bureau of Internal Revenue regulations.

20

Executive Compensation
Programming

In establishing a plan and program, it is noted that there are many systems for establishing and administering compensation, but all have common denominators. The elements found in the preceding chapter are basic to any plan. The range of approaches cover complete mathematical ones, which seek to measure the impossible human equation, to some rather simple, direct but highly successful methods of achieving results.

One successful approach, which has been employed in determining how executives and department managers may be adequately compensated, follows. Underlying policies and methods which aided in reaching objectives successfully are also examined.

Hotel "X" Corporation is a single hotel, not affiliated as part of a chain, with an annual sales volume of $4,000,000. The position of the hotel is one of several leading hotels in a prospering industrial and commercial city in the United States.

It has three separate eating establishments, aside from room service, a bar and the usual services found in a hotel, such as a barber shop, valet, laundry, beauty salon, newsstand, and various concessions.

The organization of the hotel consists of the general manager, executive assistant manager, comptroller, assistant manager, night manager, front office manager, catering manager, executive chef, executive housekeeper, sales manager, chief engineer, and executive secretary.

Functions of the hotel organization are: sales, accounting, maintenance, production (rooms, food, liquors, facilities, services), purchasing, and personnel.

Just as in any other business, this hotel gave considerable thought to the problem of adequately compensating its executives. The program here was designed to attract, retain and motivate the particular type of executive needed in this hotel.

In planning the program, there was an awareness of the different kinds of executives needed in different hotels, particularly in considering chains as against independents.

However, it was also readily apparent, right at the start, that regardless of the type of hotel or activity, executive compensation is strongly influenced by three important considerations:

1. The market price for executives. How much they are being paid and where. This is the keystone on which planning any program of executive compensation must be based.
2. The degree and kind of responsibility, as may be measured by such objective criteria as the volume of sales, invested capital, and very important, the degree to which the executive or department manager is accountable for profit and/or loss. Some call this the *responsibility over money,* which is affected by the judgment of the executive.
3. Equity in the internal salary relationships within a hotel. To a large degree this often is more important from a standpoint of morale, than what the job is worth in the open market. Prestige within a hotel and related to a community often means more than what the job is worth.

The Market for Executives

Most everyone observes the principle that executive salaries, as well as salaries for non-executives, must be in line with the market. But getting this principle to work is often more difficult with executive salaries than with the non-executive salaries.

In some non-supervisory jobs, such as the garde-manger in the kitchen, or even the room clerk in the front office, it is difficult to make comparisons to the market, simply because the job functions differ so greatly. But in supervisory and executive jobs, there is a definite degree and range of comparability between hotel companies.*

---

*The Executive Compensation Survey, covering 2000 hotels, prepared by the author's organization for hotels, as an example, shows this to be true, and a great number of hotels make direct use of the information, applying the ranges (median, highest, lowest, upper, and lower quartile) to their particular operations with excellent results.

Effect of Corporate Growth on Executive Rates

The trend toward corporate growth in hotels, such as Hilton Hotels Corporation, Sheraton Hotels, ITT, Western International, Loews Hotels, Holiday Inns, Ramada Inns, Sonesta, and Marriott, to name a few, has had a pronounced effect on rate comparability.

In many instances rates have been held down by reason of the overall company rate structure, almost disregarding different areas of the country.

The corporations involved in most instances, whether knowingly or not (but most probably with a direct awareness of it), have created individual centers of accountability, and responsibility within spans of control. And, with corporations establishing the overall corporate policies, only direct adherance to established requirements of performance need be observed by executives.

The survey rate information developed for comparative purposes, has also proved valuable in establishing the areas of accountability. Chains, as a reason or by-product of their existence, have slightly lower rates of pay as a result. The practice is not incongruous with the lesser degree of accountability required by such executives.

Executive Responsibilities

It is not enough to know whether a position is profit accountable or involves budgetary accountability in management. One must know the degree of responsibility (risk) of the positions or position in question.

In trying to measure the scope and depth of a job, a practical yardstick for all positions that established the magnitude of executive responsibility along with budget and/or profit accountability was developed. This measure is found in four parts:

1. The number of people employed in the hotel and the span of control over them.
2. The number of rooms in the hotel.
3. The type of hotel—luxury, commercial, residential.
4. The gross volume of business and the profit volume relationship of the property.

It was also found in the Executive Compensation Survey, that in strong contrast to companies outside of the hotel industry, the volume of sales had no major effect on rates paid in executive and/or major classifications. There is no relationship between volume of sales and salaries paid.

Let us examine the large hotel of more than 1,000 rooms where sales volume may be between 18 and 20 million dollars a year. The assistant manager's average earnings are between $4,800 and $5,800 a year there. In a hotel operation of 100 to 250 rooms, he earns from $4,200 to $5,600 a year. Surely a sales volume of about $600,000 in a smaller hotel, being about 30 times smaller, would not find the salary about 30 times less. The salaries in fact, are only slightly affected. In fact in the smaller hotel, the assistant manager may have even more benefits than in a larger hotel.

Equity in Internal Relationship — The Team Concept

This new concept, applied in the measurement and establishment of a program for Hotel X Corporation, is principally for use with executive positions. That was until a further approach was developed which was called "The Team Concept of Executive Compensation". It can be explained and defined as follows:

1. A team consists of a group of five, or more persons who are held jointly responsible for the successful performance of the function for which the head man is accountable. This can be a manager—division or chain manger, sales manager, comptroller or accountant, personnel or assistant manager, food manager or catering manager.
2. The head man is automatically high man for compensation purposes. A low man is also needed to provide the range into which all other salaries will fall. The low man is defined as the one whose functions are the least necessary, but still needed by the group. The compensation levels of the team are determined in accordance with an estimate of the relative contribution each person makes to the success of the team.

Relationships Often Not Simple

Using the normal compensation rate for the head of the group, it is necessary to determine if there is in industry a normal percentage ratio and relationship existing between the managers and the salary of the highest contributor, regardless of his function.

Some fairly constant percentages are required. For instance, the highest man under the manager should receive 80% of the manager's compensation while the low man should receive 40% regardless of size of the hotel.

These relationships are complex. Percentages tend to change with salary levels of the individual. However, it is apparent that in any given salary schedule of a principal executive, there is a very typical schedule of percentages of that level representing appropriate salary relationships for the high and low members of the team.

In hotels, as stated earlier, sales volume of a hotel is not a determining criterion. Most often a top man (manager) does not get more than the median being paid in the industry (a few exceptions do not really alter the picture).

Salary Comparisons

The survey discovered, for example, that managers who receive $30,000 per annum, usually see their second highest man receiving 80% of this figure or $24,000. But, sometimes the range is from 65 to as much as 95%. The low man averages about 40% in a 25% range.

It was determined that in setting up manifold compensation plans, no rule can be established as to what allowance must be made for different situations.

Personal ability often carries emphasis here, as does the wide difference in what one man can do and accomplish as compared to another who does less.

This approach is a new one based on historical methods of job evaluation, and the executive level (profile method) of job evaluation. It is not uncommon in its purely historical state, but the improvements in rate determination, using this joint approach offer a sounder, firmer basis from which to work.

21

About Management Pay
and Profit Sharing Plans

One frequently reads of the high salaries paid to top executives in various industries. These published figures are developed from available material on record with the Securities and Exchange Commission and they are easily accessible to anyone interested in verifying the rates.

In the sales field for example, 275 top paid sales executives earned an average of $42,500 before taxes one year. In addition, 65% received additional benefits by company contributions to retirement plans.

One may ask, "Is there some unique service which management renders that makes an executive more valuable than a rank and file worker?"

Perhaps a look at statistics may reveal reasons why 50 of every 100 businesses fail within two years. Only one-third last as long as five years. Why do so many fail? Some of the reasons are:

1. Underpricing products and services.
2. Underestimating products, services, and competition.
3. Underestimating time needed to build a market.
4. Starting with too little capital.
5. Using capital carelessly.
6. Expanding too rapidly.
7. Overextending borrowing.

There are many more. But, as one examines the list, it will be found that the basic reason for such failures is common throughout — errors in judgment.

Classic Errors in Judgment

Let us examine the Ford Motor Company, a classic example. It started as a one-man operation in a shed. In the 1920's it had cornered two-thirds of the automobile market. At the start of World War II, it had dropped to one-fifth and was near collapse.

Henry Ford, Sr., was undoubtedly a mechanical genius, but in later competitive years he did not keep up with modern management techniques and methods.

Henry Ford II on gaining control of the Company promptly hired top flight management. In ten years the comeback was phenomenal. From 1952 to 1956 sales actually increased 100%.

Essentially, management must plan, organize, and be responsible for men, machines, materials, money, methods and markets, as well as its products and services. It must satisfy the public, the stockholders, and the employees—a tricky job indeed.

Statistics show that only three percent of the *total* population have the opportunity and ability to run business successfully. The qualifications for most any executive position include technical knowledge, business "know-how," skill in directing and managing people, building a work team, courage, reliability, hard work, and a willingness to accept responsibility. But, high on the list and hard to find is a talent for using business facts followed by sound decisions which are of advantage to the enterprise.

Another classic example is the case of Harlow Curtice, who started as a bookkeeper in 1914. In the middle of the depression, Curtice turned Buick into the second biggest money maker in General Motors. Of course, this is an outstanding example. But the same responsibility and opportunity is in the hands of countless hotel and motel executives, managers and department heads throughout the country today.

To buy and attract "know-how" presents a problem to the hotel-motel industry, which is now facing serious competition from other industries seeking talent.

Earnings: Executives vs. Professionals and Workingmen

A close look at the earnings of wage earners and teachers compared to hotel industry professionals, shows the following (see tables):

AVERAGE YEARLY EXECUTIVE EARNINGS
(For All Sizes of Hotels)

Job Classifications	Low	Median	High
Vice President & General Manager (chain or group of hotels)	$36,000	$40,000	$45,000
General Manager	15,000	28,000	36,580
Resident Manager	˙11,400	16,700	17,600
Executive Assistant Manager	10,000	15,000	16,750
Assistant Manager	7,200	8,900	12,000
Comptroller	10,750	15,000	18,500
Auditor	8,600	10,500	14,400
Analyst Operations, Payroll, Other	6,900	8,400	8,900
Credit Manager	7,200	8,900	10,500
Front Office Manager	8,100	10,000	15,000
Superintendent of Service	5,900	6,200	6,600
Chief Telephone Operator	5,000	6,400	7,900
Security Officer	6,400	7,400	7,800
Executive Housekeeper	7,200	8,400	11,000
Executive Chef	9,800	12,000	18,750
Assistant Chef	7,800	8,600	10,400
Chief Steward	7,200	8,000	9,800
Sales Manager	8,000	12,000	17,500
Publicity Manager	6,000	7,500	9,800
Advertising Manager	8,000	8,700	13,500
Food and Beverage Manager	11,500	17,500	22,000
Catering Manager	6,500	15,000	18,000
Banquet Manager	7,900	11,000	14,000
Restaurant Manager	7,500	10,200	13,000
Headwaiter	6,500	7,500	11,500
Purchasing Agent	6,800	11,000	15,000
Building Superintendent	9,300	11,000	17,300
Chief Engineer	10,000	14,500	18,500
Laundry Manager	8,000	11,000	12,000
Social Director	4,800	5,700	6,500
Personnel Director	8,400	11,800	14,000
Executive Secretary	5,200	7,400	9,600

WAGE EARNERS*

	Average Weekly Pay before Taxes
Electrical-construction workers	$293.75
Plumbers and heating workers	267.81
Steel-mill workers	265.56
Soft-coal miners	258.13
Construction workers	257.26
Petroleum-refinery workers	250.58
Auto workers	246.02
Tire-factory workers	232.92
Electric-company employees	231.30
Metal miners	222.71
Meat packers	218.95
Aircraft workers	213.86
Chemical workers	202.25
Telephone workers	193.91
Local transit workers	188.78
Furniture workers	130.28
Apparel and textile workers	106.15

* Source: U.S. Department of Labor

TEACHERS' SALARIES*

Average annual salary for teachers in elementary and
secondary public schools

School Year	Salary	School Year	Salary
1960	$4,995	1968	$7,423
1961	$5,275	1969	$7,952
1962	$5,515	1970	$8,635
1963	$5,732	1971	$9,269
1964	$5,995	1972	$9,705
1965	$6,195	1973	$10,114
1966	$6,485	1974	$10,675
1967	$6,830		

Teachers in big-city schools earn more than the nationwide average. In New York City, for example, pay for a beginning teacher starts at $9,700 and moves up to $20,350 for a teacher with an advanced degree and 7½ years of experience.

*Source: National Education Association; American Federation of Teachers.

Successful Profit Sharing Plans

Hyatt Corporation alleges that a part of its reason for success is the clear outline of benefits from its motivational profit sharing plan. Shortly after it was inaugurated by the late then President, Donald Pritzker, he with other key executives flatly declared: "The right kind of profit sharing plan provides employees with a vested interest in the success of the property for which they work."

Every Hyatt employee from pot washer to president is eligible to participate in the Hyatt Employees Profit Sharing and Retirement Investment Trust. All employees are eligible one year after employment, to contribute from 3% to 10% of their salaries or wages for deposit to their individual accounts in the Trust. Hyatt Corporation's contribution is determined each year by its Board of Directors.

Corporate contributions plus forfeitures and the income from management's investment of funds produce substantial growth for employee dollar interests. For example, during 1971, employees received a 31% return on their investment.

An example of what this means to an individual employee — assuming he earns only a 2% increase in wages each year is as follows:

> An employee earning $9,000 per annum, who enrolls in the program at the age of 25 and at a 3% rate, which is $5.22 per week, would accumulate $250,000 at the age of 65.

The trust is tax exempt, and invests in stocks, bonds, real estate, buildings, and any other authorized, IRS-approved investments. All income taxes are deferred on the employee's account-share of the company profits, trust earnings, and forfeitures.

The plan also permits borrowing, and withdrawals for any reason. It is payable on regular retirement, early retirement, disability, death, or for any other reason. Trust funds cannot be used by the Corporation, and contributions by Hyatt are non-returnable to the Corporation.

The following outline describes the General Development Corporation's Non-contributory Profit Sharing Retirement Plan:

1. *Who Participates.* Each General Development employee who has completed one year of continuous full-time employment, automatically becomes a Participant in the Plan on the first anniversary of his employment. As long as he remains a full-time employee of the Company, he continues to be a Participant in the Plan.
2. *Rights of Participants.* A Participant does not make any contribution to the Plan. Each Participant shares in the Company contribution according to a formula spelled out in the Plan which

takes into consideration both his length of full-time, continuous service with the Company, and the amount of his earnings up to $10,000 per year.

3. *How Length of Service Counts.* In order to determine an employee's yearly share of Profit Sharing, his earnings up to $10,000 per year are multiplied by a factor of from one to four, depending on his/her length of service. These factors are as follows:

Continuous, full-time employment for more than one, but less than three years on Dec. 31,	= factor of 1
Over 3 years and up to 6 years	= factor of 2
Over 6 years and up to 10 years	= factor of 3
Over 10 years	= factor of 4

If the employee's date of employment is June 20th, then the following June 20th he becomes a participant and as of December 31st that year, he would be entitled to 6/12th of a participant's share.

4. *"Vesting."* After four years of participation, an employee's cumulative share in the Plan as of that date is permanently "vested." This means that whenever or however the employee leaves the Company, he will receive his share of the Plan as of preceding December 31st.

If the employee leaves prior to "vesting" (i.e., before four years of participation), his share is forfeited and redistributed among the other Participants. At no time does the Company recover his share.

5. *How Much the Company Contributes Each Year.* The Company does not make any contribution unless it has a profit for the year. In 1963, there were no profits and thus no profit sharing. Beginning with 1964, the Company has made an increased profit each year, and has made a proportionate contribution to the Plan.

The Plan requires that the Company contribute 5% of its profit before taxes to the Plan each year. Thus in 1967, the Company earned approximately $12,000,000 before taxes and contributed $600,000 to the Plan. In 1969 the Company contributed approximately $1,500,000 to the Plan.

6. *About Withdrawal of Shares by Employees before Retirement.* An employee may withdraw his share prior to retirement, but *it is not* to his advantage to do so. He may withdraw his entire share at any time after vesting and still remain with the Company. However, if he does so, he can *never again* participate in the Plan. There are income tax disadvantages to withdrawal.

Also, in cases of "serious need," the Trustees may in their sole discretion, grant a partial withdrawal—which does not disqualify you from future participation, again, a tax disadvantage. Partial withdrawals will be granted only in circumstances of a true emergency nature where no other sources of financing are available.

Shares in the Plan *may not be pledged, assigned to creditors,* or *otherwise transferred or used as collateral for loans.*

7. *Tax Treatment.* One of the principal advantages to employee participation in the Plan is the favorable tax treatment afforded by current federal tax laws and regulation. The General Development Corporation Plan is a Qualified Trust by ruling of the Internal Revenue Service.

What does this mean to the employee?

(a) The employee's yearly share in the Plan is not taxed to him in the year earned. No tax is payable until the employee actually receives a distribution.

(b) Upon retirement or other separation from employment with the Company, the employee's entire distribution is taxes as a long-term capital gain — which means that his tax rate is no more than 50% of his ordinary tax rate, perhaps lower, depending on the size of his eventual distribution.

(c) None of the earnings of the investments of the Plan are taxed until distribution, and then only as long-term capital gain.

(d) However, if a partial or total withdrawal is made at any time prior to retirement or separation, such distribution is considered part of the employee's ordinary income for that year and is taxed at high tax rates.

8. *How Funds Are Safeguarded.*

(a) All funds contributed to the Plan are kept separate and apart from the funds of the Company, in special custodian and trust accounts at The First National Bank of Miami. The Company has no control over these funds and cannot use them for any corporate purpose.

(b) The Plan is administered by four Trustees, none of whom is a participant in the Plan. These Trustees invest and reinvest the funds of the Plan for the benefit of the employees.

(c) Yearly reports are required by law, to the Internal Revenue Service and the Federal Department of Labor.

(d) Each year, the Company's independent auditors compute and certify to the Company, the amount of the contribution to be paid for that year.

9. *When Reports of Employee Funds Are Made.* Each participating

employee will receive a Statement of Account on his share in the Plan, as of December 31st, during the following month of April. This time is needed to close the Company books, then compute and audit the Profit Sharing Plan Funds.

Compensating Hotel-Motel Executives

Salaries alone do not satisfy hotel or motel executives who wish to spread compensation over the longest period of time, to avoid paying unnecessarily high income taxes, and to get other benefits, in the form of supplementary compensation, which permits setting aside part of their regular income.

To satisfy these major objectives, maintain executive interests in the work at hand, and preserve wherever possible, the stability of the organization, many managements today provide other methods of compensation which, in whole or in part answer these questions of security.

Types of Compensation

Cash Bonus. The first and most widely used type is a straight cash payment given annually, semi-annually, or at other specified periods. It is usually based on company earnings and the relative weight of the executive in the organization. It is used by many organizations, such as resort hotels, who are subject to seasonal changes. In many firms comparatively low salaries are reinforced by large proportionate bonuses. Bonuses, of course, are directly taxable, and are unsheltered tax items not popular with executives.

Pension Plan. This well known form of added compensation consists of two major types:

(a) "Future" Service Pensions. According to his salary classification, the executive and company jointly contribute to a pension fund, with the employer usually bearing about 75% of the cost.

(b) "Past" Service Pensions. This type of arrangement is usually made with an executive in recognition of past contributions and service to a company. Often an executive is provided with half pay for a a number of years for which he may be called in as a consultant from time to time.

Annuities. This is the provision by the company of an annuity purchased for the executive. It may also be of the mutually contributory type. Payments are considered as regular income by reason of 1942 Bureau of Internal Revenue decision that they consist solely of company funds.

Life Insurance. This may be provided solely by the company or again be mutually contributory, with the executive paying a small part.

Tax Free Compensation. Here the company agrees to either reimburse the executive for all income taxes paid by him, or it may provide a fixed amount in net income each year. This arrangement is valid except in New York State, where the law requires a taxpayer to pay his own taxes.

Deferred Payments.

(a) The Adequate Level Plan. Here the executive is paid an adequate rate, but less than he normally would receive. The extra money is accumulated for a future period.

(b) Consulting or Part-Time Basis Plan. Under this plan, executives reaching a certain age (presumably retirement) receive a percentage (usually about one half) of their last regular pay for certain specific periods, during which they are to provide advisory help and be available part time and for consultation.

(c) Deferred Bonus Plan. Under this plan a portion of the bonus or profit-sharing payments are put into a special fund to be paid out at some future time.

Other Insurances. These cover flight, automobile, accident, hospitalization, surgical, medical, public liability, property, theft, and sometimes blanket insurance. A new type of insurance used by some organizations is known as "key man" insurance, which actually makes the company the beneficiary, but the company in turn makes a part of this available, either in other insurance or direct cash payment, to an executive's estate. With the exception of "key man" insurance, these benefits are often wholly, or at least part paid for by the company.

Trade, Club, and Association Membership. A large number of companies allow reasonable memberships that are helpful to business to executives. In some instances initiation fees are paid personally by the executive, with the company carrying the continuing charges.

Health Examinations. Most companies provide some form of physical checkup (usually annually). This, of course, benefits the company as well as the individual; arrangements and costs are paid by the company.

Company Transportation. Some hotels allow executives automobile mileage (a few provide company cars) for business and, to some extent, personal use. Some allow for flight transportation for business and family vacation purposes, paying all costs:

Entertainment and Expense Allowances. Entertainment and other incidental expenses that benefit business are generally covered. Some companies even go so far as to stipulate a budgeted amount which may be spent. One hotel company allows its executives $250 a month for entertainment (below rank of managers), as long as such expenditures are for sound business reasons.

Housing and Maintenance. Complete housing and maintenance are usually limited to certain industries where hardships would be met if individuals were to try to locate themselves. Hotels and primarily resorts, provide complete housing and maintenance, either in the hotel proper, or in separate buildings.

Vacations—Leaves—Travel. There is a growing tendency among hotels to provide longer "split" vacations to executives. Various types of "special" leaves for periods of time, with full or part time pay are used by some organizations where such leaves can be granted without affecting the operation.

Miscellaneous. Trade and purchase discounts, executive dining privileges, paid magazine subscriptions, company scholarships, paid educational programs (either all or part paid by the company) are other benefits.

Profit Sharing Plans

Many large and small companies have successfully carried out some sort of profit sharing arrangement. This in the past few years has also appeared among hotels. With the exception of providing bonuses, however, profit sharing has not gained in usage by hotel companies. Over the past two years, as found in the Annual Executive Compensation Survey, only 0.13 percent reported having actual profit sharing plans.

Four Participating Types. There are four main types of profit sharing which run from simple to involved methods of distributing earnings, or that portion thereof available for distribution.

1. *Straight Percentage Profit Sharing.* This is simply an agreement by a company to pay an executive a fixed percentage of the profits, and is commonly used for managers in hotels.
2. *Group Profit Sharing.* There are generally two types most commonly used: Straight Cash Distribution—bonuses paid into a trust fund—and Straight Cash Accumulated—bonuses paid into a fund for reinvestment in stocks, bonds, or savings.
3. *Stock Bonus Plans.* This covers a wide variety of plans. It may consist of a bonus plus stock, or all stock. The latter provides further earnings and dividends, unless the stock has to be sold to cover tax payments.
4. *Stock Option and Purchase Plan.* This growing practice consists of giving executives options to buy stock, or may merely be an arrangement to buy a specified number of shares within a given period of time. Stock warrants may also be provided, but, if sold and not exercised, are subject to regular income tax payments. However, if stocks are purchased as prescribed, long term capital gains may be realized.

Indirect Compensation

There are other intangibles which attract and hold executives. The prestige or title of a position, working conditions, location and area, travel conveniences, attractiveness of the office, prominent associates, special privileges, etc., all are factors worth considering in compensating executives.

The Future

Obviously the problem of satisfying executive needs within a given situation can be resolved rather successfully. But just how this may be related to the earnings of others in other groups and particularly in terms of purchasing power, relative economic, social and professional standing, is yet to be answered.

It offers a challenge to tomorrow's society of managers, i.e., the age of the professional manager is upon us.

Emerging is a great middle class of various levels. The society of tomorrow is the educated society. It will be the age of the professional manager, the scientist, the planner and the specialist. The intellectual level is rising, and the rewards to individuals for performance and contributions made, are by the very nature of the system we live by, moral, social, and professional rather than financial.

23

Executive Salary Plan through Job Evaluation

Modern industry has long recognized the drawbacks of straight-line pay plans without periodic increases according to a fixed schedule and plan. While wage administration programs are well established in industries other than hotels and motels, some management experts and a handful of owners who have tried such programs have noted gains, not only in job satisfaction through regular progressive increases and a promotional ladder that is available to management aspirants, but also savings and economies through simplification and better job organization.

All wage administration programs usually start with the evaluation of jobs in an organization, determining the worth of each position. Step by step, this is how it is done:

Job Descriptions

Each executive and department head draws up a description of his duties and responsibilities (see *Functional Analysis* at the end of this chapter). This is somewhat different from the standard job description in that it is of the functional type. The drafted descriptions are usually reviewed, and rewritten by a trained staff member or outside specialist.

Evaluating Positions

Positions are then evaluated by either of three methods:

1. Factor comparison.
2. Job ranking.
3. Point scoring.

The first of these, factor comparison, recognizes that there are certain common factors which are found in all jobs. Usually five or more factors are chosen such as skill, effort, working conditions, etc. Then 15 or 20 positions are selected for evaluating the plan. These are generally considered to offer a fair wage, not over or under market salaries and rates paid, and are known as key jobs. They vary from the highest to the lowest in rank. Each of these jobs is then broken down into factor worths or values. Each factor is worth a part of the total salary for the job.

As a final step the other positions are fitted in between the key jobs. This system has some disadvantages. First of all, too much depends on the opinion of the evaluator. It also requires a very thorough knowledge of the subject matter by the person using this method.

Job ranking, the second method, is used by many government agencies and is popular with many companies. It grades, classifies and rates positions into money values. But this is not always satisfactory because it has no point scoring device, and, therefore, again depends too much on judgment and personal opinion.

Many experts consider the point system as the best, as it is generally the most thorough. It serves best where the greater degree of accuracy is desired.

The Area Study

To make sure that rates determined in the evaluation are objective and do not fall out of range with local and general industry rates, a local area study is advisable. This consists of mailing a questionnaire to other hotels to determine what their rates are for comparable jobs. For similar positions in related industries, a comparison should also be made for the few positions which are similar to make sure that rates are in line with those in the local area. National comparisons may also be made to see how much of a difference exists. In the South, East, West and North and subdivisions of these regions such as middle, upper and lower as applied to each region, were noted.

Differences in meals, accommodations and other service benefits are also to be considered in making such comparisons.

Setting Up an Evaluation Committee

The next step is to appoint a committee consisting of a chairman who is responsible for the total effort, and two or three others who are key operating executives, such as the Food and Beverage Manager, Executive Assistant Manager, Comptroller, and/or Assistant Manager, or any other principal who is concerned with wages.

Each member uses a factor breakdown sheet which lists each of the factors.

This enables him to assign values to each factor being noted. Each sheet is then totaled to determine the rank of the position being evaluated.

This process may take several weeks or longer depending on the number of jobs being rated and the time spent on the program each day. Once this work is completed, yearly or other increments or amounts of increase are assigned to each position.

Ranges generally depend on the total ranges, industry, real experience, and on the minimum and maximum rates the company decides it can pay over a period of time.

Putting the Program into Effect

A simple record card is sufficient for controlling the program. Next, a policy on when to review executive salaries must also be established. Usually, annual increases for executives is the general pattern.

Whether or not an increase is in order is largely determined by a number of factors: what the hotel industry pays, the major contribution the executive has made during the past year towards increasing hotel earnings and profits, the size of the operation as to the number of rooms, and the position of the hotel in the community and industry.

Of value in making such a comparison is the survey which provides hotel highs, lows, medians, upper and lower quartiles, for hotels under 100 rooms, between 100 and 250 rooms, between 250 and 500, 500 and 800, and over 800 rooms. Many hotels use this alone as a yardstick and guide for establishing their individual rate ranges. The survey also provides finer definition in terms of areas of the United States and of indirect benefits paid to executives.

Once a job evaluation program is completed, it results in establishing fair and equitable wage ranges that offer stability as well as economy for the hotel or motor hotel. Generally, payroll savings are realized through the process. As the analysis develops, it discovers duplication

Executive Personnel Rating

	EXCELLENT	GOOD	AVERAGE	FAIR	POOR
1. KNOWLEDGE OF JOB Familiarity with the various procedures of the work	☐ Exceptional mastery of all phases of his work	☐ Thorough knowledge of practically all phases of his work	☐ Adequate knowledge of particular job	☐ Insufficient knowledge of some phases of job	☐ Inadequate comprehension of requirements of job
2. EXPERIENCE Skill and practical wisdom gained by personal knowledge	☐ Broad background and training for particular job	☐ A comprehensive background	☐ An adequate background	☐ Has some background, but requires direction	☐ Inexperienced or unsatisfactory progress
3. GENERAL COMPANY INFORMATION Knowledge of major and minor company policies	☐ Thorough understanding and appreciation of all company policies	☐ Knowledge of practically all company policies	☐ Acceptable knowledge of company policies	☐ Limited knowledge of company policies	☐ Does not have enough information to be efficient
4. HEALTH Soundness of body and mind, and freedom from physical disease or disability	☐ Robust, energetic	☐ Sufficiently healthy and energetic to handle the job	☐ Sufficiently healthy to handle job but not overly energetic	☐ Frail, affected by pressure	☐ Sickly. Affects his work
5. ENTHUSIASM A positive, ardent, and eager response	☐ Believes wholeheartedly in the company and expresses both orally and in his attitude that belief	☐ Works enthusiastically, not too expressive	☐ Matter-of-fact attitude	☐ Definitely passive or indifferent	☐ Negative in attitude
6. PERSONALITY The external mannerisms consciously or unconsciously adopted in meeting situations	☐ Radiant, confident, poised, courteous	☐ Pleasant, forceful	☐ Likeable	☐ Ill at ease, not too forceful	☐ Negative colorless person
7. APPEARANCE Outward impressions made by a person	☐ Superior style, grooming, taste and a sense of the fitness of things	☐ Well dressed and neat	☐ Neat, but not particularly striking	☐ Intermittently careless	☐ Slovenly and untidy
8. CHARACTER Integrity of an individual	☐ Has the courage of his convictions and unquestioned habits	☐ Morally sound. Tolerant	☐ An average human being possessing average personal weaknesses	☐ A person whose behavior harms no one but himself	☐ A person who is a bad influence on the behavior of the group
9. MENTALITY Quality of mind, mental power and creative intellectual ability of a person	☐ Superior ability to think clearly and arrive at sound conclusions	☐ Worthwhile ideas of his own, and ability to make useful decisions	☐ Well informed on certain subjects useful in his daily work	☐ Little ability to comprehend, interpret or grasp new ideas	☐ Unable to reason logically
10. SOCIABILITY Sense of mutual relationship, companionship, and friendliness with others	☐ A genuine interest in people and extremely well liked by others	☐ A friendly, pleasant person, happy in a group	☐ Willing to be a part of a group but makes little contribution	☐ Poorly adjusted to the group	☐ Unwilling to be a part of any group activities
11. ABILITY TO GET THINGS DONE Ability to perform, execute, and achieve an assigned task	☐ Completes assignments in the shortest possible time	☐ Completes assignments in unusually short time	☐ Completes assignments in a reasonable time	☐ Slow in completing assignments, or does not complete them	☐ Takes a long time to accomplish little
12. COOPERATIVE An appreciation of collective action for mutual profit or common benefit	☐ Greatest possible cooperativeness	☐ Very cooperative	☐ Cooperative	☐ Difficult to handle	☐ Obstructive
13. ACCEPTANCE OF RESPONSIBILITY Willingness to assume duties	☐ Greatest possible sense of responsibility	☐ Very willing	☐ Accepts but does not seek responsibility	☐ Does assigned tasks reluctantly	☐ Irresponsible

These essential factors in a department manager's and supervisor's performance should be periodically rated on a form such as this. This type of rating should be subjective with an idea of trying to help with corrective action through interviews and discussion, so as to improve the efficiency and value of the person being rated, thereby also adding greatly to executive effectiveness.

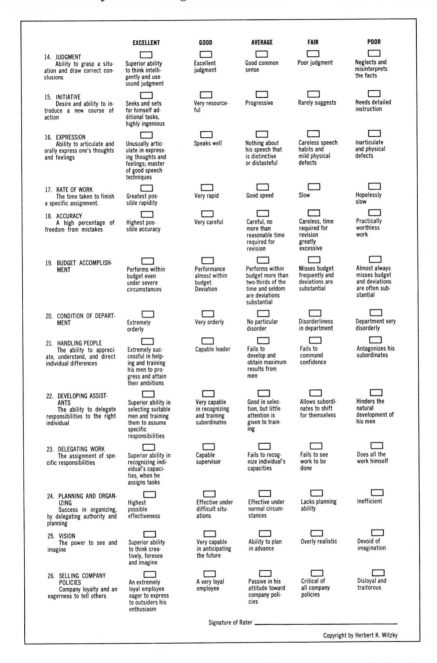

	EXCELLENT	GOOD	AVERAGE	FAIR	POOR
14. JUDGMENT Ability to grasp a situation and draw correct conclusions	Superior ability to think intelligently and use sound judgment	Excellent judgment	Good common sense	Poor judgment	Neglects and misinterprets the facts
15. INITIATIVE Desire and ability to introduce a new course of action	Seeks and sets for himself additional tasks, highly ingenious	Very resourceful	Progressive	Rarely suggests	Needs detailed instruction
16. EXPRESSION Ability to articulate and orally express one's thoughts and feelings	Unusually articulate in expressing thoughts and feelings; master of good speech techniques	Speaks well	Nothing about his speech that is distinctive or distasteful	Careless speech habits and mild physical defects	Inarticulate and physical defects
17. RATE OF WORK The time taken to finish a specific assignment.	Greatest possible rapidity	Very rapid	Good speed	Slow	Hopelessly slow
18. ACCURACY A high percentage of freedom from mistakes	Highest possible accuracy	Very careful	Careful, no more than reasonable time required for revision	Careless, time required for revision greatly excessive	Practically worthless work
19. BUDGET ACCOMPLISHMENT	Performs within budget even under severe circumstances	Performance almost within budget. Deviation	Performs within budget more than two-thirds of the time and seldom are deviations substantial	Misses budget frequently and deviations are substantial	Almost always misses budget and deviations are often substantial
20. CONDITION OF DEPARTMENT	Extremely orderly	Very orderly	No particular disorder	Disorderliness in department	Department very disorderly
21. HANDLING PEOPLE The ability to appreciate, understand, and direct individual differences	Extremely successful in helping and training his men to progress and attain their ambitions	Capable leader	Fails to develop and obtain maximum results from men	Fails to command confidence	Antagonizes his subordinates
22. DEVELOPING ASSISTANTS The ability to delegate responsibilities to the right individual	Superior ability in selecting suitable men and training them to assume specific responsibilities	Very capable in recognizing and training subordinates	Good in selection, but little attention is given to training	Allows subordinates to shift for themselves	Hinders the natural development of his men
23. DELEGATING WORK The assignment of specific responsibilities	Superior ability in recognizing individual's capacities, when he assigns tasks	Capable supervisor	Fails to recognize individual's capacities	Fails to see work to be done	Does all the work himself
24. PLANNING AND ORGANIZING Success in organizing, by delegating authority and planning	Highest possible effectiveness	Effective under difficult situations	Effective under normal circumstances	Lacks planning ability	Inefficient
25. VISION The power to see and imagine	Superior ability to think creatively, foresee and imagine	Very capable in anticipating the future	Ability to plan in advance	Overly realistic	Devoid of imagination
26. SELLING COMPANY POLICIES Company loyalty and an eagerness to tell others	An extremely loyal employee eager to express to outsiders his enthusiasm	A very loyal employee	Passive in his attitude toward company policies	Critical of all company policies	Disloyal and traitorous

Signature of Rater _____

Copyright by Herbert K. Witzky

PLAZA PERSONNEL RECORD

DATE BEGUN	ASSIGNMENTS					DATE LEFT	REASON	RATING
	DEPT.	DEPT. HEAD	CLASS	POSI-TION	RATE			

PHOTO

BP.17523a

TEST RESULTS

DATE	NAME	SCORE

PHYSICAL EXAMINATION		INSURANCE AND PENSION		FOLLOW-UP		
DATE	RESULT	UNION EFF.	TERM.	RATED BY	DATE	RATING
DATE	RESULT	NON-UNION EFF.	TERM.			
DATE	RESULT	LIFE ACC. HOSP. AMT.				

DATE REF. SENT	RESULT	TEL. NO.	AGE
SOC. SEC. NO.	TIME NO.	LOCKER NO.	
NAME	ADDRESS		

RATING & LOWER: 1 2 3 4 5 6 7 8 9 10 11 | NO. OF WARNINGS UPPER 12 13 14 15 16 17 18 19 20 | UNION LOCAL
0 10 20 30 40 50 60 70 80 90 100
U YR.EMP SEX M S   DEPT.   EMP. DATE   OUT

FRONT

		WARNING RECORD				SUGGESTION PROGRAM		
DATE	REASON	REMARKS			REASON CODE	DATE	SUBJECT	RESULT

REASON CODE:
1 CONDUCT
2 CARELESSNESS
3 POOR WORK
4 DISHONESTY
5 TARDINESS
6 INSUBORDINATION
7 INDIFFERENCE
8 ABSENCE
9 TROUBLE MAKER
10 PHYSICAL

GRIEVANCE RECORD

DATE	NATURE	DISPOSITION

UPPER-COMP.	ACCIDENT RECORD	LOWER-FIRST AID		TRAINING AND EDUCATION			
	JAN FEB MAR APR MAY JUN JUL AUG SEP OCT NOV DEC	SCHOOL	COURSE	STARTED	FINISHED	GRADE	
19							
19							
19							

SERVICE INFORMATION

BP.17523a

BACK

This multiple purpose personnel record card was designed for the Plaza Hotel in New York and is still in use. The face of the card shows a record of wage and position assignments necessary in carrying out a Wage Administration Program. Additional card sections may be stapled to assigned portions of the card as needed. Because increases and promotions are based on performance results, length of service and other factors such as interest, ability to innovate and suggest new methods, as well as training and education, the reverse of the card is useful for personnel purposes. Note that a photo may be taken only after a person is employed. In most states, it is illegal to request a photograph from an applicant, but as everyone knows, a good photo and likeness will greatly aid an applicant in getting placed.

and overlapping of functions. And it also results in staff changes, transfers and combinations, not only as the evaluations are made, but as each check and review is made of the actual descriptions.

Once it is established and begins to function, the program requires maintenance and follow up. Experienced judgment and a general familiarity with the steps involved in the process are necessary.

To be successful, the plan must be sold to the management every step of the way and be accepted. This requires skill, time and patience, and an objective and not subjective management.

Using the Point Plan

The first step is to arrange and agree on the factors that make up a job such as education, experience, complexity of duties, supervision received, chance and cost of errors, contacts, and kind and degree of relationships with others, confidential data reviewed, mental and/or visual demands, working conditions, character and nature of supervision, and the scope of supervision. The factors are then broken down into degrees as shown in the example at the end of the chapter.

A typical point plan which assigns values to each of the degrees is shown on the pages 199 to 209. This plan is adaptable to staff and employee ranks as well as executive.

FUNCTIONAL ANALYSIS

PRESENT TITLE: Sales Manager
DEPARTMENT: Sales
RESPONSIBLE TO: General Manager

GENERAL FUNCTIONS:

Responsible for sales promotion for the hotel/motor hotel. Develops and directs sales efforts, through methods and procedures, maintains liaison with other hotels, travel agencies, and business organizations.

DETAILED FUNCTIONS:

1. Supervises, directs and coordinates internal and external sales efforts.
2. Follows up sales efforts personally and through correspondence.
3. Establishes and supervises direct mail program to promote sales.
4. Contacts travel agents, business organizations, old and new guests in developing business.
5. Makes arrangements with various rooms in the hotel/motel hotel for small parties.
6. Maintains liaison with Front Office Department on reservations, the Housekeeping Department concerning table setups on furniture and equipment changes, and the Auditing Department concerning invoices to be paid.

7. Prepares various reports on the conduct of his department as to getting business, results obtained, forecasts of sales and percentage of antici- pated occupancy of banquet room space.
8. Handles extensive correspondence with travel agents concerning com- mission payments, and personally transmits such payments in covering letters.
9. Trains and develops his staff.

OCCASIONAL FUNCTIONS:

1. Prepares copy for a direct mail purpose, special letters, and internal merchandising including menus, tent cards, and other attention-getting devices.
2. Works with advertising agency in the handling of campaigns in news- papers, trade journals, and the production of all printed materials including stationery and business cards.

MINIMUM REQUIREMENTS:

Scholastic Training. Four years of college or the equivalent with special- ized sales promotion is desirable.

Business Training. At least five years of experience in hotel sales, with a thorough understanding of hotel operations with emphasis on food and beverage presentation, a knowledge of general business organization, and contacts with principals in companies and associations helpful to the achieve- ment of the sales manager's objectives.

EDUCATION OR BASIC KNOWLEDGE

Education appraises the basic knowledge or "scholastic content" (how- ever, it may have been acquired) essential as background or training pre- liminary to learning the job. This background may have been acquired by formal education, by outside study, or by experience on related work. The rating is expressed in terms of equivalent formal education for convenience. In rating job on education *analyze the requirements of the job,* regardless of the formal education of the person or persons on the job.

1ST DEGREE:

Knowledge of simple arithmetic, English and grammar. Accuracy in checking, posting, and counting. Mental alertness and adaptability to office routines. *Equivalent to 4 years high school.*

2ND DEGREE:

Knowledge of stenography; operation of office equipment such as book- keeping or calculating machines, tabulating equipment; simple blueprint reading, etc., however acquired. *Equivalent to 4 years high school plus short specialized training.*

3RD DEGREE:

Knowledge of a specialized field (however acquired) such as cost account- ing, drafting, foreign trade, statistics, time study. Equivalent to 4 years high school plus night, trade, extension or correspondence school specialized training. *·Equivalent to 2 years college.* Or broad shop trade knowledge involving complicated drawings and specifications, advanced shop mathe- matics, and manufacturing methods. *Equivalent to 4 years high school plus 4 years apprenticeship.*

4TH DEGREE:
Broad knowledge of a general technical field such as chemical, civil, electrical or mechanical engineering; accounting and finance or business administration, however acquired. *Equivalent to 4 years of college or university.*

5TH DEGREE:
Broad knowledge of an advanced and specialized field. *Usually equivalent to 1 or 2 years of post-graduate work.*

6TH DEGREE:
Intensive knowledge of an advanced and highly specialized field, requiring independent research and creative work. *Usually equivalent to over 2 years of post-graduate work.*

EXPERIENCE

Experience appraises the length of time usually or typically required by an individual with the specified educational background, to learn to perform the duties effectively. In rating a job on this factor, it should be kept in mind on some jobs, that experience is of two kinds:

1. Previous experience on related work or lesser positions, either within the organization or outside.

2. The "breaking-in time" or period of adjustment and adaptation on the specific job itself. On such jobs, the job specification may show both periods, which should, however, be added together to secure the overall rating on experience.

1ST DEGREE:
Up to and including 3 months.

2ND DEGREE:
Over 3 months up to and including 12 months.

3RD DEGREE
Over 1 year and up to and including 3 years.

4TH DEGREE:
Over 3 years up to and including 5 years.

5TH DEGREE:
Over 5 years up to and including 7 years.

6TH DEGREE:
Over 7 years up to and including 10 years.

7TH DEGREE:
Over 10 years.

COMPLEXITY OF DUTIES

This factor appraises the degree of independent action, the exent to which the position is circumscribed by standard practice, the exercise of judgment or the making of decisions, and the creative effort in devising new methods or products.

1ST DEGREE:
Simple routine duties, requiring the use of only a few definite procedures, and little individual judgment since the work is either done under immediate supervision or involves little choice as to methods of performance.

2ND DEGREE:

Routine duties involving the application of clearly prescribed standard practice, requiring the use of several procedures and the making of minor decisions requiring some judgment.

3RD DEGREE:

Semiroutine duties involving an intensive knowledge of a restricted field, requiring the use of a wide range of procedures and the analysis of facts in situations to determine what action should be taken within the limits of standard practice.

4TH DEGREE:

Semiroutine duties involving general knowledge of company policies and procedures and their application to cases not previously covered. Duties require working independently toward general results, devising new methods, modifying or adopting standard procedures to meet new conditions, making decisions based on precedent and company policy.

5TH DEGRFEE:

Difficult work on highly technical or involved projects, presenting new or constantly changing problems. Duties require outstanding ability to deal with complex factors not easily evaluated, or the making of decisions based on conclusions for which there is little precedent.

6TH DEGREE:

Participation in the formulation and carrying out of company policies, objectives and programs for major divisions or functions. Direct and co-ordinate work of subordinate department heads in order to attain objectives.

SUPERVISION RECEIVED

This factor appraises the degree to which the immediate superior outlines the methods to be followed or the results to be attained, checks the progress of work or handles exceptional cases. Consider the proximity, extent and closeness of supervision in rating this factor.

1ST DEGREE:

Under immediate supervision with short assignments of work at frequent intervals and a regular check of performance.

2ND DEGREE:

Under general supervision where standard practice enables the employee to proceed alone on routine work, referring all questionable cases to supervisor.

3RD DEGREE:

Under direction where a definite objective is set up and the employee plans and arranges his own work, referring only unusual cases to supervisor.

4TH DEGREE:

Under general direction, working from policies and general objectives. Rarely refers specific cases to superior unless clarification or interpretation of company policy is involved.

5TH DEGREE:

Under adminstrative direction, setting up own standards of performance. Virtually self-supervising.

ERRORS

This factor appraises the opportunity for, and the probable effect of errors on the job. Consider the degree to which the work is verified or checked, either in succeeding operations, by the routines themselves, or by supervision. Consider the probable monetary loss and the frequency with which opportunity for loss presents itself.

1ST DEGREE:
Probable errors can be easily and quickly detected, and would result only in minor confusion or clerical expenses for correction.

2ND DEGREE:
Probable errors usually detected in succeeding operations, and generally confined to a single department or phase of company activities. Correction involves some trouble in back checking by others. Most of work is verified or checked.

3RD DEGREE:
Probable errors may be serious involving loss of production, waste of material, holding up production, and damage to equipment. Effect is usually confined within the company. Most of work is not subject to verification or check.

4TH DEGREE:
Probable errors are difficult to detect, and may adversely affect outside relationships. Work is not subject to audit or check, requiring considerable accuracy and responsibility.

5TH DEGREE:
Probable errors may involve major expenditures for equipment, material, products, or loss of important customer accounts. Duties may involve the preparation of data on which top management bases important decisions.

6TH DEGREE:
Probable errors may involve a continuing influence on future operations of the business.

CONTACTS WITH OTHERS

This factor appraises the responsibility that goes with the job for meeting, dealing with, or influencing other persons. In rating this factor, consider how the contacts are made, how often, whether contacts involve furnishing or obtaining information only, or whether they involve influencing others.

1ST DEGREE:
Little or no contacts except with immediate associates and own supervisor.

2ND DEGREE:
Contacts with other persons within the department on routine matters or occasional outside contacts, furnishing or obtaining information only.

3RD DEGREE:
Regular contacts with other departments, furnishing or obtaining information or reports, requiring tact to avoid friction. Outside contacts where improper handling may affect results, but where the primary responsibility rests with the next higher level of supervision.

4TH DEGREE:
Outside or inside contacts involving carrying out company policy and programs and the influencing of others, where improper handling will affect operating results. Or contacts with persons of substantially higher rank on matters requiring explanation, discussion, and obtaining approvals.

5TH DEGREE:
Outside and inside contacts requiring a high degree of tact, judgment, and the ability to deal with and influence persons in all type of positions.

6TH DEGREE:
Continuous outside and inside contacts frequently involving difficult negotiations which require a well developed sense of strategy and timing.

CONFIDENTIAL DATA

This factor appraises the integrity and discretion required in safeguarding confidential data. In rating the job, consider the character of the data, the degree to which the full import of the data is apparent on the job in question, whether disclosure would affect internal relationships only, or external, competitive relationships.

1ST DEGREE:
Little or no confidential data involved.

2ND DEGREE:
Occasionally works with confidential data, but the full import is not apparent and the effect of any disclosure would be negligible.

3RD DEGREE:
Regularly works with some confidential data which, if disclosed, might have adverse internal effect.

4TH DEGREE:
Regularly works with some confidential data of major importance which, if disclosed, may be detrimental to the company's interests.

5TH DEGREE:
Full and complete access to reports, records, plans, programs, where utmost integrity is required to safeguard the company's competitive position.

MENTAL OR VISUAL DEMAND

This factor appraises the degree of concentration, and coordination of mind and eye. Consider the volume or flow of work, the requirement for coordinating manual dexterity with mental or visual attention, and the sustained character of the visual attention. This factor should not be used to appraise the qualitative requirements of the job for "headwork".

1ST DEGREE:
Flow of work or character of duties is intermittent and requires attention only at intervals.

2ND DEGREE:
Flow of work and character of duties involve only normal attention.

3RD DEGREE:
Flow of work and character of duties involve the coordination of manual dexterity and normal mental or visual attention.

4TH DEGREE:
Must concentrate mental and visual attention closely on work, coordinating mental and manual dexterity for sustained periods.

5TH DEGREE:
High degree of concentration where the volume and character of the work require unusual coordination of mind and eye.

WORKING CONDITIONS

This factor appraises the surrounding or working conditions under which the job must be done.

1ST DEGREE:
Usual office working conditions.

2ND DEGREE:
Good working conditions. Occasional exposure to noise, dust, heat, etc. Some disagreeable factor present in office working conditions.

3RD DEGREE:
Somewhat disagreeable due to exposure to noise, dust, heat, fumes, etc., but where they are not continuous if several conditions are present.

4TH DEGREE:
Continuous exposure to several disagreeable conditions.

CHARACTER OF SUPERVISION

This factor appraises the degree or kind of supervisory responsibility involved. Consider what place the job would occupy on an organization chart, the degree to which accountability for results goes with the job measured in terms of responsibility for costs, methods, and personnel.

1ST DEGREE:
Part-time, immediate supervision over several employees in the same occupation performing the same work most of the time as those supervised. No responsibility for costs, methods, or personnel.

2ND DEGREE:
Immediate supervision over a group of employees where most of time is spent assigning, reviewing, checking work, and eliminating ordinary difficulties where procedure is standardized. Or act as understudy to a job rated third or fourth degree on this factor, though no supervision is involved most of the time.

3RD DEGREE:
Direct supervision of a section, unit, or department where accountability for results rests primarily with the next higher level of supervision or, if accountability does go with the job, where the complexity of duties itself warrants a rating of not more than the third degree.

4TH DEGREE:
General supervision of a department involving accountability for results in terms of costs, methods, and personnel where the complexity of duties itself has been rated higher than the third degree.

5TH DEGREE:
Direct and coodinate the operations of two or three departments, through subordinate supervisors who, in turn, are responsible for supervision over individual departments. Set up standards of performance, check progress, and see that company policies are carried out.

6TH DEGREE:
Direct and coordinate the operations of a major function or division, such as Accounting, Engineering, and Production. Organize work, set up standards of performance, shape and interpret company policy.

SCOPE OF SUPERVISION

This factor appraises the size of the supervisory responsibility, expressed in terms of the number of persons supervised.

1ST DEGREE:
Assist and direct one or two persons in the same occupation.

2ND DEGREE:
Supervise a small group or unit, seldom over 10 persons.

3RD DEGREE:
Supervise a section or department, seldom over 25 persons.

4TH DEGREE:
Supervise a department from 25 to seldom over 50 persons.

5TH DEGREE:
Direct and supervise one or more departments, usually from 50 to 100 persons.

6TH DEGREE:
Direct and supervise the operations of a major division, usually more than 100 persons.

POINTS ASSIGNED TO FACTORS AND KEY TO GRADES

FACTORS	1st Degree	2nd Degree	3rd Degree	4th Degree	5th Degree	6th Degree	7th Degree
Education	15	30	45	60	75	100	
Experience	20	40	60	80	100	125	150
Complexity of Duties	15	30	45	60	75	100	
Supervision Received	5	10	20	40	60		
Errors	5	10	20	40	60	80	
Contacts with Others	5	10	20	40	60	80	
Confidential Data	5	10	15	20	25		
Mental or Visual Demand	5	10	15	20	25		
Working Conditions	5	10	15	20	25		

FACTORS TO BE USED FOR SUPERVISORY POSITIONS ONLY

	1st	2nd	3rd	4th	5th	6th	
Character of Supervision	5	10	20	40	60	80	
Scope of Supervision	5	10	20	40	60	80	

Grade	Point Range	Grade	Point Range
1	100 and under	9	311 - 340
2	101 - 130	10	341 - 370
3	131 - 160	11	371 - 400
4	161 - 190	12	401 - 430
5	191 - 220	13	431 - 460
6	221 - 250	14	461 - 490
7	251 - 280	15	491 - 520
8	281 - 310	16	521 - 550

MANAGEMENT SALARY PLAN

GROUP	POINTS	NORMAL INCREMENTS	SALARY RANGES
1	131 - 160	$10 - $20	$936 - $1,296
2	161 - 190	20	969 - 1,434
3	191 - 220	20 - 25	1,032 - 1,521
4	221 - 250	20 - 25	1,095 - 1,644
5	251 - 280	25 - 30	1,158 - 1,734
6	281 - 310	25 - 30	1,239 - 1,836
7	311 - 340	25 - 30	1,317 - 1,941
8	341 - 370	25 - 30	1,398 - 2,031
9	371 - 400	30 - 35	1,476 - 2,136
10	401 - 430	30 - 35	1,557 - 2,220
11	431 - 460	30 - 35	1,635 - 2,343
12	461 - 490	30 - 40	1,698 - 2,430
13	491 - 520	35 - 45	1,764 - 2,532
14	521 - 610	35 - 50	1,842 - 2,022

MANAGEMENT SALARY PLAN: JOB DESCRIPTION

POSITION: Assistant Administration and Planning **GRADE:**   4
DEPARTMENT: IHC
DUTIES:

GENERAL FUNCTIONS:

Under direction of Administration Director and Planning Department and acts for him in his absence; conducts research, expedites purchases and follows up shipments, reviews related correspondence, screens and interviews visitors and job applicants, maintains office supplies, and supervises preparation of copies of important documents.

DETAILED FUNCTIONS:

1. Conducts research as requested.
2. Checks incoming purchase orders against requisitions and control sheets.
3. Checks and files correspondence related to purchases.
4. Maintains invoice register.
5. Maintains budget and schedule control sheets, entering purchasing and shipping status information.

6. Expedites and follows up purchases, shipments, and investigates and speeds up delays.
7. Compiles status reports issued biweekly to all hotels.
8. During absence of principal, interviews and screens salesmen, vendors, and job applicants.
9. Maintains office supplies inventory.
10. Supervises preparation of copies of letters, documents, applications, and invoices.
11. Knows French, German, Spanish, and English.
12. Operates varied office machines.

RATING SHEET

Factor	Degree	Rating	Basis for Rating
Education	3	45	Knowledge of a specialized field, equivalent to 4 years' high school and 2 years college.
Experience	3	60	One to three years' related experience.
Complexity of Duties	3	45	Semiroutine duties involving an intensive knowledge of the hotel administration field, requiring the use of a wide range of procedures and the analysis of facts in situations to determine what action should be taken, within the limits of standard practice.
Supervision Received	2	10	Under general supervision, standard practice enables the employee to proceed alone on routine work, referring all questionable cases to supervisor.
Errors	3	20	Probable errors may be serious, effect usually confined within the company. Most work not subject to verification or check.
Contact with Others	3	20	Regular contacts with other departments, furnishing or obtaining information or reports, requiring tact to avoid friction. Outside contacts where improper handling may affect results, but where primary responsibility rests with the next higher level of supervision.
Confidential Data	3	15	Regularly works with some confidential data which, if disclosed, might have adverse internal effect.
Mental and Visual Demands	2	10	Normal.
Working Conditions	1	5	Usual office conditions.

Character of Supervision	1	5	Part-time, immediate supervision over several employees in the same occupation, performing the same work most of the time as those supervised.
Scope of Supervision	1	5	Assists and directs one or two persons in the same occupation.

POINT TOTAL: 240 (4)   RANGE: From $795.00 to $1,344.00

24

Executive Incentive Systems and Profit Sharing

Wallace George in his classic paper said, in support of incentives for indirect workers: "The wise management applies direct incentives where there is a measurable correlation between the output of the direct workers and the physical efforts of the indirect workers, and merit rating increases for all others whose work merits higher wages than the basic occupational rates."[*]

This theorem has been the practical basis for most all of today's incentive plans and systems. It simply means that incentives must be geared to work and performance that can be measured.

In no instance can incentives be expected, nor should they be, to take the place of good management. For it is precisely through the use and application of skills, tools, and tested techniques that incentives can be made to work effectively. It is one thing to say "be more efficient" to a man who is neither so constituted nor so learned, and entirely another to expect and be able to demand peak performance from a man who knows how to manage—how to get results through people—and who can apply the latest and most successful techniques in order to achieve results.

---

[*]"Extending Wage Incentives to Jobs Which Cannot Be Accurately Measured," *Management Review*, American Management Association, May 1947.

Types of Incentives

An examination of incentives results in the following three categories:

1. Direct financial incentives.
2. Indirect financial incentives.
3. Nonfinancial incentives.

Direct Financial Incentives. These are specific methods that directly tie a worker's pay to output. Piece rates are a form of direct incentive, and there are many methods of measuring such rates for incentive purposes.

Indirect Financial Incentives. These are not plans purposely set up to directly increase productivity, but rather policies which have a bearing on morale as related to productivity.

Some examples are:

1. A system of fair rates of pay.
2. A sound promotional plan (if good work means promotion, that is an incentive.)
3. A suggestion system.
4. Fringe benefits.
6. Morale-building devices (of which there are many).

Nonfinancial Incentives. These are different in that there is absolutely no relationship between them and pay received. They may include any company action or policy to benefit employees in other than financial ways, such as a supervisor's attitude, recognition, competition, and working conditions.

Nonfinancial Incentives

1. *Weekly, Biweekly, Monthly Staff Conferences.* The agenda would include a reviewing the week, forecasting the next week, complimenting employees, covering and reviewing complaints, examining new methods, polices and ideas, and handling mistakes.
2. *Work.* Provide enough work to keep people fully occupied instead of not completely busy. Pressure is better than no pressure, psychologically and physically.
3. *Periodic Talks.* Periodic talks, pep talks and pats on the back, providing criticism in private.
4. *Special Privileges.* A popular fallacy is that all employees want *equal* treatment. Actually they want *fair* treatment, and the grant-

ing of special privileges to certain employees can have great incentive value. This can be based on seniority, and can take the form of special clubs, luncheons, buttons, or vacation awards. A wise manager can give the conscientious employee special tasks, let him help with keeping confidential records, or give him special social responsibilities, such as having charge of organizing his group in a charity fund-raising campaign, or organizing a dinner or picnic for a retiring member of the group.

5. *Placement—Follow-Up—Ratings.* Most important is the following up of a new employee on his job. Job performance ratings are of great value in this effort. They make employees feel that management is interested in them.

6. *Suggestion Plans.* Many work well, but require time and skilled administration. And the use of prizes and not cash, generally is even more of an incentive.

7. *Development of Group Spirit.* This is an attitude of teamwork that can be fostered and should be, for the benefit of the employees as well as management, all leading to greater efficiency and improved service. A system of service awards, pins, savings bonds awards, and the use of a simple newsletter or other publication, greatly aids in the development of this spirit.

8. *Working Conditions and Equipment.* Good, clean working conditions, good lighting, acoustical treatment, air conditioning where needed, color dynamics—all stimulate and aid the work effort.

9. *Competition.* Developing competition among employees by praise, stimulation, records of attendance (lateness and absence avoidance), safety, maintenance and cleanliness—these are good morale builders.

10. *Worker Recognition.* Name plates near work stations, praise in front of others, constructive discipline, knowing people's names and using them, are all vitally important. All of this simply adds up to effective supervision and good management.

Principles for an Incentive System

The Organization of Wage and Salary Classifications.

1. Establishment of basic wage rates for each job classification—as a low, median, and highest rate for all positions including the managerial levels.

2. Adoption of the policy of adhering to this classification and making all promotions from within the organization. This establishes a very decided promotion incentive for each employee.

3. A statement that, when an employee starts in a new group, his compensation will be at the minimum rate for that group; that by performing his job satisfactorily, he can increase his compensation while still remaining within that classification. It should be made clear that his earnings can be increased further by his becoming familiar with the duties and the work involved in other higher paid groups so that he will be given such a position, if eligible, when an opening occurs.

4. Assurance that it is basic company policy to employ all new personnel in the lowest classification proper to their experience, and to make all promotions from within the organization.

5. Recognition that this plan does not provide for the promotion of every individual one step upward every time a vacancy occurs. Certain individuals can never rise above certain minimum levels of ability or capacity. This makes it inevitable that some employees will eventually supersede their former supervisors. Such practice is perfectly in accord with good management policy and actually becomes an added indirect incentive for every employee to develop himself for promotion.

The Basis of the Manager Incentive Plan

Savings Incentives. An incentive may be applied to various groups or departments by establishing a budget of expense for each group or department. The personnel within these units are then paid additional compensation in direct proportion to the savings in actual expense as compared to budgeted expense.

Generally the incentive established by this procedure is not sufficiently great to warrant its universal application. If the budgets are correctly and accurately established, it will be difficult to gain on them unless an allowance is arbitrarily made in the budget for such incentive. There is always the danger that economies will be made at the expense of satisfactory work.

There is also the added hazard that, if the budgets are established on the basis of past performance only and not on a basis of careful analysis and measure, certain departments will be able to better the budget by a considerable amount. In this case the departments which have been operating most inefficiently will receive the largest amount of added compensation, and a premium will be paid for poor performance in the past. This means that a very careful analysis must be made and the savings paid out in incentive must be only a small or proportional part of the total amounts saved.

Profit Sharing Incentive. A profit sharing plan is considered to be generally the most suitable form of incentive for the management and administrative groups. It is impossible to formulate a single profit sharing plan that will be applicable to all types of businesses. Instead, each one must be established for the particular conditions existing in order to be equitable to both the company and the employee. Certain general principles can be outlined, however. These include:

1. Establishing all salaries in accordance with the classification method previously mentioned, but with the compensation rates set at a low level so that they can be paid during bad business periods as well as good.
2. Determining the amount of profit the company should earn before additional compensation is paid to employees. The amount to be set aside for the company before distributing a proportion of the profit to employees should not be too excessive. Instead, the current rate of interest that invested capital can realize should be determined. This percentage is applied to the amount of profit that should be set aside before paying added compensation to employees.
3. Making a projection of the profit possibilities of the company under various conditions and various volumes. This determines the maximum profit that may be realized, as well as the normal profit to be expected. (Example, 1% savings on food—$40,000.) Once the amount of profit that may be realized has been determined, there should be deducted that amount of profit which is to be used as wages to capital before added compensation is paid to employees.
4. The remaining profit will then be available for profit sharing, for company reserves, and for additional disbursements to capital accounts. For a company that is not contemplating extensive capital expenditures for expansion or other development purposes, it has been found practical to divide the remaining profit in about the following proportions: (1) one-third in the form of profit sharing to employees, (2) one-third to be retained by the company for future developments, and (3) one-third to be paid to stockholders as additional compensation on their investment.
5. Analyzing the classification of positions to determine how many employees there are in each classification. Each classification of employees should then have a factor or a percentage established for that group. This factor will indicate what percentage of each employee's salary he will receive as additional compensation for a certain amount of profit. For example, a certain classification may reveal that there are six employees normally in that group, and that

the compensation rate is from $750 to $900 per month, per individual. The profit sharing factor for this group may be established at 1% for each $10,000 of profit earned over and above that portion of the amount to be set aside before any profit sharing. This means that each employee in this group will receive 1% of his salary for every $10,000 of profit earned over and above the amount to be set aside as wages to capital.

6. Calculating the total amount of the profit to be disbursed when the established factors are applied. If it is found that too large a proportion of the total profit is used for profit sharing, all of the factors must be adjusted. These factors must continue to be adjusted until the total amount disbursed is in proper proportion to the amount paid out in profit sharing.

Surveys have also shown that where a profit sharing plan has been soundly conceived, it has become completely accepted by the organization as an established policy of the company operation and plays an important part in the industrial relations phase of the business.

The advantages of a profit sharing plan may be summarized as follows:

1. It encourages every employee to make the company's earnings as large as possible.
2. It avoids the disastrous effects of possible future salary reductions, because compensation is directly related to profits.
3. It makes expenses variable and proportionate to income.
4. It gives greater job security.
5. It establishes minimum pay levels which can be maintained in bad times as well as good.

Applying Principles to Typical Plan Operation

Following is an example of a monthly efficiency rating plan, rating factors as follows:

Savings.

Food Cost (1% savings = $40,000 per year)	Payroll Cost (1% savings = $40,000 per year)
Heat—Light—Power	Restaurant Supplies
Maintenance Supplies	China—Maintaining of Inventory to Par
Glass—Maintaining of Iniventory to Par	Flatware—Maintaining of Inventory to Par

Under this plan a standard would have to be established as to what is the desirable standard of performance on labor cost, food cost, and all other costs in percentage and not in dollars.

Business Volume

Dollar Sales

Food   Bakery

Liquor   Catering

In the category of volume of business, a percentage of the net profit over and above the standard or target volume in terms of dollars (taking into consideration any price increases or decreases) is to be agreed upon.

Maintenance and Service

Sanitation Practices   Customer Service

Store Facilities Maintenance

Under the Maintenance and Service ratings category, perfect scores would add a bonus factor, which for example, could be 10% of the amount allotted under savings and volume to the total. Thus a perfect score on all three (sanitation, store facilities maintenance, and service) would equal 100%, which is equal to 10% of the amount to be added to the total amounts of savings and volume. A 50% score would equal 5% and so on.

Operation of the Typical Plan

The plan should first be carried out on a quarterly basis, with three months of experience to bring forward *the first payment* on the first month. This permits capital accumulation and also provides a better experience accumulation.

After the third month, a monthly efficiency report (to the manager) is issued to each store group consisting of the day and night managers. Cash payments, however, would be made quarterly.

The efficiency report to the manager gives ratings in percentages, and provides an overall score, the multipliers of the total amount to be made available that month to that store by Top Management.

This total amount made available is based on the savings and volume results in the amount of one-third to be set aside of the total. It is out of this one-third that incentive payments are to be made. The other two-thirds, as already explained, are set aside as profits for capital improvement and return on investment (either to be accumulated, tax laws permitting, or paid out).

The efficiency report should be prepared by the central office, and the maintenance and service reports by the division managers, who sign and submit them to the central office for review and final approval.

A dry run of the program is always suggested, consisting of three months to iron out any and all difficulties, before it is formally put on a payout basis.

A Word about Bonuses

Repeated studies at Harvard University and Carnegie Tech, have shown that bonuses do not provide any incentives whatsoever.

Unfortunately, the word bonus has been confused with incentive payments in the modern industrial vocabulary, partly through lack of an accepted definition, and partly because management has frequently used it to designate some form of profit distribution.

A bonus is correctly defined as an arbitrary gift made at the discretion of the giver, without regard to an established measure of award. It is based on the personal relationship existing between the giver and the receiver.

PROFIT SHARING INCENTIVE SYSTEM

	NUMBER OF SEATS			MONTH OF _____ 1976 Percent	MONTH OF _____ 1976 Percent	YEAR TO Date, 1976 Percent	YEAR TO Date, 1976 Percent
Counter	Rest.	Total					
SALES — Food							
Liquor							
Bakery							
Merchandise							
Cigars—Cigarettes							
Other							
Catering							
NET SALES				100%	100%	100%	100%
Less — Cost of Goods Sold							
Opening Inventory							
Plus-Purchases/Acquisitions							
Minus—Closing Inventory							
Total Cost of Goods Sold							
GROSS PROFIT							
Less — Controllable Expenses:							
Operating Wages							
Other Wages							
Payroll Taxes							
W/C Insurance							
Insurance Plan—Employees							
Total Payroll Expense							
Electricity							
Gas							
Fuel							
Water							
Sewerage							
Telephone							
Maintenance							
Cleaning Services							
Repairs							
Supplies							
China and Glassware							
Flatware							
Menus & Flyers							
Laundry							
Uniforms							
Advertising							
Travel							
Miscellaneous							
Total Controllable Expenses							
PROFIT AFTER CONTROLLABLE EXPENSES							
Maintenance and Service							
Sanitation Practices							
Store Facilities Maintce.							
Customer Service							

Part V

Business Promotion
and Executive Development

25

Measuring Sales and Promotion Effectiveness

The American Management Association in New York has conducted many programs for executives explaining how companies can measure the profitable acceptance of their products and services by the public they serve and seek to serve.

It is not a new subject but one that was first introduced under the heading of *Market Research*. Essentially, it is the predetermination of a product's or service's acceptance and appeal by various publics. Such research points out the need for proper pricing, planning, promotion, and helps to insure profitable marketing.

Today this research has been greatly extended and decentralized into various categories. *Product Planning* is one of these. Briefly, it determines the needs for a product and what it must do to meet public acceptance This covers styling, color price, packaging, copy style, design, and many other factors.

Comparatively little has been done in industry using this type of research. Individuals or groups of individuals will decide what is to be done. Sometimes figures or statistics are used to help make a decision. But these statistics often give a limited answer. Effectively measuring and interpreting public opinion and reaction gives the only true answer. And the value of this has long been recognized.

Expressed this way—"rather spend a little in advance and be sure of results, than guess and lose lots more"—makes sense.

A list of questions developed from case studies in hotels has resulted in the following list of test questions which aid in checking the marketing effectiveness of a hotel's products, services and facilities.

MARKET EFFECTIVENESS
EVALUATION SHEET

1. Do you know to what extent all of your various types of advertising is attracting *and selling* your present as well as potential guests? Yes? _____ No? _____

2. Do you know to what extent your merchandising and sales promotion is attracting and selling your guests? Yes? _____ No? _____

3. Do you know to what extent your services are satisfying and selling your guests? Yes? _____ No? _____

4. Do you know to what extent your facilities are satisfying your present markets? Are they holding these markets? Yes? _____ No? _____

5. Are new markets being developed from these sources, or is business holding its own? Yes? _____ No? _____

6. Have you measured and determined the potential markets within your present reach? Yes? _____ No? _____

7. Have you measured and defined new future sources of business? Yes? _____ No? _____

8. Do you know the reasons lost business has gone "elsewhere" and to what extent? Yes? _____ No? _____

9. Do you know the value of such business in direct and indirect revenues? Yes? _____ No? _____

10. Has your advertising, merchandising and promotion been based on what present and new publics want, or what one or more persons who "know the business or the field" have decided are necessary? Yes? _____ No? _____

11. Are you aware of, and have you determined what the pulse of your public is thinking as to preferences, likes, dislikes on any phase of services, facilities, products sold such as food, beverages and others—now, and in the future? Yes? _____ No? _____

12. Have you defined the reasons for competitive growth from motels, hotels, and other competition? Yes? _____ No? _____

13. Has a program of positive action (carefully aimed at objectives) been developed and carried out, which would reach these competitive markets and return or bring them to you? Yes? _____ No? _____

14. Has any study been made to determine to what extent present services (which mean more or less revenue to you)? Yes? _____ No? _____

The number of *yeses* or *noes* scored are not critical, but it has been found in auditing 46 outstandingly successful hotels thus far, that over 90% of them had less than three *noes*, and carried a continuous program of interest and attention getting devices (sales, merchandising, publicity) directed at the effective selling of a hotel's services and facilities to many publics.

More Business through Research

For many years the hotel and motel industry has been using a technique that has been positively paying dividends where it has been applied. It is based on the simple fact that business is not merely obtained by offering the public what is available, and trying to have it accepted. And it is also not the thinking and opinions of one man, or group of men in an organization, but is based solely on what people want.

That a new technique is important now, with hotels facing severe competition, will not be questioned by anyone. Look at the latest Directory of AAA Tour Books covering approved hotels, motels, and resorts:

TOTAL NUMBER OF HOTELS, MOTELS, AND RESORTS

United States	12,629
Canada	1,670
Mexico	436
Central America	70
Grand Total	14,805

Yet in comparing the values of hotels to motels, dollar for dollar the hotels offer and provide much more with every convenience in one location, at a guest's desire, than do the majority of motels. New motel construction, however, is meeting the challenge effectively and is either on a par with, or ahead of, hotels.

Reconcile these facts with the tremendous growth in population, greater every year, and wonder where the people are going. There is an annual average increase of approximately 4,000,000 people, and by 1967 the total population should reach 200,000,000 which is a 20% increase over 1957.

The decline in hotel occupancy means many things. First, obviously the buying public is going elsewhere. Second, and most important, it means that hotels collectively are not interpreting public reaction and changing interests, and not telling the hotel story. Word-of-mouth advertising is not enough, although it helps.

The approach to this problem is time tested by modern industry. Essentially a hotel's operations and approach is directed to its publics so as to satisfy basic wants, interests, and desires.

Early in 1950 the trend of decreasing occupancy in hotels was noted, and it was observed how in other industries successful research techniques, properly applied, were used to build and develop business. It was recognized that the best hotels regarded the guest in terms of what can be done to influence him favorably toward a hotel's services and facilities, and not what he might like, or in what he might be interested.

The new concept recognizes the hotel guest as an important, changing source of information. By properly utilizing such information, hotels conduct their operations accordingly. Those hotels, and there are quite a number that have followed this approach, are well ahead of the market.

Modern business today has gone far beyond the stage of merely auditing its accounts, inventories, buildings and personnel; it is taking a close look at just about everything it does, and particularly it considers the consumer (what the potential publics are thinking, wanting and seeking); it profits thereby.

Many hotel operators who believed that all you had to do was to provide clean rooms that are comfortable, and good food, and who did not keep abreast, let alone ahead, of the market changes are either out of business or close to it. Where are some of yesterday's giant hotel companies? Gone with winds generated by changing market conditions.

Toward a New Concept

Principals are aware that there are other essentials in pleasing guests necessary to woo and capture the business and professional traveler's dollar.

There is a recognition of the need for progress. Management realizes that guests can be influenced, but due to greatly increased communications and through wide associations in both business and personal life, they are subject to influences that make any hotel-motel effort short-lived, particularly if it doesn't tie in with, or take advantage of, outside stimuli. Unfortunately, in a period when the government is increasing expenditures for research and development, and when private business research budgets have risen sharply, the industry's American Hotel Association budget has not increased its research appropriations.

The Applications of Research

The results of research findings require interpretation. They are studied and appraised, and objectively applied to specific situations. New operating methods are developed and used as a direct result.

But the use of such methods is ruled solely by basic findings, which must clearly indicate their use. How are new methods of service developed along with determining facilities, their location, type, size and need? They are accomplished by using basic information and associating it with the results of experienced observation and contact with present practices in a large variety of situations.

The method of science is observation and interpretation. Ideas for change that are new are based on such observation and association. Practices in other industries are observed and compared with those in hotels; such items as fashion, taste, and opinion regarding anything from cars to foods, fads, styles, designs, colors, as well as social and economic thought are observed.

Sometimes it is possible that an idea or change in operations may be ready for guest acceptance; it may be too early or not have been presented in an acceptable form. Presentation is vitally important, because many good ideas have failed not because they were not perfectly workable, but because they were presented at an inopportune time and perhaps in an unobjective manner.

The Techniques

We have already explained the method of developing ideas and emphasized the importance of tying them into basic public opinion. How such opinion is gathered and refined is done in a number of ways.

1. Individual personal interviews.
2. Letters to persons asking for a reply.
3. Questionnaires.
4. A combination of questionnaire and interview.

5. Association testing, the newest form.
6. Experienced objective sampling.

Most of these techniques are self explanatory. Perhaps *association testing* requires clarification. It connects the habits and thinking of people and their reactions to stimuli of a similar nature to the problem situation, which is observed and then interpreted. It is not an exact scientific procedure, but it is used primarily by experienced, objective, experienced analysts. It is, however, a most effective method of research and analysis because it utilizes the experience and abilities of the person conducting the research.

The Publics

The great *public* of a hotel and motel is a collection of publics, each with its own particular interests and problems. It includes the following groups:

1. The employee public.
2. The owner or stockholder public.
3. The consumer public.
4. The supplier public.
5. The community public (most important to a hotel).
6. The government public.
7. The trade and competitor publics.
8. The distributor public, consisting of dealers and suppliers.

Each of these are important collectively and individually to any operation's success, and require objective understanding and interpretation of research findings.

What to Find Out

Actually, it is no trick to get the answers to questions like these:

1. What kinds of competition are there, and to what extent are they affecting a hotel or motel business?
2. What should be a hotel or motel potential if such competition, or part of it, were analyzed?
4. If a decline in business has been gradual or severe at certain periods, have reasons been analyzed?
5. What research has been conducted to cultivate and develop new markets?

6. To what extent are guests using various services and facilities?
7. Has a study been made to determine whether the ways of merchandising of facilities and services are satisfactory?
8. What are the changes in the habits, thinking and preferences of people today?
9. Should rates be lowered or increased — and what effect would this have on volume?

Manufacturers are constantly sampling consumer reaction to keep ahead of competition, or to recapture their share of the market. A growing number of innkeepers have taken advantage of statistical studies, to determine the cause for lost or diminished business. They have been enthusiastic over the results.

Low Food Sales

In one case food volume was half that of room sales, and guests were eating with competitors.

A guest opinion sampling was taken. Interviews with transient and local guests revealed the following:

DEGREE OF GUEST SATISFACTION

Transient Guests

Service	Percent Satisfied	Percent Unsatisfied	Percent Not Using Services
Food	53	46	1
Beverages	77	13	10
Waiter Service	78	15	7
Parking	22	2	76

Local Guests

Service	Percent Satisfied	Percent Unsatisfied	Percent Not Using Service
Food	21	79	0
Beverages	93	7	0
Waiter Service	64	36	0
Parking	43	7	50

Reasons given by guests for not using facilities or being dissatisfied were:

1. Prices too high, 92%
2. Food not up to standard, 64%
3. Disliked items on menu, 79%
4. Poor service and wrong orders, 36%
5. Facilities cold and unfriendly, 80%

A complete evaluation of guest comments was made. It pointed the way to changes in policy and operation. The menu, style, format and color were changed; new dishes were introduced; and correctly-aimed merchandising and publicity were used to dispel the idea that prices were too high.

A complete remodeling of the room with added local touches of color, design and artwork satisfied not only transient, but local guests as well. Gradually sales increased. Six months later food volume had doubled.

Guest Questionnaire

Often a questionnaire is sent directly to a sampling of recently registered guests. Shown is one that was successfully used by a large midwestern hotel.

Results are more positive when the guest receives his questionnaire covered by a letter signed by the manager or other responsible executives.

In the case of this hotel, results were excellent. Over 72% replied. A great majority were favorable in their comments. Helpful suggestions and valuable criticisms were given. As suggested, corrections and changes were put into effect, and guests wrote in thanking management for putting their suggestions into effect; not an uncommon occurrence.

Lack of Evening Patronage

In another case, the guests failed to use the main dining room in the evenings. Here the survey brought out that the public disliked seeing the same style and format of menu evenings as was used for luncheons, even though the principal dishes served were different.

Service was reported to be slow, there was no entertainment, and interior decoration proved uninteresting and lacked warmth. The quality of the food was below standard to that served elsewhere at less cost.

Further analysis into the tastes, habits, and economic status of guests with preferences as to type of menu and service, brought about a separate dessert menu and service, a revised wine list, and a large, three-color menu with pen and ink drawings of dishes (now a collector's item).

WHAT I LIKED ABOUT THE
_____
_____
_____

WHAT I DIDN'T LIKE ABOUT THE
_____
_____
_____

ONLY FOUR EASY
QUESTIONS

JUST ANSWER AND
MAIL

and thanks
a great
deal!

PLEASE CHECK THE SERVICES USED AND HOW YOU REGARDED THEM:

	Satisfactory	Unsatisfactory	Comment
Front Desk	—	—	_____
Your Room	—	—	_____
The Bell Boys	—	—	_____
Elevator Service	—	—	_____
Telephone Service	—	—	_____
Food	—	—	_____
Beverages	—	—	_____
Waiter Service	—	—	_____
Laundry	—	—	_____
Valet	—	—	_____
Barber Shop	—	—	_____
Beauty Salon	—	—	_____
Other Services (Specify)			
_____	—	—	_____
_____	—	—	_____
_____	—	—	_____

I SUGGEST THE FOLLOWING_____
_____
_____
_____

Service checklist.

Entertainment tastes revealed that a sophisticated musical trio would satisfy. In less than three months capacity business resulted, and the room became one of the most popular in town.

Diminishing Function Business

In still another case, banquet business was dropping at an alarming rate. Research revealed:

1. A lack of a uniform price policy.
2. Different prices charged for the same type of function.
3. Certain rooms rented more frequently than others, primarily because of sales habits of sales representatives.
4. Generally, the same type of menu was offered again and again without variation.

Recognizing that the low banquet-function space ratio might be based on attitudes, opinions and preferences unknown, of course, to the operator, a series of interviews designed to get below-surface opinions (depth interviews) were arranged with recent banquet guests and those who had not used such services for more than a year.

One-hundred interviews, with a sampling from each economic group, were conducted. Findings completely changed management policy:

1. 80% of banquet groups failed to return because of poor menu representation, merchandising, and what was believed to be excessive pricing.
2. 64% believed that overall charges had varied with other groups.
3. 23% felt that they should have had more choice of menu.
4. 96% indicated that facilities were too warm, and were not air conditioned.
5. 100% indicated that a ballroom was important, and 46% stated they would be able to use such facilities.

The result of these findings was twofold:

1. It pointed the way to more objective selling as well as follow-up.
2. It indicated the kind and type of changes in facilities and services that were necessary.

Had this information been known when the plant had been built, time money and effort could have been saved. A ballroom could easily have been constructed; air conditioning would have been cheaper to install at the time.

An intensive sales campaign aimed at new types of functional business and the installation of a wedding consultant in a small office, doubled business within a year.

Low House Count

Examine the case where room occupancy hovered between 55 and 60%. Guest opinion sampling disclosed that rates were considered too high for accommodations offered.

GRAPHIC ANALYSIS

Hotel _____ Date_____

Your Services	Superior 100	Excellent 90	Good 80	Satisfactory 70	60
Reservations					
By Letter _____					
By Telephone: "Telephone Sales Sense Test" ___					
Arrival Outside and On Way Into Hotel _____					
At the Front Desk _____					
On the Way to the Room _____					
On Arrival at the Room _____					
Elevator Service _____					
Telephone Service _____					
Room Service _____					
Restaurant Service _____					
Bar Service _____					
Laundry _____					
Valet _____					
Porter _____					
Mail and Information_____					
Cashier _____					
Barber Shop_____					
Beauty Salon _____					
Manicurist _____					
Cigar Stand—Newstand—Gift Counter _____					
Public Stenographer _____					
Gentlemen's Lounge _____					
Powder Room _____					
Bootblack _____					
Florist _____					
Other Services _____					
Departure _____					
Your Facilities					
Guest Room _____					
Desk _____					
Bathroom _____					
Bathroom Supplies _____					
Public Rooms and Spaces _____					
Outside of Building _____					
Your Merchandising					
Sales Department Techniques Audit _____					
Internal Promotion _____					
Other Factors					

Graphic Service analysis.

A public relations program indirectly aimed at exploding this myth, consisting of sales letters, brochures, and news stories about the low cost of vacations and business visits, reversed the trend. New sources of business increased reservations and occupancy 11% in three months, reaching 26% in seven months. The program, with techniques for further business development, is still in effect, and is paying handsome returns.

How to Conduct a Survey

For a comprehensive analysis four major areas should be explored: (1) services, (2) facilities, (3) merchandising, and (4) guest relations.

In each category a questionnaire like the sample shown below covers the various phases. A complete survey may cover as many as 750 to 800 questions. Results are then tabulated and transferred onto a chart which shows at a glance how the operation can be analyzed, repeated observations should be made at regular intervals by a person unknown to operating personnel.

A constructive report should contain suggestions and practical tested ideas. It should suggest merchandising and service aids, and outline cost cutting and profit making approaches.

Any operator armed with knowledge such as is made available through such research can maintain and improve his position in today's highly competitive, ever-changing market.

Typical Work Form

Restaurant Service

This analysis is based on the folowing concepts:

Complete guest satisfaction — what the guest wants, and how he wants it served.

Serving the guest items he wanted and selling him those from which the hotel makes the greatest profit.

Maintaining the hotel's policies of service standards.

1. Were the headwaiter, captain, host or hostess on hand on entering the room? _____
2. What greetings were extended? _____
3. Was the number of persons in the party immediately ascertained?
   _____
4. What was the reaction on stating a choice or change of table? ____
   _____

5. Depending on the size and importance of the party, and whether or not the dining room was busy, did the headwaiter, captain or waiter, after allowing patrons to become settled, hand them a menu, step back to a respectful distance and watch when he was needed or wanted? _____

6. Did he make suggestions with proper timing? _____

7. Were the suggestions explained in detail as to content and makeup? (The true test of a good waiter lies in his ability to judge what a patron desires and to sell him a well-rounded meal with which he is pleased and from which the hotel obtains a profit. _____

8. In taking the order, were special directions requested for such items as: Tea — *lemon or cream?* Hearts of lettuce or any other salad — *what kind of dressing?* Steak or lamb chops — *well done, medium, medium rare, or rare?* _____

9. Did the captain or headwaiter look over the table to see that everything was in order? _____

10. Did he check guest satisfaction during the meal? _____

11. Did he appear to make suggestions or criticisms and follow them up? _____

12. How long a wait was there between courses? Give the times _____
    _____

13. Was the table set attractively? Were all necessary utensils present?
    _____

14. Were the conventions of good table setting observed? Knives with blades in? Spoons following also at the right of the plate, evenly spaced, in the order in which they are to be used, beginning with the one nearest the plate? Forks on the left? Oyster fork on the right? Glass above knives? _____
    _____

15. Were items served and removed from the left? Glasses from the right? _____

16. Were the following conventional services observed?
    (a) Baked potato — if the patron wants it prepared for him, the waiter should open it, butter it, and sprinkle paprika on it _____
    (b) Hot asparagus — place the tips toward the center of the plate so that the dressing may be placed on it _____
    (c) Bottled sauces — waiter should know each of these by name. On serving care should be taken to see that the bottles are clean. In serving Worcestershire sauce, the cork must be left in the bottle, since many people have the habit of shaking it. _____
    _____

(d) French pastry — This should be passed on a tray or pastry wagon and served as the patron wishes. _____

(e) Correct garnitures — lettuce with cold meat, lemon with sea food. _____

(f) Coffee, tea, cocoa, and chocolate — many people like to serve these themselves. The waiter should aid in passing and, if directed, serve. Milk should be brought to the table, poured out and the bottle or carton removed. _____

17. What was the condition of the china, glassware, silverware, chinaware, linen? _____

18. Was food attractive, tasty and fresh? Hot food *hot?* Cold food *cold?*
_____

19. A good salad is crisp, cold, and has color. Was it that way? _____
_____

20. Did the waiter or busboy, depending on the service, say "Do you wish butter?" or "Do you wish more butter?" _____

21. Were ash trays emptied before and during the meal? _____

22. What was the waiter's apparent knowledge of dishes, wines, liquors, and service? _____

23. How was the check presented? Describe _____

24. Show costs of meal, give check and waiter number _____

25. On leaving, did someone (who?) assist you drawing chairs, helping ladies with coats and bags, and checking to see that personal items were not left behind? _____

26. Was there a pleasant farewell, appropriate to the time of day, and an invitation to return? _____

27. What was the general appearance, cleanliness, grooming, manner, attitude, dress, deportment, position, and station of personnel? _____
_____

28. Were there any objectionable noises either in careless handling of dishes, or from the kitchen present? Explain _____

29. Comments and Observations _____
_____
_____

Analyzing the Employee

A major airline, recently surveyed, showed unusual absence and turnover among stewardesses. Analysis revealed odd-hour work scheduling and poor food quality of meals as the cause. On correcting these conditions, both absences and turnover fell off sharply. Passengers got much better service, too.

There are two good ways of making such a survey. One is to distribute a questionnaire to employees. This usually covers a series of from 50 to 100 questions, depending on the scope of the problem and size of the organization. Questions fall into the following patterns; whether or not employees are satisfied with their working conditions, salary, possibilities of promotion, general company policy, extent and quality of supervision, security, recognition, and the work itself. Employees are invited to add their own comments.

The following is a sample taken from a typical questionnaire:

1. What do you think of your job at _____?
2. Do you feel management is well thought of by other employees?
3. Do you feel that there is enough opportunity to get ahead?
4. Does your supervisor treat you fairly, and does he know how to get along with people?
5. Do you think management really wants to improve working conditions?
6. Do you think management is doing a good job in running the hotel or motel?
7. Do you feel employees are doing their best to help the hotel? Why? Why not?
8. What do you like best about your job?
9. Do you think your hotel or motel is making headway against competition?
10. What do you think about management cutting costs?
11. Is it done fairly, does it make you insecure?
12. Is there favoritism?
13. Why do people quit?
14. How is the feeling between the management and employees?

Returns can run 90 to 100%. Questions and answers are generally grouped, then carefully reviewed and discussed with management. They may also be tabulated in percentages for quick comparative analysis. This helps to show up trouble spots, unsatisfactory conditions, and the relative positions of various departments.

Another method of measuring morale, that is both thorough and direct, is through the use of confidential "depth interviews" with employees. This often results in obtaining more information than what employees normally will commit to writing.

This has proved particularly valuable in special situations such as changes in management, as was recently the case of a 1500-room hotel.

There, confidential talks proved the turning point in selling the new organization to employees. It also enabled management to promptly correct unfavorable conditions. In later follow-up interviews, management's viewpoints were explained and successfully sold to employees, something which would normally have taken months to accomplish.

27

Developing New Products
and Services

Modern business today is constantly researching into *What Makes People Buy?* And it is spending millions annually finding out. Armed with the answers, it systematically and earnestly redesigns and restyles its products and services to meet public interest and demand.

Some 80 different research firms, specialists in engineering public consent, and shaping, styling and building objective appeal into their clients' products and services, are successfully serving clients now.

The Consumers—the many publics—have become complacent today. And as market research people say, "Their appetites must be whetted with new products, new services, new styling, and harder selling."

The years ahead will be hard selling ones, highly competitive, with the consumer and guest having many opportunities to pick and choose from competition. Selling and offering services and facilities to guests in the previous manner will be risky, particularly in attracting new business. People are simply more choosy now. They are attracted by things that are new, different, exciting, unique, comfortable and so on. Words like these are effectively planting mental images of guest satisfaction every day, which acquire business.

Public Must Be Pleased

Tomorrow's management, large and small, are pinning their hopes on pleasing the public more than ever before, because the fight for the dollar will be intense. More important, those companies that can retain and build business now will be ahead and are almost sure to capitalize on the next upward sweep in the economy.

In the industry, competition for the pleasure and business publics' dollar has already reached the critical stage. Hotel occupancy has been dropping for some years now. The industry is now talking about the "low sixties" and some are really in the "low fifties."

The practice of increasing guest charges to offset declining sales, also cutting costs and services has been one answer to the problem. But it has also helped build many new motels and modern hotels.

A successful approach to meet this problem which has paid dividends where applied, is:

1. Developing greater public appreciation for existing services and facilities through effective merchandising and insuring through research that these services and facilities are effectively and satisfactorily meeting public demand.
2. Planning and introducing new services, facilities and products, to capture public imagination, interest, attention and business.

Hotels vs. Motels

At one time the public believed that the best value for the dollar was offered by the hotels. Today, however, that viewpoint has changed, and the public believes that the motel offers the best value.

Actually, this was once true. Hotels, until quite recently with the advent of *modern* motor hotels, offered greater service value to the traveler, and at a lower cost. All in one area, available to any guest, were a veritable array of services, facilities and conveniences not available in yesterday's motels.

Space alone, the convenience of the lobby with accompanying facilities, offered much more than the old motel room. Space doesn't permit a listing of all the motel, motor hotel comforts and services available to a guest but here are the major ones, which are well known.

Lobby and accompanying conveniences	Garage and Parking
Assistance with baggage	Registration, Mail and Information
Experienced Telephone Service (local and long lines)	Guest Room Conveniences, Maid Services
Room Service	Elevator Service

Laundry	Valet
Barber Shop	Beauty Salon
Cashier and Credit	Medical Services
Food and Beverage (restaurants and bars)	Entertainment
Public Stenographer	Radio, TV
Shops	Bellmen's Service
Cigar Counter and Newsstand	Banquet and Meeting Facilities

In *Evaluation Audits of Services, Facilities and Merchandising*, objective recommendations on shaping, changing, adding and improving services to insure maximum public appeal, with resulting high profit volume relationships are offered.

Proprietors are thus able to keep not only abreast, but ahead, of public taste, usage, interest, and can recognize early both profitable as well as unprofitable services, in order to hold as well as develop clientele.

As one client so aptly put it recently: "We seem to be constantly changing, adding, dropping or altering services, all for the better, also modernizing, painting, correcting here and there, and spending in order to come out ahead with a profit. But we are well ahead of the game!"

In evaluating and objectively proposing new services or facilities, even products that will succeed at a profit, a checklist, covering 10 points, to pre-test and pre-tell whether or not and how successful or how saleable a new service or product will prove to be follows:

CHECKLIST FOR
MARKETING A NEW SERVICE OR PRODUCT

1. The market for the new service — or if it is a product: Is there a market and how big is it?
   (a) How big is the potential market in terms of units (covers, etc.) and in terms of dollar volume, both immediate and long term?
   (b) Who is the potential market (characteristics in terms of sex, age, socio-economic, education, occupation, income, home ownership)?
   (c) Where is the potential market located (geographically, by region, city size, urban, rural)?
   (d) Is this market immediately identifiable? How can it be identified?
2. Why consider a new service? Should there be one? Why?
   (a) Can it be introduced through our own sales efforts?

(b) Will it keep the morale of our employees?

(c) How will this service or product affect our other services?

(d) How much money is required to develop it? Get it started?

3. What are the present buying habits, usage and attitudes of the publics regarding products and services which are similar to what is being thought of? Who will buy?

    (a) What do guests like and dislike about this type of service or product?

    (b) What improvements do they feel could be made on this type of service or product?

    (c) What is the seasonal pattern of buying?

4. What is the competition for this new product or service. Who is offering it now?

    (a) What competing businesses are offering similar products or services? (Hotels, restaurants, motels, clubs, etc.)

    (b) What are consumers' opinions, buying habits, usage habits of other competition?

    (c) What are the physical and psychological attributes of these products or services — size, presentation, amount, color, current appeal, sensory qualities?

    (d) What changes in the competitive picture can be expected? Will there be much competition?

5. What are the difficulties which may be encountered in getting out this new service and/or product?

    (a) What research and development is required?

    (b) How long will it take before the public is ready?

    (c) How much will it cost?

    (d) How will it be financed?

6. Merchandising the product or service. How will it be sold?

    (a) What types of merchandising are being used by competition?

    (b) What type of merchandising will bring the greatest sales and profit?

    (c) What have tests of merchandising shown as to consumer preference? How do these compare with competition?

7. The new service or product: Is it better? Who can affirm or deny?

    (a) What are the new services?

    (b) In what ways is this an improvement over similar or comparable products?

    (c) What were the results of guest service tests? What was liked and what was disliked? How does it compare with competition?

8. Pricing the new service? Can you sell it at a profit?
   (a) What are the prices of competitive service?
   (b) What are the production costs?
   (c) What are promotion costs?
   (d) What other costs are there?
   (e) What is the break-even point, and what margin is needed for profit?
   (f) What changes in sales effort are needed?
9. Promoting the new service or product.
   (a) How much should be spent on promoting the new service, in advertising, merchandising, etc.?
   (b) Where should this money be spent? In which markets?
   (c) Which media should be used?
   (d) What is the best copy theme to use?
   (e) How much should be spent on each media? How can prospects be reached at the lowest level of cost?
   (f) What is the size and nature of competition's advertising efforts?
10. Evaluating results for future marketing? Will and does it take (after testing)?
    (a) What volume has been achieved?
    (b) What share of the market has been obtained?
    (c) What advertising or promotion has proved most successful?

A quick review of the list will show that it starts out with examining the reason and need for a new service or product, and all from the guests' viewpoint. (Mr. and Mrs. Consumer.)

It determines the full nature and extent of the market, and whether it is large or practical enough to make it worthwhile.

It permits the spotting of a potential success or failure in advance. And it can save hundreds of dollars, and greatly cut down errors.

Long before a product or service hits the market, it is given what we call a "dry run" on paper. This checklist is used as a guide in research. Its basic principle is simply this: Think first about the market, the user and his needs and requirements, then decide whether the service is saleable and will stand the test of repeat business.

Should there be no data on the actual market, before starting to use this checklist, additional research and outside help are worth consideration.

28

Increasing Advertising Effectiveness

Every experieneced sales and advertising man knows that there are two good basic ways to increase the impact and effectiveness of an advertisement:

1. Using larger sized advertisements.
2. Increasing the frequency of advertisements.

Tests conducted recently by the Laboratory of Advertising Performance of the McGraw-Hill Book Company showed the following:

Readership of an advertisement increases with size in the following proportions:

Size of Space	Noted Readership Index per Page
2 pages	142
1 page	100
2¾ pages	67
⅓ page	28

There are some factors that must also be taken into account, all of which go with a larger advertisement: better physical area in which to tell a more complete story; more attention-getting artwork, pictures and headlines; better composition to get reader attention; more prestige; and greater impression of stability and leadership.

Size alone is impressive!

Here is how the frequency of advertising affects readership:

Number of Insertions	Read Most Readership Index per Insertion	Cost per Reader Index per Insertion
12	121	76
7 to 11	114	83
6	105	92
2 to 5	100	100

Increased frequency builds readership for each insertion at a lower cost per insertion. For example: 12-time advertisers average 21% greater readership per advertisement, and 24% lower cost per reader than advertisers using two to five insertions per year. It should also be noted that advertising rate discounts increase as frequency increases.

There are other important inherent factors which make an advertisement successful and effective. *The Advertising Guide*, which contains advertising that has successfully sold the public, developed and applied a checklist which aids in making selections and insertions into the Guide.

Effective ads have these factors in common:

Pictures:

1. A big, dominant picture adds emphasis, interest and readership to the ad.
2. A good, big picture showing the service or facility of the hotel in actual use is best to use.
3. Small inset pictures tend to increase interest and readership.

Headlines:

1. The headline should be definite and specific.
2. The best headlines are tied in with a good picture.
3. Putting good clear type in the headline adds to its attention getting power, and readership.

Copy:

1. Testimonials with glamour type copy, telling the fun and benefits to be gained from use of services or facilities get best readership.
2. Straight descriptive copy gets fair attention from women.
3. When a good subhead is used, it generally gets as much readership as the headline, sometimes more. This incidentally shows the importance of using good type.

Special Note:

Simplicity in the handling of the layout, no matter the size, with a central, focal point of interest and activity is vitally important to the effectiveness of the ad.

Some factors and observations made recently have also emphasized that reaching the largest audience through the mediums you wish to employ has a bearing on effectiveness. But, it is not necessarily the largest circulation of a medium alone which counts. It may be that the medium you employ reaches the highest percentage of the market you are seeking to sell and wish to reach. This is what counts.

A good rule to observe is to expand your advertising investment in the publications which now reach and contact the greatest proportion of your market at the lowest cost to you.

Major Areas of Hotel Advertising

The possibilites of increasing sales through advertising have been found to cover 15 major areas. Two years of review of more than 200,000 hotel-motel advertisements in 1700 newspapers and 50 magazines in the United States have enabled us to classify hotel advertising under the following divisions:

1. Reservations.
2. Rooms.
3. The executive.
4. Good eating and fine food.
5. The family dinner.
6. Dining and dancing.
7. The cocktail hour.
8. Smorgasbord, buffet, special dinners.
9. Sophisticated entertainment.
10. Popular entertainment.
11. Breakfast, brunch and coffee time.
12. Banquets, parties, meetings.
13. Father's Day.
14. Especially for women: weddings, accommodations.
15. Christmas and holiday parties.

It has also been found that the great majority of hotels-motels have not fully utilized many additional possibilities for advertising their services and facilities. Anyone knows that advertising builds business but the full nature and extent to which it may be employed for increasing business lies virtually untapped.

29

Increasing Merchandising
Effectiveness

The purpose of the development of effective merchandising for hotels-motels is obviously to increase sales. Just how this is done is no mystery. Merchandising, as a term, has been given various definitions. The general opinion is that it refers to all the devices and methods whereby sales internally in a hotel or motel can be increased. Another is the total of all efforts to help move the sale of all services offered by an enterprise. Some operators include the efforts of their sales departments in this definition.

In practice, merchandising represents the total of all efforts including sales and advertising that aids in the sale of the product, whatever it may be.

Occasionally consultants say to a client, "If through objective merchandising, you can increase your sales 5, 10 or 15 percent or more, aside from increasing prices, would you be interested?" The obvious answer is *yes*, and often this has proved the minimum increase for some.

Somerset Hotel — A Dramatic Example

There are some recognized successful merchandising operations in effect today. Among the great leaders and pace setters for the industry are the now legendary Sonnabends. Anyone who remembers the Somerset Hotel in Boston, Massachusetts, in the late 50's and 60's, will immediately recall the wide range of effective merchandising that covered practically every conceivable service and facility that can be offered to today's

246

sensitive public. True masters of marketing, the Sonnabends, in a relatively short time, gained for the Somerset, prominence, distinction and prestige, plus a great deal of business.

The very effective dramatization of services, utilization of space (imagine a successful open air swimming pool in sedate Back Bay Boston, as only one example) established a distinctly different impression and atmosphere which, with the hotel's wide recognition for outstanding traditional as well as exotic foods, outstanding service, and smart facilities, met practically every pocket!

Brunswick — A Remarkable Example

Another almost legendary and quite remarkable achievement was the Brunswick Hotel, Lancaster, Pennsylvania, guided by the late Paul Heine, a master of merchandising. Practically every point of sale was covered in some way. A guest received repeated reminders and stimuli to buy with excellent results. This was a 200-room hotel with six different food operations, all of which were thriving and successful.

Anyone who saw the Brunswick will recall the extremely clever use of copy, color, style and format of menus, tent cards, decor, and all the other little items—matches, stickers, stationery, place mats, postcards, lighting, and subtle suggestions. At every turn in the great challenge of pleasing the guest, this master effectively reached the points of sale.

Dorset Sets Successful Tone

Here is another example of successful merchandising, where a sense of *oneness* prevailed. At the Dorset certain changes in decor, rooms, rehabilitation, and carefully planned merchandising built into menus, tent cards, matches, stationery, and postcards developed a concept of superior service and tone at a relatively small outlay.

This Bing and Bing property in New York City came under the hotel division headed by the late James D. Fuller, and it has not only been highly successful by every service standard in the business, but also profitable, with occupancies far exceeding the averages. Steady local, transient, and top-level commercial guests make up this hotel's clientele.

The Carlyle Is Unique

Robert F. Huyot's highly successful direction of New York City's Hotel Carlyle had no peer in its day when it came to combining modern living with the charm and dignity of the finest in services and facilities catering to an exclusive clientele.

Being gifted with outstanding talent as an artist of note enabled Robert F. Huyot to produce an extremely skillful blend of balanced merchandising, aimed at subtle suggestion and truly aiding a guest in making the best possible use of the services available.

Color and design were in balance: gold, white, and a blend of soft, warm, gay tones, an atmosphere of dignity, warmth, sincerity and welcome that denoted a character of style and service has succeeded to attract, hold, and develop an audience equalled only by those few traditionally great hotels in the world.

Merchandising Checklist

Good merchandising, in order to be effective, must meet a strong positive response on the following questions:

1. Are display cards, consisting of various sized frames in lobby and other areas, featuring various services and facilities offered? Are they effective? Are they remembered?
2. If frames are used, are they changed frequently? How often are they changed ?
3. Are frames in passenger elevators changed for meals? Do they contain cards that mention or refer to other services, laundry, valet, and special events? Are these cards changed also? Are they effective, and easy to remember? Short messaged? Well balanced with dramatic color combinations? Fit the hotel/motel?
4. Are there frames in corridors? Do they perform equally well as do those in question 3? Are they appropriate and do they fit the hotel/motel?
5. Are there frames in restaurants, or outside them? Do they get attention by reason of simplicity? Color combination? Lighting? Do they show prices? Special items? Changed often? Remembered?
6. Are there clip-ons on˙menus? Do they feature foods, drinks, leftovers, and children's dishes? Do they take advantage of the times, days, seasons, special events, and daily features? Are they effective? Remembered?
7. Are menus fit for rooms, clientele? Readable? Accurate? Priced correctly? Good color? Striking? Offer the reader easy-to-follow through courses? Sell with copy, color, and style? Create interest? Fit the times?

8. Are there Tent Cards? Do they sell, and effectively get attention, and are they remembered? Special events, fashion shows, entertainment, other rooms and features, special services — are these offered? What about color? style, form, novelty?

9. Is there advertising placed in guest rooms? Directory? Menus? Special services? Story of hotel/motel? Selling hotel/motel features? What about color, style, remembrance value and novelty? Is advertising changed? (Guests find the same things wearing.)

10. Is there a house magazine? Interesting? Readable in type, style, content, and color? Or is there a housegram, newsgram, or other informational piece?

11. What about bottle neckties? Coasters? Stir sticks? Napkins? Glasses (cresting, type, style, shape)? Napery? Flatware? Holloware? Hallware? Decor? Color and atmosphere to blend with these?

12. Is there merchandising copy on laundry shirtbands, wrappers, and cellophane wrap? Shirt boards? Collar stays? Cuff holders? Are there well organized, attractive laundry and valet lists

13. Are there Display Cases? Shadow Boxes? Are they inside and outside of lobby? Attractive, lighted, well balanced, complimenting hotel?

14. What about stationery? Original? Crested? Design effective? Good color, layout, typography, engraving where helpful, various sizes, or social size, airmail, paper weight? Are there envelopes to match? A modern post card, in color — is there one? Stickers for baggage, air mail stickers, hotel stickers? Balance, color and style to fit hotel atmosphere is all important. And what impression is created and left with guests? Such impressions affect present and future guests.

15. Outside lighting: is it attractive, fitting the hotel. Is color used? Neon or straight? Check these points: travel desk; all facilities (men's and ladies' rooms, shops, sales and banquet departments, room clerk, reservations, information, mail, restaurants, etc.); marquee, outside frames, lighted with easy-to-see-and-name plaques or show cards on services, facilities, etc.

Based on the responses to these basic questions, experienced judgment determines what changes, improvements, and additions or deletions should be made.

The general effectiveness of such a program is vitally important. Guests can be influenced favorably or unfavorably. Once in the hotel/motel, it is essential that good international promotion, as we have defined it with a partial and sample set of basic questions, must be ready to attract and sell the guest at every point of contact.

Business Promotion Checklist

1. Entertainment, if any. Define the policy as it should be to fit your operations.

2. Principal sources of business. Answers to write-ins, personal calls, clippings, direct mail, and reservations service (Warner, Hicks, Utell, Turner).

3. Mailing lists: local, state, civic associations; clubs; fraternities, sororities; fraternal, church and political organizations; business groups and organizations; selected names of business peoples; unions; and names recommended by guests.

4. Room business sources: guest registration, inquiries, selected list from commercial list compiling agencies, travel agents, associated and corporation lists.

5. Restaurant business: announcements of special events or services, regular periodic mailing of postcards listing special dishes, mailing of menus, and mailing copies of publicity items.

6. Letter warmups: departure or thank-you letter to first-time guest, follow-up letter six months later if guest has not returned, credit card offer after third visit to hotel, letters to prospects received from current guests, letters to guests not back in 12 months, and series of letters and mailing pieces to travel agents.

7. Radio: spot announcements, publicity; news releases; and list of wire, press, newspapers.

8. Sales Incentives:

   (a) Room Sales: bottle give-aways for highest sales per week, awards to clerks and assistant managers, and awards to room clerks.

   (b) Food Sales: headwaiters, captains, etc.; awards for greatest number of advance registrations; greatest number of orders; and greatest dollar value.

   (c) Beverage Sales: awards for greatest amount of cocktails, wines, total liquor sold; and high markup on low beverage cost items.

   (d) Banquet Sales: awards for full night ballroom rentals; awards for sales personnel making greatest number of calls for new business on convention or group business; and award for record in dollars per person on week-ends, resorts, slow seasons.

   (e) Miscellaneous: awards — doorman for special orders for car storage, gasoline, washing, etc.; and awards — bellman for valet, laundry, television rental.

9. Development of sales kit, mailing brochures, colored slides and establishment of sales quotas files: develop and maintain national, state and local (Kardex) trace files.

10. Inside Merchandising:
    (a) Reduce menu items, and establish leaders.
    (b) Standardize stationery to one size wherever possible.
    (c) Develop midnight snack menus.
    (d) Develop hors d'oeuvre items on 10¢ to 15¢ basis.
    (e) Develop tent card specials to be placed in guest rooms and on restaurant tables.
    (f) Develop event card frames for elevators, lobbies, hallways, etc.
    (g) Develop advertising material on the laundry box, bag, shirt envelope, etc.
    (h) Develop handkerchief cellophane bag envelope with merchandising message.

11. Menus:
    (a) Change menu format with each meal.
    (b) Realign price ratios to fit each dining room or restaurant.
    (c) Develop clip-ons and specials.
    (d) Use sufficient white space on menu for easy reading.
    (e) Feature individual rooms in menu design.
    (f) Use art work and color as needed.
    (g) Include name of hotel/motel restaurant and address.
    (h) Use Du Jour specials.
    (i) Provide attractive printing.
    (j) Develop special items: July 4th, Washington's Birthday, and historical or community items.

12. Supervision:
    (a) Provide personal attention.
    (b) Follow up of banquets personally by sales representatives and others appearing at function.

13. Use geographical analysis of guests to determine advertising and letter campaigns.

14. Banquet Department
    (a) Prepare standardized menus to eliminate continuous menu makeup changes.
    (b) Make effort to sell flowers, cigars, beverages, incidental services.
    (c) Have the Maitre d'Hotel, Catering Manager or Personnel Manager head up training program of lectures on service and guest relations.

30

Developing Tomorrow's Manager

The hotel and restaurant industry is quietly facing one of its most crucial problems. The much heralded 1970's and 1980's are clearly pointing up the critical shortage and need for new managerial talent required to fill key positions in the industry.

The Role of Education

The growth of hotel and restaurant education, due in large measure to a handful of truly visionary educational pioneers, has made an immeasurable contribution toward advancing the total concept of hotel and restaurant management.

Obviously then, the first stage in the development of the professional manager is in the college or university. Hotel and restaurant organizations both large and small look there first for candidates, and then fit them into their specific organizational environment.

This first step is an exposure to theory and, fortunately in our industry, practice. It is a development process that considers not only academic needs and requirements, but also an intellectual conditioning that takes into consideration the very practical demands of our business. Included is an inquiry of what business is and does, which seeks to accomplish something in the development of standards, goals, and objectives peculiar to our industry. Because the subject is truly international, curriculums include an appreciation of and exposure to global social and corporate concepts.

Once the graduate has completed his work and is ready to enter a field of endeavor, he is also ready for the recruiter, the organization of mutual choice, or he or she is free to start a business with enough help available to make this possible.

At this point too, the question of specialization and proper indoctrination into a company organization may be considered by the company according to mutual interests and needs. Such a course may be pursued at a much later period — even after several years — either in the organization itself, or in a special course of instruction or summer study, even returning to graduate study.

Corporate Environment of the Manager-To-Be

All organizations concerned with the growth and the management of change are aware of and usually have a growth concept of some kind — formal or informal — built into them. These vary.

First there are those companies with extremely competitive and aggressive organizations, climates and types. These do attract new talent, but they often suffer from unusually high attrition rates. Needless to say, these are turmoil centers of instability. As to people, usually such organizations attract those who are not the stablest but often the greatest risk takers, the short-term gamblers of their own futures. They are willing to risk job opportunities with the company in the long-shot hope of achieving rapid success in rank and earnings.

On the other extreme are the more secure companies, where pay and promotional practices are largely conservative. Although admirable from the standpoint of providing job security, these companies may — more often than not — fall behind in the parade of corporate expansion because management's risk element remains dormant by self-protective choice.

Obviously, the company is most attractive to young talent when it combines risk with growth and still offers a reasonable degree of security for responsible objective job performance. This fact should be obvious to the company which hopes to recruit and hold good middle and upper managerial talent to insure its profitable operation and future growth.

Corporate Education of the Manager-To-Be

Industry faces a very particular kind of problem which it also shares with the schools and colleges of higher education. It is the first responsibility of the business organization to create and develop a kind of professional competence in managers according to the individual needs of the business.

Such a job is never finished, however, as it is a never-ending task. The reason for this is simply that the standards and concepts of professional management are ever changing and evolving much as medicine and law have for 150 years.

Therefore the task of educating the Manager-to-be is two-fold, as he must:

Attain professional competence.
Continuously upgrade it.

These objectives are complicated by the fact that business has gone through severe changes.

1. The attitudes of employees have changed. They are more educated, more sophisticated, and have much stronger feelings on what is fair play and equal opportunity in business and in life.
2. Government regulation has brought about an employer-employee relationship with clearly marked lines of rigidity unknown until a few years ago.
3. The very nature of business is changing so that large companies with federal types of organizations are prevalent. A result has been antagonism among people and a lack of esprit de corps in the ranks as well as in middle management.
4. Of particular note is that management has become a dominant personality that requires special skills in administration.

In training and developing prospective managers, all of these factors should be taken into account, as they have a bearing on the success of the effort.

At the beginning, one will recognize that the development of a manager starts, of course, with his selection. And as to what the job analyses say a manager should be, aspire to be, or have to be, this is not in question; we are primarily concerned here with education. Needless to say, the objectives of what is needed in the manager, when he is at the age level where command is accepted by others, must first be determined. For almost everyone may have seen the man in one level who may look entirely out of place at a higher level, much like a fish out of water.

Facing the company and the individual destined for management is intellectual conditioning. It is a professional concept composed of moral conduct, integrity, fair play, tolerance, and objectivity. Some might sum it up as character of the individual.

Obviously, such conditioning is more of a transition, a period in a man's life consisting of experiences, partly contributed by environment and by coming to grips with situations. What is gained in the way of total information in the various fields of knowledge bears on the art of managing.

This, of course, is a continuing educational process, and one which requires both theoretical study in the abstract, as well as in the line and position of the individual in the organization. The aim of this intellectual phase of manager development is not to provide the answers, but rather to present the problem, the conditions, the issues, and the findings.

The objective is to develop the prospective manager's own perception, power of analysis, and ability to separate the relevant from the irrelevant, the important from the less important, and to provide a frame and source of reference which will enable him to develop his own answers.

A direct result of such an education will be the manager's awareness of change, new approaches to problems, new methods, and particularly that there is no one answer, and very possibly several different ones for some problems.

Management Development

When a candidate has been chosen, the first corporate stage in management development, the problem becomes one of effective orientation. This involves keeping the candidate in motion, establishing the right kind of climate to nurture growth, providing enough interested supervision, and avoiding at all costs the fencing in of the candidate. This is followed by positive, formal and informal appraisal and review, always with the long-range viewpoint of developing the candidate in mind.

Management development as a broad term embraces all the activities and functions performed by a company to assure effective management now, and successful and profitable survival in the future.

A vital function in developing the manager-to-be is the importance of total organization planning. It is futile to attempt to seek to develop a candidate in an organization unless the organization's present and future purpose is clearly in mind. At this stage organization structures or patterns are conceptualized, created, developed, and established by top management to accommodate present and future organizational requirements. From these projections future manpower needs are determined.

An important part of the development process is the regular, formal and informal, quantitative and qualitative appraisal, and the development of the potential asset value of the candidate. Planning the judicious use of manpower, and programming it for current and future organizational requirements are byproducts of the appraisal function.

Development is not the responsibility of one or more individuals but the total responsibility of top management. For example, the Chairman of the Board, and the President with the aid of the corporate staff, determine the way the organization is to be managed. Operating management then must know and utilize three-way communication — from the top to the bottom, from bottom to top, and horizontally, to assure coordinated understanding which stems from the corporate philosophy of management.

The most important catalyst in the management development process is the active support and recognition accorded this concept. It would be futile to attempt to really develop the lower levels of management, and particularly a management trainee, within the framework of a development program, unless these principles and practices are understood, practiced, and believed in at the very top. Corporations, small and large, are truly reflections of the principals or principal at the top.

Methods of Instruction

While we have herein defined the broad objectives and approaches to manager development, a treatment of methods is important. A listing of accepted methods follows:

Socratic discussion	Lecture discussion
Philosophical discussion	Guided or directed discussion
Conference leading	Role playing
Progressive role playing	Socio-drama
Case discussion	Handouts
Seminars and institutes	Chart lecture
Flannel board lecture	Indirect lecture
Films	Dinner meetings and outside
Outside lectures for inplant	speakers
meetings	Sabbatical year
Memberships in trade associations	Membership in civic clubs
Trade conventions	Night school
Correspondence courses	Reading courses

Here the point is not that the manager learns theory alone, but receives some information on policy, procedure, and the objectives of business as well. A substantial portion of this training, obviously, is pure instruction in the academics of the profession of management, and because of this, the method of teaching must fit the situation.

The instructor, where required, is either an outside authority or a specialist within the hotel company, and the manager-to-be is the student.

Executive Internship

A major area of development for the manager is directly on the job, but, of course, under supervision. This is the very core of the education of a manager. To be successful, it requires a recognition of the concept known as the "Three-Position Plan" — an old fundamental replacement device with each man knowing the position above him and below him, and where the entire organization becomes a network of development, each level responsible for developing the level beneath it. Accountability is, of course, the main important reason for its success.

When carried on, this type of training is not unlike the internship found in the training of a young physician, or even the attorney-to-be. And the advantage of this type of training is that the executive in charge of a level is also the boss. His instructions carry authority. There is continuous coaching and guidance. It is a controlled process.

The value of this type of training is that it is real, replete with genuine experiences, difficult situations, tensions and emotional conflicts. It also has the very real advantage of fixing objectives and testing them in actual competition — a most valuable advantage indeed.

Management Development Checklist

Three basic problem areas in any management developing effort are: *First,* determine manpower requirements (nothing is worse than hiring a trainee and for lack of a formal plan, letting him drift.) *Second,* keep a candidate in motion (to avoid letting him get stale and bored.) *Third,* watch his progress (if he doesn't know how he rates, the trainee may fail to develop as expected).

The checklist provided in this article will help avoid pitfalls, any one of which could upset the best laid plans of management.

The Continuing Challenge

The development of a manager never ceases. It is a continuous review, appraisal, use, disuse, discard and employment of new approaches to decision-making, all necessary to the attainment of corporate objectives. A manager's thinking is constantly tested and challenged by time itself and the many facile changes peculiar to social, political and economic developments to which even the most modest personal effort may be related.

To stand still is to fall behind. The manager in our soiety has become a self-motivating, mobile force and must remain so in order to assure his own effectiveness and that of the enterprise to which he owes his allegiance. He sublimates personal goals, giving priority to the corporate effort with which he has allied himself. To continue to do this calls for constant exposure to new insights, thinking, and practices through all of the educational means which are at his disposal.

Because this management commitment is totally human, it is also essentially creative. Managers can therefore look forward to both the constant challenge and the opportunities which management continuously provides.

Management Development Checklist

1. *Determine Requirements.*
   (a) Make manpower needs determination an item in long-range planning.
   (b) Check the estimates of department heads.
   (c) Utilize information from internal and external sources as to the number and types of management development trainees you will need.
   These include . . .
   Expected sales growth
   New acquisitions.
   Technological changes and new techniques.
   Possible changes in organization.
   Reduction in staff due to retirement, death, and job changes.
   Potential performance estimates of personnel.
   Searching out buried organization talent.
   The foregoing forecast factors will aid you in establishing the development timetable and enable you to plan management development needs.
2. *Keep a Candidate Organizationally Active.*
   (a) Challenge the candidate to use his hidden potential.
   (b) Make him accept responsibility.
   (c) Allow for his mistakes; he learns by them.
   (d) Keep him interested in making decisions.
   (e) Praise him for recognizable accomplishment.
   (f) Make failures positive opportunities for corrective action.
   (g) Keep organizational blocks out of his way.
   (h) Give him an honest face-saving appraisal of himself.
   (i) Constantly provide the challenge of new assignments.
   (j) If working under one manager is not resultful, try him under another.
   (k) When he reaches his limit, change his routine and add to his responsibilities.
3. *Watch the Individual's Progress.*
   (a) Measure his progress against clearly defined goals.

(b) Have him suggest his own near and long-term objectives.
(c) Discuss and establish a set of possible goals with him.
(d) Back up verbal commitments in writing.
(e) Check his progress informally and often.
(f) Arrange an annual formal review with him.
(g) Let him rate and score himself so that he and you know his successes and failures.
(h) Give him your opinion on how you feel he is doing.
(i) Let other department heads and executives know his weaknesses and strengths, his promotional potential, and where his next move is.

Bibliography

Executive Compensation

Books:
1. Belcher, David W., *Wage and Salary Administration.* Englewood Cliffs, New Jersey: Prentice-Hall, Inc., Revised Edition, 1962.
2. James, Casner A., *Estate Planning.* Boston: Little, Brown and Co., 1961.
3. Jones, Philip W., *Job Evaluation.* New York: John Wiley and Sons, Inc., 1948.
4. O'Neill, Hugh, *Modern Pension Plans.* Englewood Cliffs, N. J.: Prentice-Hall, Inc., 1947.
5. Stryker, Perrin, and editors of Fortune, *A Guide to Modern Management Methods: How to Pay Executives.* New York: McGraw-Hill Book Co., Inc., 1954.
6. Washington and Rothschild, *Compensating the Corporate Executive.* New York: Ronald Press Co., 1951.

Articles:
1. McDermid, Charles A., "How Money Motivates Men," *Business Horizon,* 1960.
2. Tomas, James W., "Incentive Patterns in Executive Compensation," Industrial Relations Series, Bulletin 28, Ann Arbor, Michigan, 1960.
3. Witzky, Herbert K., "Deferred Compensation for Hotel Executives and Beating the Tax Bite," *Tavern Talk Magazine* (Nov. 15, 1958), pp. 6, 8, 9, 10.
4. —————. "Establishing Cost Control in Hotels," *Tavern Talk Magazine* (Jan. 1, 1955), pp. 7-9.

260

5. ————. "Executive Compensation Policies and Methods," *Tavern Talk Magazine* (Aug. 15, 1959), pp. 10, 21, 22, 23.
6. ————. "14 Ways to Compensate Executives," *Tavern Talk Magazine* (Sept. 13, 1958) pp. 10, 20, 21.
7. ————. "Is Management Paid Too Much," *Tavern Talk Magazine* (Aug. 3, 1961), pp. 5-6.

Reports:
1. "Executive Compensation," Survey 45, *Personnel Policies Forum*, Washington, D.C.: Bureau of National Affairs (December 1, 1957).
2. "Executive Pay Plans," New York: Institute of Business Planning, 2 W. 13th St.
3. National Survey of Professional, Administrative, Technical and Clerical Pay, Bulletin 1286, Washington, D.C.: U.S. Dept. of Labor, Bureau of Labor Statistics (Winter 1959-1960).
4. National Industrial Conference Board, Inc.:
   a. "Compensation and Pensions of Executives," (New York: the Board, 1950).
   b. "Compensation of Executives," (New York: the Board, 1946).
   c. "Employee Salary Plans in Operation," (New York: the Board, 1949).
   d. "Executive Compensation in 39 Industries," (New York: the Board, 1948).
   e. "Executive Stock Ownership Plans," *Studies in Personnel Policy No. 120*, (New York: the Board, September, 1951).
   f. "Profit Sharing for Executives," (New York: the Board, 1948).
   g. "Some Problems in Wage Incentive Administration," *Studies in Personnel Policy, No. 19*, (New York: the Board, February, 1940).
   h. "Wage Incentive Practices," *Studies in Personnel Policy, No. 68* (New York: the Board, February, 1945).
   i. "Wage Payment Systems," *Studies in Personnel Policy, No. 91* (New York: the Board, June, 1948).
5. Surveys on Executive Compensation in the Hotel Industry, Herbert K. Witzky and Associates, New Fairfield, Connecticut.
   a. First Annual National Executive Compensation Survey of 500 Leading Hotels in the United States, January 1, 1955.
   b. Second Annual National Executive Compensation Survey of 1500 Leading Hotels in all Areas of the United States, February 1, 1956.
   c. Third Annual Survey in 1500 United States Hotels on What Hotel Executives and Department Heads Are Paid, February 20, 1957.
   d. Fourth Annual Survey on What Executives and Department Heads Are Paid in 2,000 Hotels in the United States, Canada, Hawaii and Puerto Rico, January, 1959.

e. Fifth Survey on What Executives and Department Heads Are Paid in 2,000 Hotels and Motor Hotels in the United States, Canada and Puerto Rico, January, 1962.

Labor and Personnel

Books:
1. Barkin, Solomon, *The Decline of the Labor Movement and What Can Be Done About It.* Santa Barbara, California: Center for the study of Democratic Institutions, 1961.
2. Horowitz, Morris A., *The New York Hotel Industry.* Cambridge, Mass.: Harvard University Press, 1960.
3. Josephson, Matthew, *Union House, Union Bar.* New York: Random House, 1956.
4. Jucius, Michael J., *Personnel Management.* Homewood, Illinois: R. D. Irwin, 1963, 5th edition.
5. Weinland & Gross, *Personnel Interviewing.* New York: Ronald Press, Co., 1952.

How to Negotiate Labor Agreements with Unions

Books:
1. Trotta, Maurice S., *Collective Bargaining.* New York: Simmons-Boardman Books, 1962.
2. Trotta, Maurice S., *Labor Arbitration.* New York: Simmons-Boardman Books, 1961.

Reports & Services:
1. Bureau of National Affairs, 1231 24th St., Washington 7, D.C.:
   a. Collective Bargaining Negotiations and Contracts Service.
   b. Labor Policies & Practice Service
   c. Retail Labor Report.
   d. Union Labor Report.
   e. White Collar Report.
2. News Releases of the National Labor Relations Board, Washington 25, D.C.

Hotel Laws:
1. Zwarenstyn, Hendrik, *Legal Aspects of Hotel Administration.* Bureau of Business and Economic Research, Graduate School of Business Administration, Michigan State University.

Management and Control

Books:
1. Barnes, Ralph M., *Motion and Time Study.* New York: John Wiley and Sons, Inc., 1963.
2. Blum, Milton L., *Industrial Psychology and Its Social Foundations.* New York: Harper and Brothers, 1956 revised edition.
3. Broom and Longnecker, *Small Business Management.* Southwestern Monuments Assn., 1961.
4. Bursk, Edward C., *How to Increase Executive Effectiveness.* Cambridge, Mass.: Harvard University Press, 1953.
5. Dean, Burton V., *Operations Research in Research and Development.* New York: John Wiley and Sons, Inc. 1963.
6. DePhillips, Berliner & Cribbin, *Management of Training Programs.* Homewood, Illinois: R. D. Irwin, 1960.
7. Drucker, Peter F., *The New Society.* New York: Harper and Brothers, 1950.
8. ————. *The Practice of Management.* New York: Harper and Brothers, 1954.
9. Folsom, Marson B., *Executive Decision Making.* New York: McGraw-Hill Book Co., Inc., 1962.
10. Freeman, G. L. & Taylor, E. K., *How to Pick Leaders.* New York: Funk & Wagnalls Co., Inc., 1950.
11. Heinritz, Stuart F., *Purchasing Principles and Applications.* Englewood Cliffs, New Jersey, Prentice-Hall, Inc., Third edition, 1962.
12. Jerome III, William Travers, *Executive Control.* New York: John Wiley & Sons, Inc., 1961.
13. Jones, Manley H., *Executive Decision Making.* Homewood, Illinois: R. D. Irwin, Inc., Revised edition, 1962.
14. Kotschenar, Lendal H., *Quantity Food Purchasing.* New York: John Wiley and Sons, Inc., 1961.
15. Martindell, Jackson, *The Appraisal of Management.* New York: Harper and Brothers, 1962.
16. McFarland and Dalton, *Management Principles and Practice.* New York: Macmillan Co., 1958.
17. Mundel, M. E., *Motion and Time Study.* Englewood Cliffs, N. J.: Prentice-Hall, Inc., 3rd edition, 1960.
18. Newman and Logan, *Business Policies and Management.* South-Western Monuments Assn., 4th edition.
19. Riley, John W., *The Corporation and Its Publics.* New York: John Wiley and Sons, Inc., 1963.
20. Rudnitsky, Charles P. & Leslie M. Wolff, *How to Stop Pilferage in Business.* New York: Pilot Books, 1961.

21. Shefferman, *The Shefferman Personnel Motivation Program.* Engle-
    wood Cliffs, N. J.: Prentice-Hall, 1961.
22. Stryker, Perrin, *The Character of the Executive.* New York: Harper
    and Brothers, 1962.
23. Thurston, David B., *Manual for the President of a Growing Company.*
    Englewood Cliffs, N. J.; Prentice-Hall, Inc., 1962.
24. Trundle & Peck, *Managerial Control of Business.* New York: John
    Wiley & Sons, Inc., 1947.

Articles:
 1. Andrews, Kenneth R., "Executive Training by the Case Method,"
    Harvard Business Review (September, 1951), pp. 58-70.
 2. Buckley, John L., "Seventeen Years of Multiple Management," *Man-
    agement Review* (April, 1950), pp. 185-186.
 3. Foreman, Charles W. L., "Inventory, Planning and Development of
    the Management Organization, A Case History," *Personnel,* (January,
    1951), pp. 267-276.
 4. Habbe, Stephen, "Executives Go to School," *Management Record*
    (February, 1950), pp. 55-56.
 5. Ingleheart, A. S., "How General Foods Gives Management Training
    to Top Executives," *Sales Management* (July 15, 1946), pp. 37-39.
 6. Linville, Thomas M., "Professional Societies — A Tool for Executive
    Development," *Advanced Management* (January, 1953), pp. 31-33.
 7. Mandell, Milton M., "Problems in Executive Selection," *Advanced
    Management* (March 1952), pp. 14-18.
 8. Mandell, Milton M., "The Qualifications, Investigations, A Tool for
    Improving Executive Selection," *Personnel* (March 1952), pp.
    387-390.
 9. Mayfield, H., "Management Inventory," Industrial Relations Division,
    Owens-Illinois Glass Co., p. 19, 1951.
10. McCormick, Charles P., *The Power of People.* New York: Harper &
    Row, 1949, p. 136.
11. McQuaiz, J. H., "Hiring Executives," *Advanced Management* (De-
    cember 1949), pp. 15-16.
12. Moore, Harriet B., "Five Tips on Picking Young Executives," *Man-
    agement Review* (December 1951), pp. 729-730.
13. Pearson, A. M., "The Ford Program of Supervisory Development: A
    Progress Report," *Organization Planning & Management Develop-
    ment, Personnel Series #141,* American Management Association,
    1951, pp. 34-45.
14. Pigors, Paul and Pigors, Faith, "The Incident Process, Case Studies
    for Management Development" — A practical course in decision-
    making, problem-solving and handling people, Bureau of National
    Affairs, Inc., 1231 24th St., N.W., Washington 7, D.C.

15. Planty, Earl G., "Case Studies in Executive Development; II. Johnson & Johnson and Affiliated Companies," *Personnel,* (July, 1950), pp. 25-28.
16. Planty, Earl G., Beach, C.K., and Van Ark, Gordon, "Executive Development Through Colleges and Universities," *Advanced Management* (December, 1950), pp. 14-18.
17. Planty, Earl B., and Machaver, W., "Upward Communications: A Project in Executive Development," *Personnel* (January 1952), pp. 304-318.
18. Rowland, Virgil K., "A Case Study in Management Development," *Management Development: Key to Company Progress,* American Management Association, General Management Series # 16, 1953, pp. 19-29.
19. Witzky, Herbert K., "The Education of Tomorrow's Manager," *Hotel Gazette* (January 31, 1959; February 14, 1959; February 20, 1959).
20. Worthy, James C., "Executive Personnel Development," *Advanced Management* (February, 1953), pp. 5-8.
21. "Assessment of Men," Office of Strategic Services Assessment Staff, New York: Holt, Rhinehart and Winston, 1948, p. 541.
22. *Management Development: Case Studies.* New York: Metropolitan Life Insurance Co., Policyholders Service Bureau, 1950, p. 62.

Improving Communications

Books:

1. Black, James Menzies, *How to Grow in Management.* Englewood Cliffs, N. J.: Prentice-Hall, Inc., 1957 (Chapter 15: "How to Get Results From Business Writing: The Report").
2. Canfield, Bertrand R., *Public Relations.* Homewood, Illinois: Richard D. Irwin, Inc., 1956.
3. Hilton, Peter, *Handbook of New Product Development.* Englewood Cliffs, N. J.: Prentice-Hall, Inc., 1961.

Articles:

1. Jackson, Jay M., "The Organization and Its Communications Problem," *Advanced Management* (February, 1959).
2. Janis, J. Harold, "Writing Skills Cut Management Waste," *Nation's Business* (April, 1958).
3. Pigors, Paul, "Effective Communication in Industry," National Association of Manufactures of U. S., New York, 1949.
4. Rogers, Carl R., and Roethlisberger, F. J., "Barriers and Gateways to Communication," *Harvard Business Review* (July-August, 1952).
5. Bureau of National Affairs Reports:

a. "Communications to Employees," *Personnel Policies Forum Survey #15* (November, 1952).
b. "Downward Communications," *Personnel Policies Forum Survey #35* (February, 1956).

On Building Business
Books:
1. Brodner, J., Carlson H., and Maschal, H., *Profitable Food and Beverage Operation.* New York: Ahrens Book Company, 1959.
2. Coples, John, *Tested Advertising Methods.* New York: Harper and Brothers, 1961.
3. Dichter, Ernest, *The Strategy of Desire.* New York: Doubleday and Co., Inc., 1960.
4. Heine, Paul L. H., *Food Sales, Unlimited.* New York: Ahrens Book Company, 1952.
5. Patrick and Spitzer, *Great Restaurants of America.* Philadelphia: J. B. Lippincott Co., 1960.
6. Thompson, Willard M., *Salesmanship: Concepts, Management and Strategy.* John Wiley and Sons, Inc., 1963.
7. Watkins, Julian, *The Readers Digest, The Best Advertisements From Readers Digest 1955-61,* New York: Random House, 1962.
8. Witzky, Herbert K., *Hotel Advertising Guide.* New Fairfield, Connecticut: Herbert K. Witzky & Associates, 1958.

Automation in Hotel and Restaurant Operations
Books:
1. Brady, Robert A., *Organization, Automation and Society.* Berkley, California: University of California Press (Publication of the Institute of Business and Economic Research), 1961.
2. Brooks, Frederick C. Jr., *Automatic Data Processing.* New York: John Wiley and Sons, Inc., 1963.
3. Gregory and Van Horn, *Automatic Data-Processing Systems, Principles and Procedures.* Belmont, Calif.: Wadsworth Publishing Co., Inc., 1961.

Articles:
1. Bright, James R., "Does Automation Raise Skill Requirements?," *Harvard Business Review* (July-August, 1958).
2. Ferber, Robert C., "Space Age Innkeeping," *Hotel Gazette* (April 25, May 9, May 23, June 6, and July 4, 1959).
3. Witzky, Herbert K., "Automation May be the Key to Economies," *Hotel Gazette* (July 5th, 1958).
4. "Company Experiences With Automation," *Personnel Policies Forum Survey #46,* Bureau of National Affairs, Washington 7, D.C.

Index